Brown University

THE CAMPUS GUIDE

Brown University

AN ARCHITECTURAL TOUR BY
Raymond P. Rhinehart

WITH PHOTOGRAPHS BY WALTER SMALLING JR.

FOREWORD BY CHRISTINA H. PAXSON

INTRODUCTION BY DIETRICH NEUMANN

PRINCETON ARCHITECTURAL PRESS
NEW YORK

PUBLISHED BY
Princeton Architectural Press
37 East 7th Street
New York, New York 10003

Visit our website at www.papress.com

All photography by Walter Smalling Jr. except the following:
Tom Gastel: 267; Brown University: 85, 98, 217; Toshiko Mori Architect: 182.
Archival photographs and illustrations used courtesy Brown University
Library: 12, 19, 40, 41, 66, 76 (top), 79, 88, 109, 243, 244, 252–53.

SERIES EDITOR: Jan Hartman
PROJECT EDITOR: Dan Simon
LAYOUT: Benjamin English
MAPMAKER: Tom Gastel

This book has been made possible through the generous support
of the Brown Alumni Association Board of Governors.

SPECIAL THANKS TO: Meredith Baber, Sara Bader, Janet Behning,
Nicola Bednarek Brower, Megan Carey, Carina Cha, Andrea Chlad,
Barbara Darko, Russell Fernandez, Will Foster, Jan Haux,
Emily Johnston-O'Neill, Diane Levinson, Jennifer Lippert,
Katharine Myers, Margaret Rogalski, Elana Schlenker, Rob Shaeffer,
Sara Stemen, Andrew Stepanian, Paul Wagner, and Joseph Weston
of Princeton Architectural Press —Kevin C. Lippert, publisher

LIBRARY OF CONGRESS CATALOGING-IN-PUBLICATION DATA
Rhinehart, Raymond P., 1940–
Brown University: an architectural tour / by Raymond P. Rhinehart;
with photographs by Walter Smalling Jr.; introduction by Dietrich Neumann.
pages cm.
Includes bibliographical references and index.
ISBN 978-1-61689-073-5 (pbk.: alk. paper)
1. Brown University—Guidebooks. 2. Brown University—
Buildings—Guidebooks. I. Title.
LD639.R55 2013
378.745'1—dc23
                    2013002048

Contents

And this our life, exempt from public haunt,

Finds tongues in trees, books in the running brooks,

Sermons in stones, and good in every thing.

— William Shakespeare, *As You Like It*, Act 2, Scene 1

Buildings speak. If you stop to listen, they have many stories to tell about themselves, about those who designed them, and, in the end, about us. This guide reflects several years of eavesdropping on the architecture of Brown, College Hill, and Providence. Perhaps there is not good in everything, but the stories they tell are never dull; they are sermons in stone—and brick, glass, wood, metal, and poured concrete.

The larger narrative of Brown's architecture is divided into nine chapters, or Walks. The first is the most comprehensive, a curtain raiser that introduces the reader to the University's oldest and most historic buildings, as well as some of the newest developments transforming the twenty-first-century campus. Walk One also brings onstage the major player in this narrative, the Hill. It is this quirk of geography, called Prospect Hill by the first English settlers, that determined what was built, how it was built, and who built it. More than any other actor, the Hill is what gives Brown a sense of place unique among its Ivy peers.

The remaining Walks propel the story forward chapter by chapter—the College Green, the creation of Lincoln Field, Pembroke, "The Walk," the athletic precinct, and much more. The groupings are not arbitrary. Although they all contribute to the larger mosaic that is Brown, each, like the Pembroke campus, has a distinct history and personality that deserves its own focus. Where possible, these Walks unspool chronologically; however, the guiding principle has been to construct Walks that are in fact walkable. A strictly chronological guide would have the reader or the person on the ground darting from one often widely separated building or quad to the next. Each building may have a separate voice, but together they constitute unique choirs and are treated as such.

VISITOR RESOURCES

The Stephen Robert '62 Campus Center (Faunce House), Haffenreffer Gallery, John Hay and John Carter Brown Libraries, Annmary Brown Memorial, Sarah Doyle Gallery, and John Nicholas Brown Center for Public Humanities and Cultural Heritage are open to the public. Hours vary and follow the academic calendar. For specific times, reference the "A to Z Index" on the University's website: www.brown.edu/a-to-z

Maddock Alumni Center, 38 Brown Street
Weekdays, mid-August – June, 8:30 AM – 5 PM;
July – early August, 8 AM – 4 PM

Brown University Bookstore, 244 Thayer Street
Weekdays, 7:30 AM – 8 PM;
Saturdays, 10 AM – 8 PM

Directions and parking:
www.brown.edu/about/visit/driving-directions

Online tours:
www.students.brown.edu/bruin/vtour

ADDITIONAL RESOURCES

Providence Preservation Society
21 Meeting Street #2, Providence
(401) 831-7440; www.ppsri.org

Rhode Island Historical Society
110 Benevolent Street, Providence
(401) 331-8575; www.rihs.org

Building Brown: A Guide to Construction Projects
www.brown.edu/Facilities/Building_Brown/

Manning Hall through the Van Wickle Gates

My office, in the heart of Brown's oldest building, occupies a formal position in Brown's architecture, a center within the center. Although it is a modern office, with all of the technology I need to work, it retains some of the formality and sense of tradition that Brown's original architects wanted to invest in University Hall.

And yet, standing in front of University Hall and looking toward the Van Wickle Gates, it is clear that there is nothing static about the Brown campus. The students and faculty who walk through the gates, deep in conversation, are much more diverse than were members of the Brown community in the eighteenth century. Just down the hill, one can see the John D. Rockefeller Jr. Library, built to celebrate Brown's bicentennial in 1964 and now approaching a fiftieth anniversary of its own. The List Art Building, very modern when it was built in 1971, which could not look more different from its neighbor, the John Hay Library (1910). Like the students, the buildings seem to be enjoying a lively conversation with each other.

The Brown community feels a rightful pride in the beauty of this campus, which offers some of the most charming university architecture in the United States. The structures display an eclectic range of styles, and yet there is still a feeling of unity. Generations of architects and builders did their work well, and within a walk of a few minutes, one can stroll through nearly two and a half centuries of the loftiest aspirations about what a college building should look like. There is both seriousness of purpose and playfulness, and the combined effect, atop College Hill, with its magnificent views of Providence and Narragansett Bay, is guaranteed to make a strong impression on first-time visitors.

Eclecticism subsumed to a larger purpose strikes me as highly appropriate for Brown University, where constructive irreverence remains the prevailing spirit. In a similar way, Brown's famous New Curriculum (soon to be fifty as well) offers more freedom of choice than most but demands coherence at the same time. To take diverse elements and combine them into one; that is not a bad purpose for a university. Indeed, it is the very origin of the word, which derives from the Latin *universitas*, or "the whole," which comes from *universus*, "combined into one."

In riveting detail (sometimes you can almost see the rivets), Raymond P. Rhinehart (Class of 1962) has told the story of our campus and how it came together as a whole. It is absorbing to read about the ways in which certain buildings have changed functions over the years—surely, a sign of Brown's dynamism. Robinson Hall, adjacent to the College Green, was the university library when it was built in 1878, and is now home to Brown's Department of Economics. Manning Chapel (1835) has contained a chapel, a library, and now a collection of Native American artifacts. Even University Hall is not immune to change; or perhaps it is more accurate to say that we ourselves change,

University Hall, The College Green

A S.W. view of the COLLEGE in Providence, together with the PRESIDENT's HOUSE & GARDENS.

University Hall, c. 1795

as we look at it from new angles. Thanks to the *Slavery and Justice Report* (2006), we now know more about the laborers who built it, including those who were enslaved.

I hope that this publication will appeal to a wide range of readers, from students eager to deepen their knowledge about the special place in which they are learning, to parents, casual visitors, and general admirers of beautiful buildings. Brown University is fortunate indeed to call Providence and Rhode Island its home, and the eclecticism of our campus dovetails nicely with a local architectural tradition that knows few rivals for its spirit and charm. With this book as a guide, I encourage all to do what generations of Brown students have done: take a walk outside and encounter the world around you.

Christina H. Paxson
Nineteenth President, Brown University

The American college campus is a place apart, yet a part of the larger community in which it goes about the business of preparing young minds "for discharging the Offices of Life with usefulness and reputation." These words are found in the charter that established the College of Rhode Island and Providence Plantations in 1764. With this ambitious mission, the College began preparing young minds in the small town of Warren, Rhode Island, but soon moved to Providence, the equally ambitious settlement at the head of Narragansett Bay. The far wealthier town of Newport would have seemed to be the more logical choice. Certainly, Newport worked hard to land this honor. But the merchants and businessmen of Providence, led by the extraordinary Brown brothers, worked harder still, and at the end of the day, Providence prevailed.

What inspired the town fathers of Providence to lobby so aggressively was as much a matter of practical considerations as the love of knowledge. An institution of higher learning would provide an educated class that served the economic and political interests of Providence in its drive to dominate southern New England. Thus, from the very beginning when James Manning, Brown's first president, moved his household to Providence, the fortunes of the city and the college were intertwined.

The pages that follow focus on the growth of a great university as seen through the prism of its buildings and landscaping, a prism that reflects many colors, including the tension between Brown's vision of itself and its evolving relationship with the city that became its home. In the first Walk, which is something of an overview, the architecture tells us that Brown was conceived as an urban institution. Although at a small distance from what was then the heart of the emerging downtown, on the brow of what was then called Prospect Hill, the campus nevertheless began to line up as if along a street. Its front door led directly out to the city below. This pattern continued into the first half of the nineteenth century when facilities were built to house the study of the sciences or what then was called "natural philosophy." Their construction was supported by a business community whose wealth was increasingly rooted not in commerce, but in finance and industry. Even the architects who built the new buildings dedicated to research and science hailed from Providence.

The benefits of this mutual dependence were not lost on the struggling College. Francis Wayland, one of the University's greatest presidents, understood the importance and value of a healthy dialogue between town and gown, a point made clear when he complained that the typical American college was "isolated to a great extent from connexion with the community around it," and thus from the "salutary restraint of public observation".[1] In his mind, Brown was exceptional in its embrace of the larger community it served.

Succeeding Walks, however, show a growing tension between the city and Brown. As Providence expanded up what was now called College Hill, and as

Students catching up on the steps of Sayles Hall

the city became a great industrial center, Brown gradually turned in on itself as a place apart. Walls and gates went up; the center of the campus was no longer the lawn in front of University Hall, but on the other side at the emerging College Green. The most stunning early twentieth-century building on campus, the new John Hay Library (1910), literally turned its back on the city. William Faunce, Brown's ninth president, may have protested that the erection of the Van Wickle Gates was not meant to "shut out our friends," but the message was clear. As the economy of Providence began its slow decline during the Depression, Brown took on the appearance of a leafy gated community, a pleasant green oasis in the midst of urban blight and decay.

A new page in the relationship began in the final decades of the twentieth century, spurred by a number of converging forces: a growing appreciation for the unique treasure of historic architecture shared by both; the slow reverse migration of people back to the city; student activism and the rise of social media, which dissolves boundaries; new materials and construction methods;

and perhaps most important for Providence and Brown, as institutions of higher
learning create new knowledge, they must inevitably grow. Under the leadership
of Howard Swearer, Vartan Gregorian, and Ruth Simmons (Brown's fifteenth,
sixteenth, and eighteenth presidents), Brown began to reconsider its place in
the city, a process that led to a new appreciation of the mutual dependence that
binds each to the other. Brick is replaced by glass; new circulation paths are
developed that knit the city and the University more closely together; Brown's
investment in Providence increases in actual dollars, programs, and physical
plant, and the city finds new ways to help the University accommodate its need
to grow both on the Hill and in the emerging downtown area beyond College
Hill. Pages of this chapter are found in each of the Walks, but most explicitly in
the ninth and final Walk. Here, the University comes down from the Hill and
brings the promise of new life to the city that convinced the young College to
plant its roots at the head of Narragansett Bay. It is a story of a vital partnership
that has no end, but a constant series of new beginnings. It is the story of Brown.

Raymond P. Rhinehart, Hon. AIA

1   Francis Wayland, *Thoughts on the Present Collegiate System in the United States* (Boston:
    Gould, Kendall & Lincoln, 1842), 121–22.

In November 1932, Frank Lloyd Wright visited Brown University to give a lecture titled "Growth and Development of Architecture"—and, as he promised his audience, to make "all the trouble he could." His good-humored talk was the highlight of an "Institute of Art," a conference jointly organized by Brown and the Rhode Island School of Design (RISD).

The 65-year-old architect had a lot to say about the local buildings in particular and college architecture in general. "I am a modern architect who stands here ready and willing to point to the old buildings of Providence, and its atmosphere, as much better than almost anything." Of course, he told his audience in packed Alumnae Hall, this did not mean "that we ought to reproduce, or copy, the best of these Providence buildings." Rather, an understanding of their genuine qualities would lead to truly contemporary solutions "in the forms of our own life and our own day."

Wright had just visited New Haven and entertained his Providence audience with remarks about its Ivy League neighbor to the south, where James Gamble Rogers's Collegiate Gothic had redefined the campus in recent years. While modern architecture had "certain very definite forms and many definite implications," he stated, it "is very definitely not the thing that Yale has spent so many millions to commemorate in such foolish fashion, a betrayal of the youth entrusted to her care. And I can't see how any thinking man would go to a university where, especially in architecture, the spirit of youth has been denied in this fashion and senility set in its place. So conspicuously true is this perversion of a fundamental affair at Yale that I fail to see how the great university could be trusted in other matters."

Historic architecture without integrity perfectly symbolized, in Wright's eyes, the eclecticism in much academic education, which he considered a "sterilizing process" robbing "the individual of initiative." After lecturing his rapt audience (gazing up at him, as he noted, from "their worm's-eye view") some more about modern materials and the supremacy of his own organic architecture (casually dismissing the work of Michelangelo, Wren, and Le Corbusier along the way), Wright stepped down from the podium to answer a barrage of questions, which kept coming as he was finally walking down the aisle to leave the building.

Wright's fondness for Providence and its architecture was no accident. As a boy, from age four to seven, he had lived in Pawtucket, Rhode Island, where his father was the pastor of High Street Baptist Church from 1871 until 1874. In his autobiography, which had appeared only months before his visit to Brown, Wright fondly recalled clambakes on the shores of Narragansett Bay. The family lived at the corner of Cross and Hawes Streets in Pawtucket and it seems likely (although there is no proof) that Wright's parents would have taken him to Providence to see the First Baptist Church (his father being an officer in the

The College Green in autumn

Rhode Island Baptist State Convention) and the First Baptist College to which it belonged. If, indeed, young Frank Lloyd Wright had wandered onto College Hill, sometime between 1871 and 1874, he would have found a small assemblage of all but five buildings, some in dire need of repair. In fact, the *Providence Press* observed on January 28, 1876: "Brown University has always been known as the college where the instruction is of the best nature, and where the buildings are almost the poorest that could be devised." Brown had recently celebrated its hundreth anniversary and had seen little growth since Manning (1834) and Rhode Island (1840) Halls had joined University Hall and Hope College (1822) to form a modest row of buildings. Only the chemistry laboratory at Rogers Hall of 1862 (later to become the Salomon Center for Teaching) gave an indication of the future main green and the school's expanding scope. A new building campaign was about to begin as the country recovered from the Civil War. Rhode Island Hall would be enlarged in 1875, a new, spectacular library in Ruskinian Gothic (Robinson Hall) followed in 1878, and Slater and Sayles Halls in 1879 and 1888. More growth came around the turn of the century, when the main quadrangle was completed through Rockefeller Hall (today the Stephen Robert '62 Campus Center) and the John Carter Brown Library, followed by Carrie Tower and the John Hay Library.

Much had changed when Wright returned after sixty years. Expansion plans for the campus, drawn up by Frederick Law Olmsted, Charles L. Klauder, Paul Cret, and others had begun to define a sequence of well-proportioned quadrangles for Brown and Pembroke, filled out in recent years by Colonial Revival structures, such as Alumnae Hall, six years old at the time of Wright's speech, as well as Hegeman Hall, Metcalf Hall, and Littlefield Hall, built at the same time. Andrews Hall and Wriston Quad followed after the war and contributed much to the sense of casual coherence that to this day characterizes the central part of our campus. Colonial Revival architecture was, in Wright's eyes, while not entirely the answer to the needs of the time, still far superior to Yale's Collegiate Gothic. It offered a link to local traditions and its humble simplicity held the key for future developments.

Such truly modern architecture was embraced by Brown after Wriston Quad was finished. "We have a wonderful opportunity at Brown University to create a museum of the works of the most important mid-twentieth-century architects," declared Samuel Lerner, engineering professor and director of construction planning at Brown in 1964. As a result, Philip Johnson was commissioned to build the List Art Building, his only building in reinforced concrete and the best urban intervention in his entire oeuvre. I. M. Pei and Félix Candela designed major projects (an Earth Sciences and Mathematics Building and Athletics Center) that remained unbuilt (with the exception of Candela's remarkable heating plant), and the campus became decidedly contemporary. Major figures in American architecture as diverse as Diller Scofidio + Renfro, Robert A. M. Stern, and Rafael Viñoly have left their mark in recent years.

Archival image of Alumnae Hall

The enormous interest in architecture at Brown, to which the attendance at Wright's lecture testified, continued after the war, when William H. Jordy joined the faculty in 1955 and stayed for thirty years. He was one of America's preeminent architectural historians. Students in his immensely popular lecture classes often created models of modern buildings as their final projects— a tradition still alive today. Just like Wright dazzled his audience at Brown in 1932, in recent years Daniel Libeskind, Robert Venturi, Richard Meier, Steven Holl, Michael Graves, Peter Eisenman, Bjarke Ingels, and many others have lectured to a packed Salomon auditorium. The collaboration between RISD and Brown that led to the "Institute of Art" in 1932 is very much alive today. An architectural design studio has been taught every year since 2008 (following a short-lived attempt at architectural design instruction in the 1890s by Norman Isham), and the first joint urban design studio between Brown and RISD was held in the fall of 2012. Students have written and developed a smartphone app as a complement to this guide called Brown FACADES (Facts About Architecture Design Environment and Spaces).

Brown's eleventh president, Henry M. Wriston, captured the school's special sense of the importance of architecture in 1955 when he wrote: "I have often thought that no student can walk the paths of the College Green for four years—if he has any sensitivity at all—without learning something from the appearance, something from the atmosphere that the buildings breathe, something from the way history looks down upon him."

Dietrich Neumann
Professor of the History of Art and Architecture, Brown University

> Whereas Institutions for liberal Education are highly beneficial to Society, by
> forming the rising Generation to Virtue, Knowledge & useful Literature & thus
> preserving in the Community a Succession of Men duly qualify'd for discharging
> the Office of Life with usefulness and reputation.[1]

The smallest of states, Rhode Island has the longest name: Rhode Island and
Providence Plantations. The state also enjoys a large history out of proportion
to its size. Birthplace of the Industrial Revolution in America and, in Newport,
a playground for the Gilded Age, Rhode Island was settled by dissenters of all
stripes, beginning with Roger Williams, whose great experiment in the separation
of church and state lay the foundation of the future United States. Agreeing on
nothing else, those who put down roots in Rhode Island were of one accord: their
neighbors had the right to express and practice their religious beliefs unhindered
by civil law. Some outsiders remarked favorably on what they saw as a resulting
"tumultuous amity." Others dismissed the colony as "Rogues' Island." Or as one
minister in the Dutch colony of New Amsterdam wrote: "All the cranks of Newe
England retire thither."[2]

That same embrace of what we today might call a "rainbow perspective"
colored not only Rhode Island's history, but also the history of the institution
initially called the College in the English Colony of Rhode Island and Providence
Plantations, that is, until Nicholas Brown Jr. in 1804 came up with the $5,000 to
earn naming rights. (What may seem like a modest sum was in fact 1,000 times
the roughly $5 annual tuition.) The tumultuous amity of Brown University's
architecture is a case in point. Whether out of an innate frugality or simply a lack
of funds, Brown seldom built many buildings in one style, with the exception
of much of what was built in the first six decades of the twentieth century. Then,
Brown, like a number of other colleges, actively pursued what today would be
called a brand, Colonial Revival.

However, Colonial Revival architecture was but one chapter—and not
the longest—in the history of architecture at Brown. For many years, buildings
emerged one or a few per decade. Each reflected the prevailing style, as well as the
most up-to-date design and technological advances of the day—from Colonial to
Federal to Italianate to Richardsonian Romanesque to Queen Anne to Classical
Revival, Beaux-Arts, and so forth. The single word that best describes the
resulting rich ensemble is *eclectic*.

Eclectic though the architecture may be, the resulting rich inventory of
buildings is not an incoherent babble. There is instead a wonderful harmony or,
to repeat the phrase, a tumultuous amity. No one building is a cross-the-ocean-
to-see edifice, even the oldest and most venerated building on campus, University
Hall. Yet weave together the various threads, as time has done, and the outcome,

John Nicholas Brown Gate, detail

like the students themselves, is a magical urban tapestry that evokes a special sense of place. For those in search of a textbook ensemble of American architecture, from colonial times to the present, no place is richer than College Hill.

Like a musical overture, this introductory stroll around the neighborhood of Brown's front campus introduces themes that emerge and recur throughout this guide—restoration and adaptive use, the relationship between ideas and their physical expression, and architectural eclecticism and design standardization or branding, as well as shifting attitudes toward the College Hill neighborhood and the city of Providence. It sets up a continuing conversation across generations. It introduces key elements of place making: green spaces, permeability, walkability, scale, texture, and the impact of site. If there is time for only one Walk, this is the one to take.

The physical energy required by this initial exploration of the campus speaks in perhaps the most memorable way of what defines Brown—the Hill. It is the experience of encountering buildings at different elevations and the views that often open up as you turn a corner that give Brown a special sense of place. Take advantage of the fact that the First Baptist Meeting House at the foot of College Hill is the halfway point of this initial Walk. Drop into one of the nearby coffee shops or restaurants on North Main before tackling the steep rise of Waterman Street.

Maddock Alumni Center

1   Maddock Alumni Center

1830; modification, Stone, Carpenter & Willson, 1882; restoration, Irving B. Hayes and Associates in collaboration with Thomas Hagerman, 1974

Maddock Alumni Center and its immediate neighbor, Nicholson House, tell an intriguing tale of two brothers, William and Francis Goddard. Together they also document a major shift in nineteenth-century residential design as well as a surprising ambivalence about the impact of the Industrial Revolution.

    The house on the southwest corner of Brown and George Streets reveals itself in the manner of Russian nesting dolls—a building within a building within

another building. The history of the shaping of Maddock Alumni Center also illustrates a fundamental difference between early and late nineteenth-century architecture, a difference we will encounter again and again in this guide. In essence, residential design in the eighteenth century and the first decades of the nineteenth was designed from the outside in: the exterior shape of the building dictated how the rooms were arranged inside. The change initiated by the Victorian builders, a change that influences architecture to this day, is that a building tends to be designed from the inside out. That is, the exterior reflects how people use the space inside; function helps drive form. But this is getting ahead of our story.

What in 1973 became the Maddock Alumni Center began life in 1830 as a late example of a Federal-style residence, its entrance directly abutting the George Street sidewalk with a view of what then was an open field. Built for Brown professor William Giles Goddard (Class of 1812) and his wife, Charlotte, the house was a typical period exercise in symmetry— what was to the left of the front door was echoed at the right, from the windows to opposing fireplaces on the end walls of the front rooms. The footprint of the building was likewise symmetrical—box-like. Also characteristic of Federal architecture, the intricate ornament of garlands and beading around the fan light and the delicate classical columns of the front entrance would have been inspired by recent archaeological digs at Pompeii. The past tense is used because the house underwent a radical transformation inside and out that altered its appearance and size; the north-facing George Street entrance is gone. In its place is a fifth bay that duplicates the window pattern on either side.

After the death of his parents, the Goddards' son William (Class of 1846 and later Brown's chancellor) hired the city's most distinguished architecture firm,

Stone, Carpenter & Willson (whose work will be encountered on almost every Walk), to rework the house, transforming the cube shape of the original into an L, whose long side runs south. Access was no longer gained by the Federal front door that faced George Street, but through today's grander one-story Brown Street entry porch recessed a few steps behind the original house. The new configuration, with its fluted Roman Doric columns, clearly anticipated an increase of visitors and a much more active social life commensurate with the owner's position as the University's chancellor. Although William Goddard's more imposing residence was doubled in size, a second glance is needed to distinguish the old from the new—at least on the exterior. The architects' radical surgery was skillfully done, even using the same red brick to make a seamless connection between old and new.

Across the threshold of the new entrance, we come upon a triumph of High Victorian design with its characteristic emphasis on opulence, texture, and comfort. Every surface is a canvas for ornament and decoration, with hardly a space for the eye to rest. Before moving past the reception desk, look up. In modern homes the ceiling is typically a solid neutral color. Not here. The foyer boasts a painted ceiling that at some point in the twentieth century had been painted over. Today the intricate detailing shines anew, having been re-created in 2004 based on physical analysis of the surface. Furnishings reflect two centuries of refined taste, including a late eighteenth- or early nineteenth-century English mahogany tall-case clock and a portrait, painted c. 1795, of the Reverend William Rogers, Brown's first graduate (Class of 1769). To the right of the entrance hall, a three-story Neo-Colonial staircase is illuminated at the first and second landings by stained-glass windows designed by a contemporary of Tiffany, John LaFarge (1835–1910), the artist responsible for the splendid windows of Boston's Trinity Church.

Linger at this staircase for a moment. The characteristic Federal plan featured a center hall and stairs from which rooms were laid out symmetrically on either side. Here and at Nicholson House next door, the architects removed the original staircase and inserted an entirely new system of circulation. Rather than subdividing the interior space into equal parts, the U-shaped staircase that rises to the third floor now functions in the manner of a spine around which the rooms are arranged. More than a space to pass through, the staircase and the hall leading to it function almost like another room. This is typical of Victorian homes built for the wealthy.

The elegant Queen Anne library (the Heritage Room) and dining room (the 1933 Room) on the south side are the crown jewels of a house not lacking in splendor. Note the fine wood paneling, especially the shell motif, which frequently appears in the furniture and decorative objects produced in "the Ocean State." With so much to appeal to the eye, it is a challenge to focus on any one element; however, by all means linger over the tiles that decorate the fireplaces throughout the house. Each carries its own design motif, each one more stunning than the next. These are the trophies of owners who have decisively abandoned the modest aesthetic of the founding Baptist colonists. Plain is elbowed aside by fancy—but all in the best of taste.

Maddock Alumni Center's 1933 Room   *Entrance Hall*

The enlarged and reoriented house that emerged is a testament to the position of Providence in the years after the Civil War as one of the wealthiest cities in the nation and a center of manufacturing and craftsmanship. The rich palette of materials (wallpaper designed to imitate embossed leather, the eighteen ceiling panels composed of four different designs, the mahogany doors with nickel-plated knobs) was for the first time easily obtainable and, relatively speaking, affordable for a rising middle class. The décor celebrates the abundance of manufactured goods made possible by the Industrial Revolution, yet at the same time reacts against it by celebrating craftsmanship and the handmade. This creative tension between manufactured and handmade goods has continued to tug at artists down to the present day.

The Victorian remodeling also reflects the technological advances reshaping America's architecture. Plumbing is only the most obvious. Consider the impact made by advances in illumination: the introduction first of gas, then electric lighting allowed rooms to be deeper and used more intensely at night. An argument can be made that wiring, plumbing, and central heating as much as aesthetic theory shaped nineteenth-century architecture.

However, the design evolution of the Maddock Alumni Center did not stop here. The Goddards' only daughter, Hope, and her husband, New York banker and accomplished yachtsman C. Oliver Iselin, put their far-different stamp on the first-floor rooms of the original, north side of the house. The path they chose did not entail major structural modifications. Instead, they turned to the emerging

The Goldberger Room

practitioners of interior design, a profession that was in large measure a response to the abundance of decorative materials made possible by the Industrial Revolution. What we see today in the Brian and Lanpher Rooms (named after the principal donors who underwrote the restoration of these spaces) is an aesthetic championed by the writer Edith Wharton and her friend, the leading designer of the day, Ogden Codman. Along with the rest of the nation, Hope Goddard and her husband succumbed to the extraordinary success of Chicago's 1893 Columbian Exposition, a showcase for Beaux-Arts planning and ornament. The aesthetic narrative set in motion by the Chicago Exposition had its roots in the transformation of Paris under Napoleon III, the city where America's most influential late nineteenth- and early twentieth-century architects received their education at the École des Beaux-Arts. From the private homes of the wealthy to the grand public buildings being constructed across the nation, Beaux-Arts architecture, with its reinterpretation of Greek and Roman forms, became the hallmark of what has since been called the American Renaissance.

Whereas the rooms on the south side of Maddock Alumni Center shout color and texture, Brian and Lanpher speak a more chaste language: bold colors relax into pastels; giddy aestheticism defers to the quiet correctness of spaces for intimate teas. Of particular interest are the fireplaces in both rooms (marble in Lanpher, wood with matching marbleized faux finish in Brian). Both are surviving pieces of the original Federal house, a tribute to New England thriftiness.

Even at that, the house had yet another act to play—the rise of the historic preservation movement. In 1940, Mrs. Iselin deeded the house to Brown in memory of her father. The University acquired the property in 1966. Four years later, Mrs. Iselin died at the age of 102. Working with the Providence architecture firm Irving B. Haynes and Associates and Newport interior designer Thomas Hagerman (under the leadership of Robert Reichley, the then–vice president for alumni affairs and external relations),

Center Stairway and LaFarge window

the University began a program of renovation and scientific restoration that continues to this day. In 1974 Brown's new alumni center was dedicated in honor of Paul L. Maddock (Class of 1933). Each May alumni gather here to form the Commencement Procession that winds its way through the Van Wickle Gates down to the First Baptist Meeting House at the foot of College Hill. The brick walkway, which begins at the front door and leads into the pleasantly landscaped garden at the south side of the house, is paved with individual bricks donated to honor Brown alumni, parents, and friends. Take note of the jolly 5-foot-plus bear sculpture tucked in the southeast corner of the garden. Of the numerous depictions of the University's mascot, this is by far the oddest, for the very good reason that the sculpture does not represent a real bear, but rather, a student wearing a bear costume (peer into the mouth). The piece was sculpted by President Howard Swearer's son, Nicholas, and was awarded to the University by the Class of 1949.

The Goddard family's contribution to the architectural legacy of Brown continues around the corner on George Street, where William's brother Francis made his own, quite different mark with the same architecture firm.

2 Nicholson House (Francis Goddard House)
Stone, Carpenter & Willson, 1878

Before her death in 1881, Charlotte Ives Goddard gave her house, which then faced George Street, to her son William, and the frame house next door, also facing George Street, to her son Francis (Class of 1854). Whereas William completely reworked his inheritance, Francis tore his down. Into a tight lot deeper than it was wide, Stone, Carpenter & Willson shoehorned one of the most noteworthy houses on College Hill, a multigabled polychromatic textured confection of stone, pressed brick, slate, and wood. Unlike his brother's house with its exterior Neo-Colonial allusions, Francis Goddard's house was built for him in a "modern" style that communicated his position as a successful, forward-looking patron of the arts and frequent contributor of essays to the *Providence Journal*. His position as something of an aesthete ensured his house would be high style, dramatic, and perhaps not a little flamboyant. Francis lost naming rights when the house was sold after his sudden death of heart disease to the president of Nicholson File, Samuel Nicholson, and his wife, who lived there in the first half of the twentieth century.

Nicholson is a textbook case of the profound impact of the theories of the English art critic and social thinker John Ruskin (1819–1900). Ruskin's essays on architecture celebrated Gothic style (individual and asymmetrically expressive) over geometrically four-square classicism, which he dismissed as forced and repressive. Whatever emotions Victorians might have repressed in their public lives, they gave full rein to passion in their architecture—and landscape design. Little dampened their enthusiasm for sensual detailing, right down to finely molded monumental chimneys and the exuberant, exotic vegetation that rioted in urban parks. Keep this rebellion against classicism in mind when we move on to examples on the Brown

Nicholson House

campus of mid-twentieth century Modern, a style that swept almost everything before it. For just as Ruskin preached a gospel of exuberance in the face of architecture that he saw as forced and repressive, many Modernists returned to what they construed as the more pure and honest geometry of classical straight lines.

If the firm's work for William Goddard next door might be called an example of adaptive use, Nicholson House is a complete embrace of a modern sensibility, at least as the term would have been understood in the years after the Civil War. As they were to do at Maddock, the architects reoriented the new house away from George Street. The front door now faces west toward the city. Note how the foundation is angled slightly away from the upper stories. This is what you would expect of a load-bearing wall; it gives the impression the full weight of the house has been absorbed by its base. The gentle slope also serves a practical purpose by directing rainwater and snow melt away from the basement. A short flight of stairs empties onto a rather grand covered stone arched porch, where guests could pause, sheltered from the elements, before being announced and admitted into the house.

Occupied since 1964 by the offices of Brown's Public Affairs and University Relations, the interior of Nicholson has not been restored like the Maddock Alumni Center. However, vestiges of what no doubt was a splendid interior do remain. The most prominent is the massive skylighted staircase, which like in Maddock Alumni Center is at the center of the house, anchored at the first-floor landing by an extraordinarily chunky newel post. Its massiveness feels like a strong spine, keeping the building upright. This feature serves more than a metaphoric purpose: the skylight illuminates the central circulation path that connects the three and a half stories, flooding the interior with daylight. Also the central staircase promotes a stack effect: as warm air rises toward the skylight, cooler, fresher air is pulled from the lower stories, especially the basement, into the house.

The number of windows should banish the notion that Victorian architecture was constructed to be spooky and dark. That illusion was fostered by years of neglect, when architectural treasures from the period were allowed to become dirty and dulled by soot. Conscious of the value of the gem it has inherited, Brown has devoted resources to repair and clean Nicholson. At least the exterior reflects the dazzling impression Francis Goddard intended when he built his new home.

Given that the homes of William and Francis Goddard literally turn their backs on one another, does the reorientation betray a family feud? A more likely explanation is that by rotating the entrance of each house by 45 degrees, the architects gained for their clients a more gracious, spacious, better lit entrance, and, not incidentally, a measure of protection from the snow and ice of the city's long winters. William's home captured the light of the rising sun, while Francis's, the light of the sun as it set. Skilled at adopting the latest technological advances in an era of rapid change, as well as adapting the various period styles for the particular tastes of its Victorian clients, the Providence-based architecture firm was for approximately a half century a popular choice for private clients and for Brown University itself.

Shortly after the house of Francis Goddard was built, High Victorian Gothic houses fell out of fashion, whereas the Neo-Colonial stirrings of the Maddock Alumni Center would grow into a flood and for many years prove to be the course of much of the architecture built on College Hill.

Before moving on to the next stop of this Walk, step into the small shaded seating area just off Brown Street between Maddock Alumni Center and Nicholson. This is the Brown Alumni Association's Alumni Garden. The attractively landscaped space (with wireless access) is one of the many green outdoor "rooms" scattered throughout Brown's bustling urban campus. Far from being random, leftover spaces, they are carefully and deliberately integrated into how students and faculty experience the University, offering opportunities for reflection and quiet conversations. More than a collection of individual buildings, a campus, like that of Brown, is revealed as an interconnected landscape.

3   Horace Mann House

Richard Upjohn, 1854; renovation, Finegold Alexander + Associates

The next building on this first Walk occupies a middle distance between the chaste lines of Federal architecture and the flamboyant, over-the-top Victorian exuberance of Nicholson. Horace Mann House is relatively restrained. Yet the rounded windows with their larger panes of glass—made possible by midcentury innovations that made plate glass commercially available and affordable—the proliferation of gables on every side, and the heavy brackets underneath the wide eaves are signs we have moved away from the severe geometry of Roman and Greek models to a more picturesque style that takes its cue from the Renaissance architecture of northern Italy. Not quite classical and not really Victorian, what has since become known as "Italianate" style straddles the middle distance between the two.

The brick double house honors a Brown alumnus (and 1819 class valedictorian) who was a pioneer in advancing the idea of universal public education, although he never lived here. A few minutes in front of this tall, rather severe big barn of a building tell us it was built less for the pleasure of the occupants than the profit of the owner. Double houses, which began to appear in Providence in the first decades of the nineteenth century, were typically built as investments, that is, for the rent they would bring. Hence, Horace Mann House eschews ornament for a sensible and

Horace Mann House

maintenance-free straightforward-ness. That said, since a house in a fashionable College Hill neighborhood would attract an affluent tenant, the owner, Seth Adams, hired one of the period's most eminent architects, Richard Upjohn (1802–1878), the designer of St. Stephen's Church a few blocks east on George Street and Manhattan's Trinity Church. The English-born architect, whose family immigrated to the United States in 1829, was instrumental in cultivating a taste for Italianate and Gothic Revival styles on these shores.

Look carefully at how exquisitely subtly the architect handled the long east and west walls. In lesser hands, these would be neglected because they are, in a sense, purely utilitarian. All the energy and creativity would be devoted to the front, rather like the application of lipstick, rouge, and eyeliner to highlight the face. But Upjohn understood that good architecture is more than a pretty face. For one thing, the brick on the sides is of the same quality as the front facing George Street. How he handled the windows deserves special attention: they are not all of the same shape, but like the notes on a musical staff change and create a pleasing rhythm. The half round window in the gable (and the gable itself) is architecture's equivalent of a musical pause or rest. All the windows are slightly recessed, allowing the play of light and shadow that further enlivens the surface of what is a lot of brick. The horizontal belt courses are not only decorative and functional (they deflect rainwater), they indicate where the ceiling joists are that tie the walls together. In studying the craft of what makes a good building, look at what the architect did behind the building's back. This same attention to what might be called design in the round will be evident when we come to the University's oldest structures at the crest of College Hill. It is why they retained their power when they became the western edge of the College Green: the architects took as much care in shaping the back of the building as they did the front.

Brown purchased the property in 1938 to house students displaced by the renovation and reconstruction of University Hall. Given its location at the corner of Brown and Magee Streets, the facility was named Megee House, until it was renamed again in 1940 for Horace Mann, the "father of American public education." The house held the distinction of being the first coed dorm in the Ivy League, a feat enabled by the separate entrances and the wall that Pyramus and Thisbe–like divided the house, ostensibly keeping the men on one side and the women on the other. Today the students are gone and the house serves as the University's headquarters for its ever-increasing Graduate School programs.

4   Howard R. Swearer Center for Public Service
Clarke & Howe, 1914

By the opening years of the twentieth century, there was not much empty land left on College Hill. It was not uncommon, therefore, to tear down older houses and replace them with new structures that were felt to better serve the needs and often the social standing of a modern family. Although arguments for keeping older buildings were beginning to be made in the opening years of the twentieth century, historic preservation as we know it was not yet a local or national passion. Up the street, Francis Goddard had razed an older building for what today is Nicholson House. Likewise, the prominent Providence physician who commissioned this house had his architects tear down a dwelling that had been constructed in the years just before the Civil War. In both cases, the new houses were larger than the ones they replaced.

    The Providence firm of Clarke & Howe, which flourished in the first three decades of the twentieth century, designed a number of significant buildings, many in the downtown. However, their work at Brown was minimal, with the important exception of Marvel Gymnasium on Elmgrove Avenue (discussed in Walk Eight), which was demolished in 2002. Like the gym—and much of Clarke & Howe's residential work—this house is a skillful, by-the-book exercise in the Colonial Revival style. Much preferred by the professional class of doctors, lawyers, and bankers, Colonial and its first cousin Federal Revival architecture represented a sober reining in of the fanciful inventiveness of Queen Anne architecture as seen a few decades earlier in Nicholson House or, across George Street, at Wilbour Hall. The conservative change in taste, which was national in scope, was inspired by the first official World's Fair held in America, the 1876 Centennial Exposition in Philadelphia. Conceived in

part as an event to bring the nation together after the ravages of the Civil War, the Centennial Exposition marked America's coming out party on a global stage. It inspired a growing appreciation and celebration of the nation's shared history, including the design legacy of the eighteenth and early nineteenth centuries, a legacy that included architecture and furniture. The ground was seeded for early American styles, in everything from teacups to the restaurant chain Howard Johnson's signature design. A more lasting consequence was the first stirrings of what would become the historic preservation movement.

Howard R. Swearer Center for Public Service

The three-story clapboard house built for Dr. James Davenport exhibits all the characteristics of Colonial Revival residential design: the balance and symmetry of the windows, the double set of stone steps leading to the small entry portico or porch centered at the front, the use of classical ornament (the matched pair of Tuscan columns that support the roof of the portico), the anachronistic but historically correct multipaned windows, and the gambrel roof. On a more practical note, Colonial Revival architecture, with its emphasis on straight lines, was easier to construct than the complex detailing of high Queen Anne style. Also the upkeep was much less expensive, which suited the relatively modest means of the owner.

After Davenport's death, Brown acquired the property and in 1987 repurposed the house as the Center for Public Service. Renamed in 1991 as the Howard R. Swearer Center for Public Service, the center honors the memory of the University's fifteenth president (1977–88), who brought new recognition to Brown in the fields of international relations and public service.

One additional footnote about the previous owner: Upon his death, Davenport endowed his collection of medical books to Brown. Included in the eclectic collection are books by physician authors in the fields of history, biography, travel narratives, and fiction, as well as many other works, including *The Adventures of Sherlock Holmes* (1892). The collection is one of the treasures of the John Hay Library.

5   Wilbour Hall
Stone, Carpenter & Willson, 1888

Built for a wealthy Providence merchant, what at the time was called the Dorrance Mansion was bought by the Delta Phi fraternity in 1920. For nearly three decades it remained the chapter house until it was purchased and remodeled by Brown in 1949 to house the University's Department of Egyptology.

Rechristened to honor the achievement and generosity of Charles Edwin Wilbour (Class of 1854), Wilbour Hall is yet another fashionable residence by one of the city's most prolific and highly regarded late Victorian architecture firms. Wilbour himself was no less flamboyant than the architecture of this striking house, which anchors the south end of Prospect Street. Among other accomplishments in a colorful career (including employment by New York's notorious Boss Tweed), Wilbour became a lifelong student of all matters Egyptian once he and his family fled to Paris to escape the law. Upon her death in 1947, Wilbour's daughter left money to Brown to start a department and endow a chair in Egyptology, which today remains the only university department in North America devoted exclusively to the study of ancient Egypt.

Wilbour Hall appears to be clutching its site, crowded by the pale modernist structure next door. Indeed, it came within a hair's breadth of being pushed off the block. Threatened by demolition in 1960 to make way for Brown's new library, Wilbour Hall escaped the wrecking ball thanks to a stroke

Wilbour Hall

of underhanded genius, as the following description lifted intact from Martha
Mitchell's *Encyclopedia Brunoniana* will make clear:

> The original plans for the Rockefeller Library [immediately next door] included the
> razing of Wilbour Hall, but the plans were changed to accommodate Professor Otto
> Neugebauer, whose office was in the building and who had been quoted as saying, if
> asked to move his books once more, he would move them to Princeton. Wilbour Hall was
> saved, and it was later revealed that Neugebauer's statement was only a well-placed
> rumor instigated by another resident of the building, Egyptologist Richard Parker.[3]

The asymmetrical two-and-a-half-story house of many gables and dormers
is a fanciful (which is redundant) example of a late Victorian style, Queen Anne. The
half-timbered two-story bay above the front door is a dead giveaway, as is the paneled and tiled recessed vestibule, a thoughtful gesture to keep guests and visitors
dry as they awaited entry to the house. Pay particular attention to the brickwork.
The vertical plane of the facade is broken and endlessly varied by the decorative
way the brick is used. It is the masonry equivalent of Bach improvising on a theme.
The same care extends to the chimneys on the southwest and northwest corners at
the rear of the house, best seen from an upper-story east-facing window of the John
D. Rockefeller Jr. Library. Like so much Queen Anne architecture, the craftsmanship
is a reaction to the impersonal machine-age aesthetic of the Industrial Revolution.
To quote from a lecture given in 1884 by the Victorian designer William Morris
(1834–1896): "It is the allowing of machines to be our masters, and not our servants,

that so injures the beauty of life nowadays." Here, the bricklayer's deft handling of his mass-produced material suggests the mastery of an artist.

Do not cross Prospect Street without looking at the sundial on the southeast corner of the building. This is one of those many extra pleasures from an era of architecture that reveled in such moments of delight. Unfortunately, little of that ethos remains in an interior that has been repurposed for offices. That said, the architecture of Wilbour Hall rewards a second glance.

6   Van Wickle Gates and Fence
Hoppin & Ely with Hoppin & Koen, 1901

> The object of a fence is not to shut out our friends, but to protect them and ourselves whenever we together celebrate any of the festivals of the academic year.[4]
> — University President William Herbert Perry Faunce

Built with the bequest of Augustus Stout Van Wickle (Class of 1876), the marvelously crafted iron gates are, together with University Hall, the iconic image of Brown. However, like much of what has been built over the years, even what appears uniquely "of Brown" sometimes turns out to have roots within the entire Ivy League. Just as the oldest building on campus, University Hall, was modeled after Princeton's Nassau Hall, and just as the row of historic buildings in which University Hall is the central element owes much to the precedent of Yale's Old Brick Row, Hoppin & Ely were inspired by the example of Charles McKim of the New York firm McKim, Mead & White, who designed Harvard's Johnston Gate and fence (1889).

The handsome cast-iron fence that radiates out from each side of the Van Wickle Gates and surrounds approximately half of Brown's original eight-acre campus was erected two years after the gates themselves were built. Each section is 21 feet long, separated by brick and stone piers, and bears the year of the class that contributed to defraying its cost. The single exception is the 1786 section, given in honor of the class of Nicholas Brown. The gates in the fence are also gifts to the University in memory of various Brown luminaries, and in one instance, a fraternity—Psi Upsilon—to commemorate its centennial.

Front of the Van Wickle Gates

Some brief comments about the iconography of the Van Wickle Gates. The meaning of the stone figures depicting an hourglass, a lamp upon a book, and a globe remind the keen observer that the time to prepare to lead a life of "usefulness and reputation," is brief and must be seized.[5] As for the owl, the keen-eyed bird is the winged companion of Athena, goddess of wisdom, although

The Van Wickle Gates, detail

The Van Wickle Gates, Athena's owl

the nocturnal creature could just as well be the student's mascot for all-nighters. The stone tablet at the right of the entrance is inscribed with a quotation from Cicero that echoes the message of the images carved in stone: "These studies fortify one's youth, delight one's old age; amid success they are an ornament, in failure they are a refuge and comfort."

The architects may have looked to Harvard for inspiration, but the students at Brown developed a rich store of traditions that transformed the Van Wickle Gates into something uniquely their own. Although the side gates are left open, the center gates remain closed all year except for two special occasions: inward in the fall to admit freshmen to the campus and outward on Commencement Day to allow a procession of graduates and faculty to pass through and down College Street to the First Baptist Meeting House—and from there to lead lives of "usefulness and reputation" in the greater world. Legend has it those students who walk through the

Commencement Procession through the Van Wickle Gates

Section of the campus fence commemorating the Class of 1812

center gates more than twice before Commencement will not graduate. The legend is noisily flaunted every year when the University's band leads the Commencement Procession through the Gates and down College Street, although many turn and walk backward through the Gates.

Two small biographical footnotes before crossing the street to the John Hay Library. The "Ely" of Hoppin & Ely, architects of the gates, was Edward Francis Ely, the son of a prominent Providence physician, J. W. C. Ely, who lived nearby in the house at the corner of Prospect and Waterman Streets, within sight of the Gates his son would design. Ely's partner, Howard Hoppin, was the nephew of Providence artist Thomas Hoppin, whose home at the corner of Benefit and John Streets is discussed at the end of Walk Seven.

7   John Hay Library
Shepley, Rutan & Coolidge, 1910; addition, Shepley, Bulfinch & Abbott, 1939; restoration, Shepley Bulfinch Richardson & Abbott, 1981; restoration of main reading room, Selldorf Architects, 2014

According to the Roman historian Suetonius (*The Twelve Caesars*), the emperor Augustus on his deathbed bragged that he "found Rome clothed in brick, and left it clad in marble." The quotation is apt for the building that took shape at the southwest corner of Prospect and College Streets. In choosing a firm to design what was arguably one of the most important buildings on College Hill—certainly from the perspective of the Corporation's goal to fashion a great twentieth-century university—Brown aimed high. The choice was the successor firm to the great Henry Hobson Richardson (1838–1886), the architect of Boston's extraordinary Trinity Church. And despite President Faunce's preference for the republican honesty of Colonial brick (see Walk Three), in this instance only an Augustan marble edifice would do.

Named for the Brown alumnus (Class of 1858) who became Abraham Lincoln's personal secretary and then U.S. secretary of state for Presidents William McKinley and Theodore Roosevelt, the library today houses most of the University's rare books, manuscripts, special collections, and archives. The lead gift of $150,000 was made by Andrew Carnegie, an unusual gesture for a philanthropist who otherwise endowed public libraries. This exceptional gift was a mark of Carnegie's deep friendship with and admiration for one of the most remarkable men in

John Hay Library

American history. The bust of John Hay in the lobby, his nose rubbed golden by generations of students seeking good luck at exam time, was one of the last works of famed American sculptor Augustus Saint-Gaudens (1848–1907).

In the run-up to the construction of the library, President Faunce corresponded with the preeminent landscape architect of the day, Frederick Law Olmsted Jr. asking, "Where should the new library be built?" This was not an academic question, since Brown was deep into the process of transforming itself from a liberal arts college into a great research university. More than with any other building, the size of a library's collection and the impression of its physical plant advertised an institution's commitment to the central purpose of the academy— knowledge and education. It was a principle first enunciated on these shores by Thomas Jefferson, whose design for the University of Virginia placed the Rotunda, the library, at the center of his great master plan.

Olmsted vigorously advised against the corner of Prospect and College Streets. Of the various sites being considered, this, in his opinion, was the least desirable. Beaux-Arts notions of sound urban planning would have dictated the new library be the focal point of a vista. This was Jefferson's approach in Charlottesville. As built, the Hay Library terminates nothing. As you walk up College Street, the library is almost invisible. In addition, the relatively tight lot left little room for the library to step back from the street. Instead, the building is set on a podium, or pedestal, that crowds the sidewalk. This raises another issue.

Late nineteenth-century view of College Hill

Earlier photographs looking up College Hill before the library was built show private residences on either side of College Street. These stepped back from the lot line, framing a pleasing vista at the top of the Hill that included Manning Hall on one side, Slater on the other, and University Hall in the middle. Think of the effect as akin to the drawing back of curtains into opposing wings to reveal a stage set or performance. The library draws the curtains tighter so only University Hall remains. The view is still dramatic; nevertheless something has been lost. One thing more that may have prompted Olmsted's displeasure: unlike University Hall, the John Hay Library turns its back on the city. To grasp the full measure of the building, it has to be seen not from the city, but from the steps of University Hall.

To be fair, there is logic to the site chosen by President Faunce. A powerful dialogue was initiated between the library and University Hall, Brown's newest and oldest buildings—the original small room that housed the College's first collection of books acknowledging the monumental state-of-the-art repository of tens of thousands of titles. The John Hay Library charts the vast distance the University and the nation had come from being a provincial echo of the mother country to a world power—brick to marble, college to university.

The architects have continued the tradition of the library as a place set apart. Gaining entrance requires climbing a set of paired stairs that twist one way, then the next, separating those making the journey from the dust and noise of the workaday world. The psychological distance from here to there is underscored by the overscaled doors. These must be negotiated before gaining entry into the hushed, somewhat clubby sanctuary where the treasures of a literate civilization are kept. What was new and welcome were the eight floors of open stacks. This allowed free access to the library's holdings—but only for students and faculty.

*Archival photograph of the John Hay
Reading Room*

Also new was the extravagance. The rich surface detail of high-style English Renaissance architecture, with its reference to classical forms, is imported *in toto* by the architects. This is seen most conspicuously, of course, at the front, which in mass and detail bears a striking resemblance to Easton Neston, an English country house designed by Nicholas Hawksmoor (c. 1661–1736). Note the ornate cartouche atop the great arched window above the entrance, complete with a carved scallop shell (a recurring Rhode Island "Ocean State" theme) and oil lamp—the light of knowledge cutting through the darkness of ignorance. All this would be fussy, except the scale is so monumental. The elements have room to breathe. The rusticated podium on which the building stands is meant to exaggerate the monumental nature of the entire composition. The contrast between the plain, no-nonsense, Baptist aesthetic that shaped University Hall and that which shaped the Hay Library could not be greater.

When the library opened, one of its most outstanding features was a 4,400-square-foot, two-story-high reading room that ran the full length of the south side of the building. Such grand reading rooms are yet another characteristic of Beaux-Arts architecture. These rooms were then, and remain today, the glory of the great public and institutional libraries built during that period. They occupied the same spiritual space as the naves of the great medieval cathedrals, only here the worship is strictly secular. Ironically, the Hay's reading room eventually fell victim to the explosion of knowledge it was built to celebrate: to meet the ever-growing need for administrative and shelf space, the room was divided into three sections in 1939. Grandeur was sacrificed to functionality.

The reading room is slated to be fully restored to its original undivided splendor by Selldorf Architects. Of course, restoration will include a complete update of the technical infrastructure in keeping with an age in which information is digital. Plans also include exhibition space in the center of the room to display the Hay's many special collections, including such treasures as the internationally renowned North American History and Literary collections, which feature the world's largest repository of American poetry and plays. The restoration will have brought back to life one of collegiate America's great reading rooms.

As impressive as the library was to its contemporaries and remains so today, even before the first shovel broke ground, President Faunce made what turned out to be an accurate prediction: no facility would be adequate beyond a single generation. Extensions and enlargements were inevitable. This is the background for the next stop, just across the street.

8 John D. Rockefeller Jr. Library
Warner, Burns, Toan & Lunde, 1964; interior renovation,
Shepley Bulfinch Richardson & Abbott, 2004

Some pleasures are best experienced by night. This might describe the visual appeal of a building students call "the Rock." Named for Brown alumnus and principal donor John D. Rockefeller Jr. (Class of 1897), the library has twice the space of the John Hay and can hold a million volumes on its seven floors.

The building we see today is the outcome of a number of false starts. At one point the University entertained the thought of a massive complex that included a lecture hall and an arts center mediated by that favorite '60s design gesture—a windswept open plaza. Entry to the plaza would be gained through the Van Wickle Gates, which would have been removed from their present location and erected down the Hill to a site closer to Benefit Street. The startling effect of this transplant can only be imagined. Also, the bundling of the arts suggests another '60s preoccupation—the shopping center. Think Lincoln Center and the Kennedy Center in New York and Washington, respectively.

The far more modest building that stands on the southwest corner of Prospect and College Streets is described thus by the man who designed it:

> We sought to match the modest monumentality of the John Hay Library, by developing a series of paired piers on the building perimeter, which incorporates air-conditioning risers with structural columns. The cantilevering of the main floor, necessitated by the need for greater area, provides a strong horizontal band, which hovers above the undulating terrain of College Hill.[6]

The John D. Rockefeller Jr. Library flaunts the latest building technology and construction, especially the use of prefabricated materials. It is a building whose standardized precast elements have been wheeled in on a flatbed truck. Victorian and Beaux-Arts architects also made liberal use of the abundance turned out by the factories and foundries of the industrial age, many of which were based in Rhode Island. But they handled the pieces in such a way as to give the illusion of being built on site by hand. The handcrafted look of the Hay or Wilbour Hall next door was a conscious reaction to the machine aesthetic of mass-produced products often derided as inferior or cheap. As inheritors of the twentieth-century International Style, which celebrated the machine, the architects of Rockefeller Library had no such reservations.

Like with most large institutional buildings built after the turn of the twentieth century, what we see at the Rock is veneer. The walls do not hold up the building; the function of the precast concrete panels that make up the exterior is largely reduced to keeping out wind and rain. As an obviously prefabricated composition hung on the cast-in-place piers, the Rock is, for better or worse, very much of its time. If the concrete does not age well (and it seldom does), the panels can simply be pulled

John D. Rockefeller Jr. Library

off. This suggests that as with a fashion runway model, at some point the costume the Rock is wearing could be pulled off for a newer, more contemporary dress, not unlike what has been happening across the country to many post–World War II buildings. This raises the issue of the legacy of midcentury modern structures and what should be preserved. After all, only a generation or two separates us from the mass destruction of Victorian architecture, which at the time was unappreciated and actively reviled.

Although the John Hay Library has a greater street presence, perhaps the Rock can claim to be the more sensitive urban design. Instead of fighting or ignoring the Hill, the Rock relaxes more easily into the slope. Also unlike with its neighbor, students working in Rockefeller Library have a more panoramic view of downtown Providence, if they put their noses up to the continuous bands of tall, narrow windows. The greater transparency of the Rock over its neighbor across the street is a sign of the changing attitude toward libraries. The Rock moves away from the library as a fixed repository of information toward a new outgoing role as connector and disseminator. It is a marker of the dawning information age in which transparency and a blurring of boundaries become a cultural and an aesthetic ideal. By allowing patrons and pedestrians alike to see into and through the building, the architects not only throw open the library to light, they reject the idea of a library as a mark of privilege and a guardian of knowledge. At night, this difference is especially apparent: the Hay is dark and cloistered, while the Rock is a bright lantern inviting entry.

A short walk down College Street brings us to the work of one of twentieth-century architecture's best known (some might say notorious) architects.

Albert and Vera List Art Building

9   Albert and Vera List Art Building
Philip Johnson, 1971; interior design, Samuel Glaser

After one of the last gasps of Colonial Revival architecture appeared on the Brown campus (Hunter Laboratory of Psychology [1958], Walk Five), a new wind began to blow. It coincided with the growing influence of yet another member of the Brown family, John Nicholas Brown Jr. (1900–1979). His nearly five-decade-long association with the University included service as secretary of the Corporation (1963–71) and several seasons as chairman of the University's Planning and Building Committee. His affection for contemporary architecture is evidenced by his commissioning one of the most significant twentieth-century Modernists, Richard Neutra (1892–1970), to design a summer house, Windshield, on Fisher's Island, New York (1938). Given his position (and his wealth), it was perhaps inevitable that with the support of the Corporation, the new chairman of the University's Planning Committee would encourage Brown along a different path. That path led, among other places, to Philip Johnson (1906–2005), an architect who over a long and productive career shed styles as often as snakes shed skins.

    Commentaries about List point out its "having-it-both-ways" qualities: broadcasting an aggressively modernist message, yet conveying the message with a distinctly classical accent. Johnson's evolution from the stripped-down style of midcentury modernism to increasing experimentation with classical forms may be traced to 1952 after a period of study and reflection at the American Academy in Rome. Frequent visits to Hadrian's Villa and Trajan's Market awakened a keen interest in Roman walls, arches, and vaults, elements that were increasingly incorporated into his work. Indeed, when seen from the bottom of College Hill,

List comes across as a playful take on a Greek temple perched high above the city, a citadel in which (depending on one's response) the Muses are either celebrated or incarcerated.

Johnson's own feelings were mixed. So many alterations were made to the interior plan by faculty and administrators that he took his name off the project, which forced Brown to call on another architect, who was caught in the unenviable position of negotiating a middle course between the conflicting demands of a strong-willed architect and equally determined clients. Johnson ultimately relented, but this leaves today's visitor with the challenge of trying to figure out what of the interior expresses Johnson's design intent and what does not, because the layout of the interior is a mixed bag.

The cheek-by-jowl proximity of List to the Hay Library is an opportunity to study what is unique or different about Johnson's use of classical motifs. Indeed, the architect seems to invite the comparison. Consider, for example, the way one enters the front door of both buildings. At the Hay, the elevated entrance is clearly the center and focus of the ensemble. It is a typical Beaux-Arts strategy. Constrained by the relative narrowness of the site, there are no flights of stairs into List; instead, the recessed entrance is really at the side at street level, approached by making a 90-degree turn from College Street into a long, covered four-story colonnade. The space underneath can feel unwelcoming and not a little off-putting, since the skinny pillars do not look like they can support the crushing weight placed on their shoulders.

If the Hay is a comfortable reference to the English Renaissance, List is something of an aggressive experiment by an architect who liked to think, literally, outside the box. On the roof, for instance, the series of north-facing sawtooth skylights are powerful exclamation points, especially at night. Unlike Victorian architects, whose interest continued above the cornice of a building, midcentury modernists often neglected roofs, save for the squat utility boxes that house the machinery for elevators and air-conditioning (see the John D. Rockefeller Jr. Library). Johnson would fully exploit the possibilities that lay above the cornice in his design for Manhattan's so-called Chippendale Building (1984), which is crowned by a monumental broken pediment.

Like with the Hay, the front of List is by far the most interesting. There is that colonnade. But there are also glass boxed balconies on the upper stories that jut out from the plane of the wall. Along the south end of the top or fifth story, which steps forward like a classical entablature from the floors below, there is a series of nonfunctional sun blinds outside the windows of what are faculty offices. Some commentators have likened these to door handles. (The resemblance is most obvious if you stand directly under them and look up.) Farther north along the top floor, there are two large rectangular voids that bring diffused light into the high-ceilinged studios and open up views from the inside to the city below. The dashes of the sun blinds and dots of the two voids read like Morse code. The effect is in equal parts functional and decorative.

Yet for all its experimentation that looks forward to postmodernism and the ironic fiddling with classical motifs, there is also much about List that's wedded to the contemporary fashion for Brutalist architecture, not the least of which is its monumental assertiveness of all that concrete. This is a building that defied the fears of a contemporary atomic Armageddon. Like other architects of the period who worked with poured-in-place concrete, Johnson liked to show off the construction process. This is most obvious in the shallow holes carefully positioned in the middle of each exterior panel. While the regular incisions on the walls come off as decorative allusions to the blocks of marble at the John Hay (rumor has it that Johnson had in fact originally specified marble for his own building), they turn out to be a practical way to allow the newly poured concrete to cure without cracking. Whatever one may think of poured concrete as a building material, this work is flawlessly done.

The location of the University's art department mediates the distance separating Brown above and the Rhode Island School of Design (RISD) farther down College Hill. In other words, List is something of a bridge between both schools. It is a nice way to acknowledge and support a creative cross-pollination between both institutions. Indeed, the building literally supports the arts: the sculpture on the upstairs terrace level is *Weathervane* by Rhode Island sculptor Jonathan Bonner. However, the narrow lot on which List stands forced Johnson to go long and high. This results in a deadening expanse of windowless concrete on both the Waterman and College Street sides. With all the attention given to one wall at the expense of the rest of the building, List comes off as something of a two-dimensional exercise. As one looks up College Hill, the sawtooth roof with its north-facing skylights does stand out on the skyline. That said, passersby encountering List up close might find the exterior surprisingly institutional, oppressive, and dour, a feeling not much dissipated when one steps inside to see an exhibition in the David Winton Bell Gallery. Some might consider this an odd way to communicate the edgy creativity of students painting, sculpting, molding, and welding inside. Johnson earlier designed a building for the University's computer program (Walk Five), this was the last commission Johnson did for Brown.

The walk down College Street lowers the temperature to a more human scale.

10   Samuel N. Gerard House (formerly Whipple-Slater House)
1838; enlargement and remodeling, Alpheus C. Morse, 1867

Macfarlane House
1845

Both houses began life as typical symmetrical, cube-like Greek Revival homes, the clapboard bracketed at the corners by crisp flat columns, or pilasters, that visually appear to bind or hold the walls in place. Both were owned by two prosperous cotton brokers, John Whipple and William J. King. In the twentieth century, the two

Gerard House   *Macfarlane House*

properties became fraternity houses—Alpha Delta Phi at Gerard (1904), Zeta Psi at Macfarlane (1917). (In the 1950s, both fraternities moved to Wriston Quad, after the properties were acquired by Brown.) Note the different way the columns are handled at the entry porticos of each house: The unknown builder or builders employ the same Greek Revival vocabulary but have the good sense to use different words. One set of columns is Ionic (that scroll, or curl, at the top, or capital—Macfarlane); the other, Doric (plain, not fancy—Gerard).

Shortly after the Civil War and in response to the new prosperity the war had brought to the city, the Gerard residence was considerably enlarged (from two and a half stories to three) and brought up to the then-current taste for Italianate design by Alpheus C. Morse (1818–1893), a leading local architect. Italianate details include the blocky quoins at the corners (which replaced the simpler flat Doric pilasters at the corners of Macfarlane House), the heavier detailing over and under the windows (especially the pedimented second-story window above the entrance), and the deeper eaves, which throw a dramatic shadow on the wall. Advances in cast-iron and pressed metal technologies allowed Morse to introduce additional, sometimes exotic decorative elements, such as the brackets and cornices. Side by side, the two houses illustrate the differences between Greek Revival and Italianate styles. The interiors of neither resemble their original state.

Other examples of Morse's work will appear throughout the guide. It was to this firm that the far more influential Alfred Stone came in 1857 to practice in the increasingly prosperous city of Providence. In 1864, Stone parted from Morse to establish his own firm with Charles Carpenter and Edmund Willson to begin an extraordinary run as the city's most sought-after local firm. Both Macfarlane and Gerard Houses are named after twentieth-century alumni benefactors who contributed to the restoration of the properties once they were converted from fraternities to academic department offices.

11 Providence Athenaeum

William Strickland, 1838; James Bucklin, 1868; Norman Isham, 1917; Warren Platner and Associates, 1978

Before turning right on Benefit Street and heading to the First Baptist Meeting House, turn left. Although the two-story Greek Revival building on the southeast corner of College and Benefit is not part of the Brown campus, there is, in fact, a connection that goes back many years. After the College moved from its first home in Warren to Providence, the Athenaeum welcomed its new neighbor by making its books available to the students. The connection has even deeper roots: the cofounder of the Athenaeum was the same Nicholas Brown who gave the family name to the young College.

Dedicated to the Greek goddess of wisdom, Athena, the Athenaeum houses one of the country's few remaining private subscription libraries, a service now provided for the general public by municipal taxes. The only building in New England designed by the Philadelphia architect William Strickland (1788–1854), the very style immediately communicates a message about its mission—enlightenment. It also brands the edifice as both an heir and steward of Western civilization, something very much on the mind of contemporary Americans after the Greeks had just won their own war of independence. Practical as well as iconic, the many large windows and ample skylight welcome natural light deep into the airy interiors of Strickland's building, where students pored over the classical canon plus the newer classics of Dante, Shakespeare, and Milton. The choice of granite was equally symbolic and practical: it identified the timelessness of the Athenaeum's mission and was eminently fireproof, essential for a repository of books and fragile paper documents.

Providence Athenaeum

Note how Strickland makes the steep slope of College Hill work for his building. Though not an exceptionally large structure, the library looks imposing from its perch above Benefit Street. The visitor walks up the broad stairs past the flanking columns that mark the entrance to the temple dedicated to wisdom. The design of the journey is deliberately choreographed to be quite literally uplifting: it is the ascent to enlightenment. Nearly a century later, the architects of the Hay Library adopted the same design strategy. In addition to an ingeniously engineered roof, Strickland incorporated a hot-air heating system (less prone to the unintended consequences of stoves or room fireplaces), which he had pioneered in Philadelphia. In 1868, the interior was reworked by Rhode Island architect James Bucklin (1801–1880), who earlier had designed Brown's Manning Hall. The main staircase is his. In 1917, Norman M. Isham (1864–1943), who is better known as one of the nation's first architectural historians and preservationists, had his own say by designing a small addition at the rear southeast corner.

In 1978, an award-winning renovation and a three-story addition at the southwest corner facing Benefit were carried out by Warren Platner Associates. The rusticated granite of the addition echoes the platform on which the Athenaeum stands and defers to the original structure by stepping back from the plane of the entry facade. These, however, are just the most obvious elements of how the twentieth-century architect engages his nineteenth-century predecessor. The void in the middle of the addition echoes the porch of Strickland's building. At the center, however, is not a door, but a large plate-glass window that allows those on the outside to look into the lower story. The knowledge inside is made to appear more accessible. In front of the window is a pleasant landscaped courtyard, yet another one of the intimate tree-shaded outdoor rooms that dot College Hill.

Providence Athenaeum, interior

Over the course of nearly two centuries, the architectural ensemble that is the Athenaeum has been enriched not only by the architects who have adapted its fabric to meet contemporary needs, but also by the products and wealth generated by the Industrial Revolution. Note the delicate iron lampstands that flank the entrance, the surrounding cast-iron fence topped with palmettes (which we will see again on Brown's College Green), and the handsome Gothic granite fountain out front, designed by the highly regarded Boston firm Ware & Van Brunt (1871). Since the fountain is fed directly from the Pawtuxet River, the welcoming words carved in the granite above the fountain's basin—"Come here everyone that thirsteth"—should be disregarded.

Not many interiors of buildings discussed in this guide are readily accessible to the general public. This one is. It is worth the trouble to step across the threshold, admire the interior, and test your skill at identifying the notables honored by the marble busts that ring the upper level. Browse a few of the Athenaeum's many treasures and add your name to the list of distinguished visitors, who include Poe, Audubon, Emerson, Longfellow, and, more recently, Archbishop Desmond Tutu. By all means do not miss the extraordinary library table on the lower level under the stairs. It is modeled after an Egyptian temple and adorned with painted hieroglyphics. It acknowledges the interest in all matters Egyptian ignited first by Napoleon, and then by midcentury German and French archaeologists. But could it also be a subtle bow to the fact that the course of Western civilization did not begin in Athens, but in Egypt? Plato, Pythagoras, and other Greek philosophers freely noted their debt to a civilization two millennia older than their own. How fitting, therefore, that the resident deity deep inside this temple to Athena should, in fact, be Egyptian.

From September through May, the library is open free to the public seven days a week. Self-guided tours may be taken by following the ravens. (The allusion to Poe becomes clear once inside the library.) From June through August, the library is closed on Sunday.

12   First Baptist Meeting House

Joseph Brown, architect, and Jonathan Hammond, master carpenter, 1775; restoration, Perry, Shaw & Hepburn, 1957

Blistein House

1857; remodeled, Stone, Carpenter & Willson, 1874

Prospect House

1871

That one of the first truly major buildings in Providence was built to house a college edifice (1770) says volumes about the city's priorities. Yet when a few years later the Baptists of Providence replaced their second meeting house, they erected one

First Baptist Meeting House

of the most impressively beautiful houses of worship in the nation, paid for, in part, by the proceeds of a lottery. The argument for the city's pride of place in southern New England (at the expense of Newport) would be advanced not only economically and not only as a seat of learning, but also architecturally.

Even though both city and colony followed the lead of its founder, Roger Williams, in maintaining a wall between church and state (a legacy adopted by the new College, which was open to men of any or no religion), it was understood that the newly established Rhode Island College would be a valuable source of an educated Baptist ministry for the growing denomination and would answer the charge that the Baptists were indifferent or actively hostile to education. The young president, James Manning (who was not incidentally the pastor of the Meeting House) prevailed upon the congregation to erect a building large enough to accommodate Commencement ceremonies. How large? Large enough to hold 1,500. To put this in perspective, at the time it was built, this represented a third of the total population of Providence.

The Meeting House and University Hall share something in common that may not be obvious at first glance. Each is in concept urban. Although both face a tree-shaded lawn, the buildings align with the street rather than a common or village green like those, for example, in Boston and New Haven. In his book on Roger Williams, John Barry explains this difference was intentional and a reflection of the unique nature of Rhode Island in the constellation of New England colonies:

> In most New England towns, the building of a church and meeting place was among the community's first acts. Despite Williams's own intense religiosity, no such meeting place would be built in Providence for half a century. People worshipped in their homes, and homes in Providence were laid out not around a town common but in a straight line. This reflected an unusual, if not unique, individualism.[7]

Built "for the publick Worship of Almighty GOD; and also for holding Commencement in," the edifice at the foot of College Hill marries two distinct American Protestant design traditions: the square, nonhierarchical, no-nonsense but finely crafted New England meeting house, and the southern tidewater Anglican church, with its steeple and primary entrance at the west end. The horizontality of a two-story 80-by-80-foot wooden box (originally bisected by a north-south aisle) meets the soaring verticality of a towering steeple and marks a step in the evolution of the colonial nonconformist Protestant house of worship from a utilitarian building or cottage plan to the familiar long nave with steeple composition that by the nineteenth century immediately reads "church." What had been a radical splinter movement that rejected Puritan theology (including infant baptism) had by the closing days of the colonial period become a respectable mainstream Protestant denomination with all the architectural trappings of success. By way of contrast, the Quakers never abandoned the simpler, nonhierarchical meeting house form.

The precedents for this remarkable structure are well known, but for the moment focus on the astonishing steeple, the first for a Baptist congregation in New England. (The large bell cast in London was also a first for the denomination.) The 185-foot spire is based on a design for London's St. Martin-in-the-Fields, which was published in James Gibbs's *Book of Architecture* (1728). This invaluable resource for eighteenth-century carpenter builders was produced by a student of the great English architect Sir Christopher Wren, and was owned by the architect of the Meeting House, Joseph Brown. (Brown went so far as to have the spire painted to imitate the grained multicolored stone of the prototype on which it was modeled. The architects working on the restoration in the 1950s chose not to be quite so jarringly authentic and painted the steeple a reassuringly New England white.) Like the notes of a musical scale, no two "keys" of the tower are the same, yet the harmonious chord that is struck by the sum of all the various elements is a wonder to behold.

The music begins at a projecting two-story pedimented entry porch. The entrance itself is framed by a freestanding pedimented Doric portico. The next stage of the tower is a square, which houses the clock. Above this stands a temple-like pavilion, pedimented on all four sides and framed by Ionic pilasters. The third and fourth stages are octagonal, diminishing in size to reinforce the vertical thrust. This time the architectural order is Corinthian, which completes the architect's parade of the three classical orders. The next and final element is the elegant cone of the tower with the weather vane on top. All this was erected in a matter of days. The feat was accomplished by ingeniously prefabricating the various sections and then hauling them up from the inside of the steeple, rather like a telescope.

Contemporaries would have seen this rifling of pattern books as neither a lack of imagination nor outright plagiarism. The modern obsession for novelty was largely unknown to a period when all the arts looked to the past in the pursuit of excellence. The government of the United States was itself patterned after the Roman Republic rather than some future utopia. In the absence of a formally trained architecture profession, talented gentlemen amateurs like Brown and Thomas Jefferson turned to the hundreds of eighteenth-century British pattern books that circulated throughout the English-speaking world. These books deserve a lot of the credit for the remarkable leap in the quality of American architecture from 1700 to 1800.

First Baptist Meeting House, interior

Nor were men like Brown and Jefferson loath to adjust or innovate in response to local conditions, including peculiarities of site and the availability of affordable building materials.

Perhaps the most striking impression inside the meeting house is the dazzling light. The large, expansive clear glass windows, the sunlight glancing off the great Waterford chandelier (given to the church in 1792 by Hope Brown Ives in memory of her father), and the white plaster of the walls augment the brightness that identifies the First Baptist Meeting House as a child of the Enlightenment, with its emphasis on the light of reason rather than the colors and shadows of medieval mystery. The architecture conveys a point of Reformation theology—that the wisdom of godly knowledge requires no mediator but is accessible to all believers. (Transparency will become a theme of twenty-first-century architecture at Brown.)

Any doubt about the centrality of the sermon, that is, the preaching of the Word as opposed to the sacramental, is removed by the size and placement of the pulpit where the traditional altar would have been found. (The wooden element suspended above the pulpit just below the three-part Palladian window is a sounding board, the colonial equivalent of modern electronic amplification.) A similar light-filled aesthetic was common to most East Coast eighteenth-century Christian churches, including Roman Catholic houses of worship. (However, the existence of a slaves' gallery at the west end suggests that even in Rhode Island the Enlightenment went only so far.)

During the course of the nineteenth century, the interior underwent a number of modifications, from the arrangement and nature of the pews (originally high boxed) and the introduction of some stained glass (one window memorialized Hope Brown Ives) to the lengthening of the sanctuary in 1884 to accommodate a new baptistery at the eastern end and the introduction of an organ in 1834. (It was President Manning who brought music into the Meeting House. Until then, music was not a part of Baptist services.) The 1957 restoration financed by Brown alumnus and Baptist John D. Rockefeller Jr. (Class of 1897) returned the interior to what preservation architects at the time believed was its original condition, right down to the palette of white plaster with sage-green trim. The organ, however, stayed. As for the dazzling white exterior, that is a bit more complex. As Bill Bryson notes in his book *At Home: A Short History of Private Life*, "The brightest white available [to the architect and his contemporaries] was a rather dull off-white, and although whites improved through the nineteenth century, it was not until the 1940s, with the addition of titanium dioxide to paints, that really strong-lasting whites became available."[8] Brown would no doubt be pleased by the stewardship shown this, his most impressive achievement as a gentleman architect; he would perhaps be surprised by how brightly shines this house of worship at the foot of College Hill.

The next stop takes us up Waterman Street back to the Brown campus. As you walk up the Hill, look across to the award-winning red-brick RISD dorms on your left. Note how the architects (1957, Cull, Robinson & Green in collaboration with Pietro Belluschi) deftly work with and are inspired by the steep slope of the site.

Blistein House

Prospect House

On the right side of Waterman, in the neighborhood of Prospect Street, stand a pair of solid mid-nineteenth-century buildings, Blistein House (1867; remodeled in 1874 by Stone, Carpenter & Willson) and Prospect House (1875, built for J. W. C. Ely, a prominent local physician and father of one of the architects who designed the Van Wickle Gates). The original architect of Blistein House makes no effort to reference the slope of College Hill but instead angles the granite foundation so that the structure on top is perfectly level. Prospect House similarly ignores the Hill: the wedge of the brick and red sandstone foundation allows the house to command the site as if it were on level ground.

Both houses exhibit a hybrid aesthetic with references to three styles popular in local mid-nineteenth-century residential design: Classical, Italianate, and Second Empire. One of the most distinguishing architectural details shared by both houses is the roof, whose style traces back to the seventeenth-century French architect Jules Hardouin Mansart (1646–1708). The steeply sloped pitch is an effective strategy to gain extra headroom and square footage in the top floor. Additional space was an important consideration on a tight urban lot. Such roofs were also the latest fashion after developments in France during the Second Empire, that is, during the reign of Napoleon III (1852–70). On the other hand, the heavy brackets underneath the wide projecting cornices of both are evidence of an earlier Italianate influence, as are the exaggerated lintels above the windows with their two-over-two glazing. If the mansard roof of the Blistein House seems less integral or organic than that on top of Prospect, the impression is well founded. It was added in 1874 for the owner, Henry L. Parsons, by the architecture firm Stone, Carpenter & Willson, which no doubt designed the enclosed room that sits on top of the entry porch.

The most striking difference between the two is the way the architects handle the entrances. That of Blistein leads directly from the sidewalk into a side hall via a classically inspired porch. The glass, which is *in* the paired doors, is an Italianate detail that replaces the narrower, multipaned side lights and fan windows common to an earlier period. When Blistein was built, larger panes of glass were cheap and commercially available. The fact that this third bay steps out from the plane of the facade hints at another feature common to Italianate design—a corner tower. Up the street, the front entrance to Prospect House is recessed, a smart gesture for a house that sits directly on the property line with no room for a porch. The recessed entry provided shelter against inclement weather for those who came calling.

Acquired by Brown around 1920, the residence at 57 Waterman Street has since 1983 borne the name of a beloved professor of English, Elmer M. Blistein (Class of 1942), as a gift of Philip Hayes (Class of 1953). If it seems squeezed into its site, the fault lies in the 1939 brick addition to the John Hay Library, which abutted the older building. Rumor has it there is or at least was a secret back entrance from Blistein House into the Hay addition that allowed for the surreptitious borrowing and return of books. Currently used by the University as offices and classrooms, both Blistein House and Prospect House are examples of Victorian residential design at its most imaginatively eclectic: ample, comfortable, accommodating large families and frequent guests, including offices (if the owner was a professional, e.g., doctor, lawyer, accountant), and capable of sustaining a wide range of household chores, from laundry to cooking, carried out by a small on-site staff.

13 Carrie Tower
Guy Lowell, 1904

The 92-foot brick and limestone tower was given to Brown by Paul Bajnotti of Turin, Italy, as a memorial to his wife, Carrie, granddaughter of Nicholas Brown. The inscription at the foundation reads: "Love is as strong as death." Carrie's sister,

Carrie Tower, detail

Carrie Tower

Annmary Brown Hawkins, was also memorialized on the Brown campus by her husband (Walk Eight). The sisters were clearly an exceptional pair.

Under the direction of John L. Thorpe of Boston, the elaborate stonework above the faces of the four clocks includes thirty-two carved urns, eight capitals, four shields, and at the very top, four urns with flames (a bit of iconography earlier encountered on the steeple of the First Baptist Meeting House, likewise symbolizing the resurrected soul—the flame—escaping the bounds of death—the urn). Steering gullible freshmen to the corner of Waterman and Prospect for a date with Miss Carrie Tower used to be a favorite sport for upperclassmen and perhaps continues to this day. Although the clock no longer works, Carrie Tower is something of an architectural folly, that is, a nonutilitarian ornament. It serves as an object of delight and a way-finder for those traveling up Waterman Street in search of Brown.

14   Corliss-Brackett House

George H. Corliss, 1882; restoration, Durkee, Brown, Viveiros & Werenfels Architects, 2002

George Henry Corliss (1817–1888) is a star of the first magnitude in the galaxy of self-taught nineteenth-century inventors who powered (literally in this case) the Industrial Revolution that transformed America's agrarian economy and propelled the United States into the first rank of nations. Having opened a grocery store in Greenwich, New York, in early adulthood, his interests increasingly shifted to engineering and mechanical matters, for which he had an instinctive gift. From his first patent on a machine for sewing boots and heavy leather, he eventually moved on to the design of steam engines, ultimately securing a patent that made their operation far more efficient and powerful.

By 1844 Corliss had moved to Providence and set up shop in a plant that at his death covered about five acres and employed over 1,000 workers. It was Corliss who supplied the great 1,400-horsepower engine that supplied the power used in Machinery Hall at the Centennial Exposition in Philadelphia. Of all the attractions at the Exposition, the mighty Corliss engine was the most celebrated and described

Corliss-Brackett House

by awestruck admirers as the new god of the Industrial Age. Supernaturally powerful in his own way, Corliss was a man who achieved whatever he set his mind to—as long as it was mechanical, which is the background for the next stop, the magnificent Italianate house that commands the southeast corner of Prospect and Waterman Streets.

When specialists informed Corliss that his second wife, Emily Ann Shaw, must spend the cold months in Bermuda for reasons of health, most husbands might have resigned themselves to solitary winters in Providence. Not George Corliss: "I will build a Bermuda for Mrs. Corliss!" The result was quite possibly the first house in America to be warmed by a radiant heating system that was thermostatically controlled. In the document prepared when the house was nominated for inclusion in the National Register of Historic Places, the engineer's report reads as follows:

> In the stable complex adjoining the house [at the rear] Corliss installed a steam boiler and a small version of his famous steam engine. This engine drove a fan which sent air, through steam-heated ducts, through a tunnel and into the main house. There the heated air was distributed through ducts built into the walls, thus heating all rooms by radiation from their walls. These wall ducts all collected in the attic, from which the air was returned to the stable and re-circulated in order to conserve and re-use any heat which it still contained.
>
> This heating (i.e., the steam engine effecting its distribution) was controlled by a thermostat—surely one of the earliest known—located in the main hall of the house. On the ceiling of this hall and running its full length was a rod of metal alloy which expanded and contracted markedly with changes in the house temperature. Through mechanical linkage, this rod regulated a governor on the engine driving the fan, and thus regulated the flow of warmed air to the radiant heating duct-work of the house.[9]

As fine as the building undoubtedly is, the asymmetrical Italianate aesthetic with its stylistically obligatory square tower was at that time a style that was no longer cutting-edge. On the other hand, this was the residence not of an aesthete, but a newly prosperous businessman establishing his position in the community. It was best to stress roots and tradition. The sumptuousness of the Corliss residence, in which no expense was spared, certainly befitted a remarkable man whose engineering skills and business acumen had propelled him to a gilded perch on

College Hill with a commanding view of Providence, a prospect gained from a sizeable roof terrace with observation platforms.

Motion picture scriptwriter Charles Brackett (1945's *The Lost Weekend*) inherited the property from Corliss's daughter, Maria, and proceeded to shut it up for most of the year, a case of preservation by neglect. Brown acquired the house in 1955. The twenty-first-century rehabilitation included a state-of-the art restoration of the exterior and museum-quality restoration of historic spaces on the first floor. The University's enlightened stewardship was recognized in 2003 by awards from both the Providence Preservation Society and the Rhode Island Historical Preservation and Heritage Commission. Corliss-Brackett is one of six Brown properties listed on the National Register of Historic Places. Although the house is not open to the general public, there is much to delight the eye from the vantage point of the sidewalk. Pause to look closely at the lampstands that flank the entrance at the top of the stairs. The way metal is rendered flowing and sinuous is characteristic of Art Nouveau style and a testament to the love of craftsmanship that gave rise to the neighboring RISD.

15   Robinson Hall
William R. Walker and Thomas Gould, 1878; partial restoration, 1991

Named for President Ezekiel Gilman Robinson during whose tenure (1872–89) it was built, Robinson Hall was the first significant University building to be sited on the north side of Waterman Street. The land, along with the cost of the building (estimated at $120,000), was contributed by John Carter Brown and his widow, Sophia Augusta Brown. Among the few remaining examples of post–Civil War Victorian Gothic in Providence done on a grand scale, the new library was also one of the College's first prefab structures. The foundries of the Industrial Revolution mass-produced the connecting metal sections that were transported by rail to cities across America. Not only was Robinson Hall modern in the method of fabrication, Robinson represented the most up-to-date thinking about library design. Apparently influenced by a similar library at Princeton (Chancellor Green Hall, formerly Chancellor Green Library, 1873), Robinson was the nation's third panoptic library (*pan*, Greek for "all"; *optic* for "observe"). With the open balconied stacks in the three wings that radiated from a central octagonal core, the librarian could keep a 360-degree vigil of the space from his desk at the center. The panoptical shape was popular during early prison reform schemes for much the same reason—surveillance.

And what a splendid building it is! If the restrained, pale marble palette of the Hay Library is the aesthetic equivalent of Kansas, Robinson inhabits the Technicolor landscape of Oz. Here the aesthetic theories of Ruskin, who believed truth in art was based on direct observation of God's work in nature, are yoked to the tidal swell of manufactured building materials. The latest advances in structural steel made it possible to span ever-larger spaces and introduced an architecture that over time

Robinson Hall

could and did grow both horizontally and vertically. The increased number of tools the Industrial Revolution put in the architect's kit is evident on every side, from the roof of wrought iron and parti-colored slate to the hothouse menagerie of carved flora and fauna at the entrance. The carvings by James C. Brierly merit special attention. They celebrate the abundance of God's creation under the watchful eye of Athena's ubiquitous scholarly owl. The claims of nature and the industrial forge pull in opposite directions, but the resulting tension no doubt contributes to the dynamic restlessness of the architecture as expressed in all the jutting angularity of a structure that seems poised to spin off the stone podium on which it stands.

Although the architects of Robinson emphatically abandoned the chaste Greek temple form as visual shorthand for "library" (compare Mencoff Hall immediately next door), there was no less a sense that a library is a sacred space akin to a church or cathedral. In other words, the design of the building as well as its contents was meant to advance a moral purpose. This is underscored by the ceremony that attended the dedication: The first book carried in was Samuel Bagster's Polyglot Bible—"polyglot" for a book that contains side-by-side versions of the same text in different languages, in this case, Hebrew, Samaritan, Greek, Latin, English, and Peshito (ancient Syriac). This was appropriately placed on the first shelf in the first alcove. Not leaving to chance what he intended by this gesture, the librarian, Reuben A. Guild, described Bagster's Bible as "the embodiment of true wisdom, and the fountainhead of real culture, civilization and moral improvement." Brown now had space for 150,000 books.

Robinson Hall, interior

Like with the Hay Library, the approach to Robinson is a matter of twists and turns as one climbs the somewhat steep stairs toward the shadowy grand entrance beneath the projecting columned porch. And like the experience at the Hay, what the ascent achieves is a quieting of those who are about to enter. Before one reaches the front door, the winged griffins on either side of the upper-most flight of stairs have to be negoti-ated. These are not casual decorative additions, but, as the iconography of the beasts—part eagle, part lion—makes clear, they are on duty to guard treasures and the priceless posses-sions inside.

The actual entrance into the library through the large double doors is reminiscent of a compres-sion / release technique often employed by, among others, Frank Lloyd Wright. One leaves the daylight of the busy urban street, passes through the quieting confined shadowy space of the porch, and then enters the cool quiet of the breathtaking floor-to-ceiling octagonal rotunda, or atrium of the library proper. Embraced by concentric circles of open octagonal wrought-iron necklaces that served as railings, the two tiers of iron balconies supported seventy-two alcoves of books, each fitted with movable shelves. The cruciform floor plan and central reading room welcome daylight through the many windows and the stained-glass skylight in the octagonal cupola. In the evening, Robinson was illuminated by six hundred gas lamps. Pierced by all those windows, Robinson Library must have been a fiery beacon in the dark of a Providence winter's night.

Beneath the exuberant decoration both inside and out beats the pulse of a finely engineered machine that makes maximum use of light and air in a three-story fireproof structure. As originally designed, there was no wood inside save for the shelves and other furnishings. Once again, innovations in product fabrication and fireproof building construction, as well as advances in lighting, heating, and plumbing, lurk just beneath a period skin that distracts the eye from the science of the builder's art. For all its rouge and lipstick, at its core Robinson Hall was in its day a functionally modern building.

As years passed, it quickly became clear the design, though compelling in theory, had a limitation of some consequence: a panoptic building on a relatively small city lot could not be expanded to accommodate the accelerating floodtide of printed materials. Sooner than the architects or the College expected, Robinson's days as Brown's main library were numbered. Although the alcoves are today walled off for the use of the Department of Economics, twentieth-century restoration work (which among other things revived the rainbow palette of the original) conveys some idea of one of the most interesting interiors on the Brown campus.

16   Mencoff Hall
James C. Bucklin, 1844; rear addition, Stone, Carpenter & Willson, 1891; restoration and renovation, Lerner | Ladds + Bartels Architects, 2003

Next to the every-which-way red-brick effervescence that is Robinson Hall stands yet another sober temple dedicated to knowledge. This two-story stucco Greek Revival building was originally known as the "Cabinet" of the Rhode Island Historical Society and the repository of books, papers, and graphic material about the Ocean State. The word refers to a small room used for a specific purpose. In Renaissance Germany, the *Shatzkammer* was a treasure room filled by various princelings with costly objects. In other words, cabinets were understood to be special rooms that housed collections not readily accessible to the public. These "treasures" could as easily be biological and geological specimens as books and finely crafted objects. As such collections expanded and grew more heterogeneous, they often morphed into museums.

After Massachusetts, New York, and Maine, Rhode Island's is the fourth oldest state historical society in the United States, and, yes, another member of the Brown family—Moses Brown—was one of the founders. After Brown acquired the building in 1942, the University embarked on a series of fairly happenstance

Mencoff Hall

Mencoff Hall, entrance lobby

remodelings intended to increase the usefulness of the facility. To serve a host of disparate activities, from the Program of Advanced Instruction and Research in Mechanics to Brown's inventory and purchasing departments, the gallery mezzanine was infilled as a new floor, and the Victorian interior dome designed by Stone, Carpenter & Willson was hidden above an acoustic tile ceiling. To say the result was something of an architectural babble of different floor levels, materials, and uses would be accurate.

The 2003 restoration removed the many interior modifications that had obscured the building's original clear layout and circulation patterns. Accommodating a new spirit of interdisciplinary collaboration, transparency and flow became the guiding principles of a remarkable design tour de force. The architects inserted interior glass walls and open staircases, placed the public spaces at the core, and uncovered and carefully restored the coffered dome of the two-story display hall on the north end of the building. This space has become the center's main conference room.

Additional square footage was found in the attic by removing part of the roof and installing a continuous ridge skylight, an intervention that exposed the original hand-hewn wooden roof trusses. A formerly windowless space was thus retrieved for open offices and meeting areas bathed in natural daylight. Perhaps the most visible sign of this new commitment to easy access can be seen immediately at the Cabinet's monumental front doors. These are now fixed in an open position, which yields a clear line of sight from the street through a new set of glass doors to the conference room at the opposite end of the two-story entry lobby. What had been architectural babble has become lyrically clear. In recognition of this achievement, the 11,700-square-foot Cabinet received a Providence Preservation Society Award for Adaptive Use in 2006.

Named for Samuel M. Mencoff (Class of 1978), the building houses the University's Population Studies & Training Center.

17   Hope College

Master mason, Daniel Hale, master builder, Samuel Staples, 1823; renovation, Perry, Shaw, Hepburn & Dean, 1959

Walk across Waterman Street, enter Robinson Gate (dedicated 1904), and pause in front of Brown's oldest residential dorm. Let your eye run down the lineup of Brown's most historic buildings, which begins here, at the northern end with Hope College, and terminates to the south at Rhode Island Hall. What you see is reason enough for a trip to Providence.

Hope College

Like its model, Yale's Old Brick Row (which used to front New Haven's historic Common but has since been demolished), these five structures engage the city across a broad lawn today known as the Front or "quiet" Campus. The row suggests an alternating A-B-A-B rhythm: the long sides of Hope and University Hall; the gabled ends of Manning and Rhode Island Halls in between. (The newest, Slater Hall, breaks the rhythm for reasons that will become clear a few pages on.) The row does not line up perfectly with Prospect Street, which in any case was not laid out until 1834. Rather, it follows the geology of the ridge as it gradually rises in a northeast direction toward the highest point on College Hill, the site of Brown's Ladd Observatory (Walk Four). One additional detail is the dominance of brick and stucco: these were locally available, durable, and relatively inexpensive building materials appropriate for a fledgling institution that had limited financial resources.

The orientation of all five buildings is no accident. Rather, it was the instinctive response of the architects and builders who had learned to work with the natural rhythms of light and air. Take the long ends of the rectangles that are Hope College and University Hall. These face east and west. In an age when candles and oil lamps were the prevalent forms of illumination, it made great sense to site residence halls to harvest the most natural light. Also, the orientation made maximum use of prevailing breezes for ventilation. Natural energy at its most elemental was a shaper of form. Once gas and then electricity became common, along with modern heating and cooling technologies, the size and orientation of buildings became increasingly less dependent on the ambient energy of light and air.

One additional point that really gets to the heart of why the overall plans, or designs, of America's earliest colleges, like Brown, evolved the way they did. The proximity of living, learning, and worshipping together nurtured something even closer than a community of scholars; it encouraged a sense of family. This was important in shaping of the whole man, who, to use the words inscribed

The Quiet Green

in Brown's Charter, would be prepared to discharge "the Offices of Life with usefulness and reputation."

Now, let's continue our tour, beginning with a stop at Hope College. Built on a lot purchased from Nathan Waterman by Nicholas Brown, the College's first exclusively residential hall was a visible sign that after a slow start, interrupted by the Revolutionary War, the College was growing. In addition to buying the land, Nicholas Brown paid for the building's cost, which was named after his only surviving sister, Hope Ives.

The design of Hope College was the first and by no means the last instance of a deliberate reference by succeeding architects to Brown's oldest building, University Hall. Although Hope clearly echoes University Hall in material, size (four stories), rooftop balustrade, and its projecting central bay with pedimented gable, the proximity of both buildings is an opportunity to make a quick assessment of what distinguishes eighteenth-century Colonial from early nineteenth-century Federal style. The most obvious difference is the delicacy of the detailing in Hope College. This is seen in the rising sunbeam tracery of the fan lights and the granite arches with their keystones above the doors, the granite lintels of the windows, and the half-moon window in the gable, which echoes nicely the arches of the doorways below.

Delicate architectural gestures notwithstanding, Hope College was no exercise in gracious living. The forty-eight rooms were heated by coal-burning fireplaces, and the ashes were collected in iron cans chained to the hall walls. In the absence of plumbing, access to water was by way of a pump, a replica of which stands at the back of the building on the College Green, though it is no longer functional. The Spartan conditions of Hope College were exacerbated by the lack of a cellar for plumbing or heating. (The cellar was not excavated until 1894.) Anything in the way of water or fuel had to be hauled into the building and the waste simply pitched out back.

Hope College room, c. 1900

The twentieth-century restoration, carried out by Perry, Shaw, Hepburn & Dean, gutted the historic core, fireplaces and all. What emerged is a thoroughly fireproof interior of steel beams, concrete block walls, and double metal doors that lead from the halls into the rooms. The result may be best described as functional and chaste. Archival photographs give some idea of the layout of typical rooms and what the students of the day considered interior design. The "trophies" have changed, but there is a comforting commitment to clutter that links one generation of undergraduates to the next.

Why is Hope called a "college"? Harvard began the custom when it called its first buildings "colleges." In this sense, the words *college* and *hall* are interchangeable. Nearly two centuries on, Hope College continues to serve its original purpose as a residence hall.

18   Manning Hall
Warren, Tallman & Bucklin, 1835; upper-floor restoration, Perry, Shaw & Hepburn, 1959

Like Hope College, the third building to be constructed on the emerging campus was funded by the generosity of Nicholas Brown Jr. Designed to house the library (on the first floor) and chapel (on the second), Manning Hall was informed by two separate but closely related contemporary events. First was a growing knowledge of classical Greek architecture fed by late eighteenth- and early nineteenth-century archaeological digs in Italy and Greece. This knowledge was communicated through pattern books to which the Providence firm turned for inspiration. In this instance, the book in question was the *Unedited Antiquities of Attica, Comprising the Architectural Remains of Eleusis, Rhamnus, and Thericus* (1817), specifically, the temple of Diana-Propylea in Eleusis, though what was built between Hope College and University Hall is twice the size of the original. Indeed, the scale of every element of the structure, from the monumental 18-foot-high entrance behind the four beefy Doric columns to the 15-by-15-foot lites (i.e., panes) of the double-hung windows at the sides and rear, as well as the height of the ceilings on the first and second floors—all this and more is meant to convey the importance of the activities housed inside and perhaps to underscore the relative smallness of mere mortals who attempt the heights of secular and spiritual knowledge.

Turning to Greek precedent suited the ideals of the new American republic, which identified its own democratic ideals with the recent Greek struggle for independence. (Brown students enlisted in the fight, the remarkable Samuel

Manning Hall

Gridley Howe [Class of 1821] being the most famous. Gridley eventually rose to be the surgeon-in-chief of the Greek navy.) As we have seen at the Athenaeum down the Hill and the Cabinet across Waterman Street, the very idea of libraries as temples of wisdom is a pedigree that stretches back to the dawn of Western civilization. One other point helps explain this appetite for Athens and especially Rome, which was more familiar. A legacy of the Renaissance was the belief that the wisdom of the ancients, from architecture to zoology, was superior to that of the moderns. *Progress* was often defined as the degree to which a poet, a politician, or an architect was successful in looking back, not forward. It is not for nothing that Virgil was Dante's guide in writing *The Divine Comedy*. This definition of progress was turned on its head by the scientific discoveries of the nineteenth century, and with it was the concept of higher education and its architecture. The outcome will be the subject of later Walks. First, the building itself.

The stucco applied to the four brick columns at the entrance and the rubble walls (that is, stones of varying shapes and thicknesses fitted carefully together to form the walls) was a durable, attractive, and weather-resistant way to unify the structure and give the appearance of expensive granite. (Indeed, the stucco is scored on the front to resemble masonry.) As a building material, stucco is much lighter than stone and easier to work with, which recommended it to the masons responsible for producing the fluting on the columns. Stucco no doubt had the same appeal for the builders of the Cabinet across the street and, later, at Rhode Island Hall.

But why would the College, the donor, and the architects turn to a clearly pagan form to house a Christian place of worship? There was a precedent at Yale. However, something far more subtle than precedent is just as likely to have guided the College and its architects. The prevailing worldview of Protestantism in the eighteenth and early nineteenth centuries did not see a conflict between reason and religion. Indeed, reason was faith's greatest ally: knowledge begat faith, and faith, knowledge. Pairing the two—library and chapel—made perfect sense in Providence as it did in New Haven five decades earlier. The lack of stained glass on the second floor of Manning (and in the First Baptist Meeting House) is not for want of money; it is a statement about the pure light of God: faith based on reason, the word, rather than ritual. Even the hierarchy of Manning's spaces is carefully calculated—library below, chapel above—knowledge of the world leading to knowledge of matters divine.

Similarly, the very orientation of Manning serves a dual purpose, both practical and eschatological. The tightness of the site demanded that the long side of the building run east-west, rather than north-south as at Hope College and University Hall. However, of equal significance is the traditional orientation of Christian chapels and churches—the altar or pulpit on the east side (the rising sun / Son and resurrection, in other words, the head of the Church), and the exit at the west end, which took worshippers back into the world.

Manning Hall portico, detail

Although the relocation of the library from where it had been in University Hall to the first floor of Manning represented a significant increase of space for books and manuscripts, the facility still was rather small. Among America's early colleges, Brown was not exceptional in this regard. Since the program of instruction relied on a small number of standard texts—the Greek and Latin classics plus the Bible and related religious tracts—large libraries were not necessary. After all, when University

Hall first opened its doors, it was still theoretically possible for an exceptionally learned and long-lived man to have read every available book. Yet as scientific inquiry came to define a new, expanding curriculum, Manning Hall as a library was dated almost from the day the first book was put on its shelves. In trying to keep up with the accelerating flood of published materials, storage and ease of access would be dominant concerns in the decades ahead. That *and* fireproof construction.

Standing in front of Manning Hall, you can see at a glance the evolution of American libraries, beginning with the small, locked space in University Hall, then Manning, on to the fireproof construction of Robinson on Waterman Street, the clubbiness of the John Hay on Prospect, and across College Street, to the transparency of the Rock. It is a case study in brick, stucco, marble, structural steel, prefabricated concrete panels, and glass that documents the radical transformation of libraries, the nature of knowledge, and who has access to it.

Once Sayles Hall opened in 1881 (Walk Two) and served Brown as a chapel, the upper room of Manning was repurposed as a space for architectural and freehand drawing. In 1959 the second story was restored and returned to its original purpose as an interdenominational chapel that seats two hundred. In 2004, the lower story became the space for objects from Brown's Haffenreffer Museum of Anthropology. Designed by the Boston architect Signer Harris, it is a nice programmatic bookend to Rhode Island Hall at the south end of the row, which houses the study of archaeology and the ancient world. Entered from the College Green, the gallery features changing exhibitions from the Haffenreffer collection of objects created by the indigenous peoples of North and South America. Open Tuesday through Sunday from 10 AM to 4 PM, the gallery has free admission.

19 University Hall

Robert Smith, 1778; extensive restoration, Perry, Shaw & Hepburn, 1939; landscape design, Mary Elizabeth Sharpe, 1939

The most impressive buildings of medieval European cities were their cathedrals. In the American colonies, that role was typically played by the facilities built for higher education. Brown was no exception. The four-story brick late Georgian building is the third of three proposed designs considered by Brown's first building committee for a structure that would be "above the smoke and stir" of the town. The initial plan called for a smaller facility that would be "one wing of the whole College edifice, when completed." The committee seems to have had in mind Harvard's existing open quad, bracketed on each of three sides by buildings. This plan was ultimately scrapped. What was built looked not to Boston for inspiration, but south to Princeton, the alma mater of Brown's first president, James Manning. The model was Nassau Hall with several differences, including the addition in Providence of a fourth story. Today the resemblance between the two is not obvious, since Princeton's administration building was given a thorough Victorian face-lift after a disastrous fire.

University Hall and the Van Wickle Gates

Which raises the question of what, if any, was the role of Robert Smith, the Philadelphia master builder who most likely designed Nassau Hall? Did he make the journey to Providence, or was his influence on what was then called the "College Edifice" exerted at a distance through correspondence and President Manning's recollection of his alma mater? The Corporation papers do record an expense of £1.04 "to postage of a letter from the Architect of Philadelphia," Smith's home and where he practiced. What in turn had inspired Smith? Was it a stripped-down version of James Gibb's design for the Fellows' Building at King's College, Cambridge, which was widely known in the broadly read and influential *Book of Architecture* (1728)? That said, it should also be noted Joseph Brown was on the committee charged with the site selection and the design of University Hall. It is difficult to imagine the talented amateur architect played no role in the design of the first building of what in many ways was a family enterprise.

What is not open to debate is that University Hall is constructed of brick, the material Smith had recommended for Nassau Hall, which Princeton's Presbyterians

deemed too expensive. (They chose instead honey-colored metamorphic rock, or gneiss, obtained from a local quarry.) Tradition has it that when Joseph's brother John laid the first foundation, it was liberally baptized with rum punch. If true, this would be a nice allusion to the source of the Brown family's wealth as leaders of the triangular trade built on slaves, molasses, and rum. The eighteen years required to complete construction of Brown's 108-foot-long, four-story building are accounted for by the interruption of the American Revolution and the appropriation of the incomplete building first as a barracks for American soldiers and then as a hospital for French troops.

The edifice that ultimately emerged served every function of the College. The north and south entryways led to the residential floors; the west center door opened to the chapel (a two-story room with a gallery), while the east center door was the common room, which also, like the chapel, featured a gallery. The central projecting pedimented bays on the east and west sides of University Hall (the first known example in Rhode Island) follow a Renaissance practice of designing buildings and vistas that had clear focal points. By stepping forward, the bays also break the planes of what otherwise would be long, unrelieved brick walls.

When University Hall opened its doors, it was the largest building in Rhode Island. It demonstrated to all who saw it rise the value the city fathers placed on education, and their expectation that those who emerged from the College would be an investment in the city's and the colony's future prosperity. Like the First Baptist Meeting House down the Hill, the College Edifice was not built to serve immediate needs but to accommodate an expansive future. This even more than the particular details of the design may be the most extraordinary aspect of both buildings. To the north, Boston was not impressed: "[The Corporation has built] a College near as large as Babel; sufficient to contain ten Times the Number of Students that ever have, or ever will, oblige the Tutors of that popular University with Opportunity of educating, or instructing them." [10]

The College Edifice was renamed University Hall in 1823, when Brown's second building, Hope College, was dedicated. By 1834, the wear and tear of six decades clearly showed. The balustrade around the roof was removed—which no doubt had the unfortunate effect of calling attention to a cupola somewhat too small for the size of the building. The exterior walls received a coat of stucco painted a neutral olive color to cover the badly deteriorated brick and mortar. The stucco also had the effect of harmonizing the appearance of University Hall with Manning Hall next door.

The next major alteration focused on the interior. As originally designed, the upper-floor residential portion of University Hall followed the precedent of Princeton's Nassau Hall by including double-loaded corridors, that is, with rooms on either side of long halls. In the 1850s, partitions were constructed, dividing the central corridor, which had run the entire length of the building. Something similar was done to Princeton's Nassau Hall, no doubt for the same reason: control of the resident students who at both institutions were prone to ringing bells at all hours of the night and rolling paving stones down the long halls. (For good reason, the top floor of University Hall had been christened "Pandemonium.")

Three decades later, a few voices (among the loudest, the students') called for replacing "a relic of the past" with a more modern facility. A diary entry by Elijah Brightman Stoddard (1847) shows the students had a point. He was reflecting on a time when *extracurricular* meant the exercise gained from carrying wood to his room from the wood pile next to the College privy:

> It was not uncommon for him to awake to find a frost on his blanket where he had breathed during the night and the water, which he also had to carry up from the College pump, frozen in the basin. University Hall, he complained in his diary, "is drafty, the windows poorly fitted, and is not designed for the comfort of the inhabitants."[11]

Instead of tearing it down, the University chose to restore its most historic building. The architects, Gould & Angell, re-created the balustrade, replaced the small-paned windows with large plates of glass, repaired the chimneys, introduced steam heating and gas lighting, and gutted the interior, including what had originally been the chapel and common room at the center of the building. Both double-storied rooms with galleries were now used for recitations, lectures, and meeting spaces. Brown's seventh president, Ezekiel Gilman Robinson, hoped these rooms would stimulate a revival of the debating societies that were popular in most American colleges in the early decades of the nineteenth century. The hope proved vain.

Among the many building projects constructed during the administration of President Faunce was yet another renovation in 1905 of University Hall. Off came the stucco and back came the small-paned windows. In the upper story, the University welcomed a station of the U.S. Weather Bureau. (The building's occupants had to wait until 1912 before bathrooms were installed.) The dormitory rooms on the second floor were taken over by the departments of English and History.

University Hall from the College Green

In 1939, Brown commissioned a comprehensive top-to-bottom restoration of University Hall by Perry, Shaw & Hepburn, the architecture firm that had honed its Colonial Revival skills on the contemporaneous restoration of Colonial Williamsburg. The crumbling foundation was replaced with steel and concrete masked by a stone face, the cupola restored to its original octagonal shape (based on remnants that were uncovered on the roof), and ceiling heights increased by the installation of thinner steel and cement floors in place of what had been wood. Almost everything was reworked for the building's new program (administrative offices) and a commitment to fireproof construction. The President's office was moved to the first floor in the central front projection, where the two-story chapel had been. On the third floor, a 50-foot-long, two-story-high meeting room for faculty and Corporation meetings was created. Designated in 1963 as a National Historic Landmark, University Hall is, like Colonial Williamsburg, much beloved, but in the end it is an almost total reproduction of the College Edifice that first arose on the Hill above colonial Providence.

Built in part by slaves and financed in part by funds derived from John Brown's lucrative trafficking in slaves, University Hall has become the subject of a more sobering narrative about the role of slavery in the shaping of America. Overlooked for many years, this chapter of Brown's history is being given the attention it deserves. A University-commissioned sculpture by Martin Puryear will acknowledge Brown's links to the transatlantic slave trade. In the words of the Corporation, the memorial will invite "reflection and fresh discovery without provoking paralysis or shame." It will be sited, appropriately, at the front door of the University on the Front Green near University Hall.

Slater Hall from the Front Green

20   Slater Hall
Stone, Carpenter & Willson, 1879

The impetus behind the construction of Brown's second dormitory was, depending on one's point of view, either a bribe or a generous inducement. The wealthy Providence industrialist Horatio Nelson Slater offered the College $25,000 if Ezekiel Gilman Robinson would give up his position as president of Rochester Theological Seminary and come to Brown. For several years, Brown had been courting Robinson, but Robinson had difficulty making up his mind until he received news of Slater's offer. Robinson came to Brown in 1872 to become the College's seventh president, and with the donor's consent, the gift was applied to the construction of a sorely needed residence hall. The gift, however, unexpectedly turned out to be a somewhat mixed blessing.

A century earlier, the College Edifice commanded a view of empty fields. This would soon change as Providence rapidly expanded up College Hill, a consequence of the city's prosperity. In time, Brown discovered that to meet its needs to grow, it increasingly had to consider the interests of its neighbors. No sooner had the College dug the foundation for a large Victorian Gothic building on the south end of the College Green than nearby residents voiced objections. Most strident were William and Francis Goddard, who did not want their view across the parklike environs obstructed, especially by a student dormitory. There was no small irony in the opposition of the Goddard brothers: the firm designing Slater was the same team that had designed their homes directly across the street. Brown ultimately backed down and sited a smaller building between University and Rhode Island Halls. (A mast from one of the objecting neighbors' yachts, C. Oliver Iselin, stands on the very site where Slater Hall would have been built. In 1941, a marble and bronze base for the mast was dedicated as a memorial to Samuel Gridley Howe by the American Hellenic Educational and Progressive Association.) In its present location, Slater Hall occupies real estate once given to the school's privy, otherwise known as "Sprague Hall." According to Walter Lee Munro's book *The Old Back Campus at Brown,* students named the school's privy after Rhode Island Governor William Sprague. The governor was accorded this dubious honor when he allegedly reneged on a promise to present a building to Brown. Indoor plumbing eventually made Sprague Hall obsolete.

Once again Stone, Carpenter & Willson showed they were as adept at changing styles as a model on a fashion runway stage. Widely acclaimed at the time for its beauty and up-to-date fireproof construction (no small amenity in a structure with working fireplaces), the French Romanesque dormitory would later serve as a model for a building designed by the same architects for the University of Maine at Orono. Even though student life had already begun to migrate to the middle or College Green, Slater's two main entrances followed the precedent of its older neighbors and were oriented west toward the city. This is made clear by comparing the relatively straightforward doorways on the east, or rear, facade with the elaborately ornamented entry porches on the west. In a little more than one hundred years, Brown had come a long way from the Spartan residential amenities of University Hall. Indeed, the two buildings not only mark the University's changing fortunes, their side-by-side positioning shows far better than mere words what is unique about each.

Although the brick of the older building is not without its decorative pleasures, the function is primarily utilitarian, and in the eighteenth century would have played a structural role. At Slater, the masonry is insistently decorative. Look up at the brickwork of the cornice and in the triangular spaces immediately below

Slater Hall, student room, c. 1890

Slater Hall from the College Green

the peaks of the gables. There is nothing like this at University Hall or for that matter Hope College. At University Hall, the roofline pretty much defines the end of the action. At Slater it is merely the pause before the fireworks of the chimneys and gables. Like that of University Hall, the central bay of Slater steps out from the plane of the building, but then so do the adjoining bays on the north and south ends of Slater. University Hall is resolutely horizontal and symmetrical; the symmetry of Slater (and it is there) is of a far different order, akin to the harnessing of horses that want to pull in different directions. The architect Frank Lloyd Wright said that buildings either sit or stand: University Hall sits on its site; Slater stands vertically exuberant.

The science or intellectual discipline that informs the worldview of those who designed and constructed the late Georgian architecture of University Hall is mathematics. The organic restlessness of Slater references the dynamic world of biology, the inevitability of the forward motion of progress, and the late Romantic embrace of nature. One of the drivers of that progress was, arguably, one of Slater's most famous residents, John D. Rockefeller Jr., whose generosity to his alma mater, as already seen across the way at the library, would figure prominently in the growth of the University through much of the twentieth century.

21   Rhode Island Hall

Tallman & Bucklin, 1840; ell added on the east side, 1874; south side addition, 1904; restoration and renovation, Anmahian Winton Architects, 2009

This final stop is something of a bookend to the journey that began across the street at the Maddock Alumni Center. Both Maddock and Rhode Island Hall are historic buildings—the former, a superb example of the art of historic restoration; Rhode Island Hall, a case study of the art and science of inspired adaptive use. But first some background.

At its September 1836 meeting, Brown's Corporation appointed a committee to "devise means for erecting a building for lecture rooms and rooms for the reception of geological and physiological specimens." In the first decades of the nineteenth century, the study of chemistry and geology captured the interest of academics and the public alike. In the rocks themselves there was evidence that challenged the biblical account of creation. Or so some thought. Others, however, believed close study of the material world would offer even more proof of God's power.

Again the College turned to the generosity of Nicholas Brown Jr., who deeded the land and pledged $3,000 for a new building devoted to the physical sciences. There was one condition: matching funds had to be secured in two months. Secured they were, mostly by contributions from Rhode Islanders, hence the name bestowed by a grateful College, which opened Rhode Island Hall to the public free of charge as a natural sciences museum with the extra bonus of a portrait gallery before the collection was moved and rehung in the newly built Sayles Hall (Walk Two).

Rhode Island Hall

Before moving on to the specifics of this new building, which marked a transformational moment in how the College viewed its mission, let us pause to reflect on a man whose patronage and generosity quite literally shaped the first images that come to mind in any conversation about Brown University. Most commentaries on the early history of the College focus on the $5,000 gift that bought Nicholas Brown Jr. naming rights. It seems like a modest sum for such an honor, but this distorts the extraordinary impact that he, his brothers, and their descendants had in the physical shaping of the University. Four of the structures on the University's historic front row were underwritten partially if not totally by Nicholas Brown Jr. Even the land on which the first buildings of the College as built was paid for and donated by the brothers John and Moses Brown. Brown University was truly a family enterprise and continued to be for over two hundred years.

Initially, the new building was to be located at the corner of Prospect and George Streets. Had Rhode Island Hall been built on this site, a precedent might have been set toward creating a closed quadrangle, with a row of buildings marching north along Prospect Street. The quiet lawn in front of University Hall might have more closely resembled the busy green space that is today's College Green. Why the College had second thoughts and built the new sciences facility on a line with University Hall and the other older buildings is not clear. What is obvious is that Brown at this point at least chose not to gaze inward but to continue to look out to the city.

Rhode Island Hall, natural history museum
c. 1890

As for what turned out to be Nicholas Brown's last direct involvement in the construction projects transforming the Brown campus, the original 70-by-40-foot building altered the typical Classical Revival plan in a number of ways. For example, unlike in Manning Hall, the gable ends of Rhode Island Hall face north–south, although the main entrance is placed, like at Manning, in the middle of the west facade. Its 12-foot projecting vestibule with boxy, squared-off outlines suggests the severity of Egyptian Revival architecture, a style briefly popular at the time. However, the shaping of the new temple dedicated to the sciences had just begun. More than any other building in this row, Rhode Island Hall was subjected to a long series of interventions, extensions, and repurposing that increasingly compromised the clarity of Tallman & Bucklin's design.

In 1874, a two-story Greek Revival ell with four flat Doric pilasters was added on the east side, facing the College Green. The second floor of the addition was used as a portrait gallery for Brown and Rhode Island notables; the first floor, for a museum of natural history, which became increasingly filled with various stuffed birds and mammals; the basement, for a chemistry laboratory. The addition, which opened to the College Green, confirmed that the center of gravity of the campus had shifted 180 degrees from a dialogue with the city to a more internal conversation. In 1885, the portraits were removed and rehung in Sayles Hall, where they hang today. The removal of the portraits led to yet another reworking of the interior, including the addition of skylights in the summer of 1886. The 1904 addition on the south side became a veritable Noah's Ark for live animals, with an aquarium, and on the third floor, a room for preparing animal skeletons.

By the end of the twentieth century, those who walked into the building confronted a warren of offices and closed-off doorways reflecting the University's attempt to find room for the burgeoning sciences faculty and program. Brown could have simply torn down the building as hopelessly ill-suited for a modern university. Yet a devotion to Brown's architectural legacy, along with the University's growing commitment to sustainability, led Brown to save the much compromised facility and reinvent Rhode Island Hall for new purposes, a commitment encouraged by Chancellor Emeritus Artemis A. W. Joukowsky (Class of 1955) and his wife, Martha Sharp Joukowsky (Class of 1958).

The result is a total reworking of the interior. Employing a thoroughly contemporary design vocabulary, the architects reintroduce us to the open, light-filled building Bucklin had in mind. Gone are the shadows and gloom perpetrated by years of haphazard alterations and interventions; in their place is light, much of size;

it brought into the interior by opening up the skylights that had been boarded up. There are many fine touches throughout, including benches made from the original chunky wooden beams removed during the reconstruction. The architects also cut through the new drywall to reveal a narrow strip of the original stacked fieldstone wall. Besides the intrinsic interest of a window into the past, this and the benches are witty allusions to the ongoing work in the home of the Artemis A. W. and Martha Sharp Joukowsky Institute for Archaeology and the Ancient World. In other words, the thorough renovation of Rhode Island Hall can be compared to a scientific dig beneath layers of history to unearth the original building. The ugly duckling revealed its inner swan.

Recycling Brown's fourth-oldest building was an act of enlightened sustainability. It earned for Brown a Gold rating for Leadership in Energy and Environmental Design (LEED) by the U.S. Green Building Council for New Construction, the first such recognition at the University. More recognition was to come: in 2012, Rhode Island Hall was awarded a national AIA Honor Award for interior architecture. In bestowing this award, the jury commented: "[T]his contemporary intervention within this historic shell challenges the notion of archaeology as a conservative and dusty pursuit."[12]

The construction of Rhode Island Hall marked the beginning of Brown's transformation from a college to a university. Built in response to President Wayland's efforts before the Civil War to realign Brown's curriculum from memorization and recitation to exploration and research, Rhode Island Hall set the stage for a second and parallel row of buildings to the east that would create a domain for the sciences. This chapter of Brown's architectural history is the focus of the next Walk, which follows the transformation of the land immediately behind University Hall from a backyard into one of the most significant greens of any American campus.

1 Reverend Ezra Stiles (future president of Yale University), from the *Preamble to the Charter of 1764*, which established Rhode Island College (later Brown), the seventh-oldest institution of higher learning in the United States, quoted in Martha Mitchell, *Encyclopedia Brunoniana* (Providence: Brown University Library, 1993), 136.

2 Evan Haefeli, *New Netherland and the Dutch Origins of American Liberty* (Philadelphia: University of Pennsylvania Press, 2012), 158.

3 Martha Mitchell, *Encyclopedia Brunoniana*, 578.

4 Brown President William Herbert Perry Faunce, quoted in R. M. Kliment and Frances Halsband, *Campus Heritage at Brown University: Preservation Priorities* (Providence: 2006), 12.

5 As stated in the *Preamble to Charter of 1764*, quoted in Mitchell, *Encyclopedia Brunoniana*, 136.

6 Mitchell, *Encyclopedia Brunoniana*, 474–75.

7 John M. Barry, *Roger Williams and the Creation of the American Soul: Church, State, and the Birth of Liberty* (New York: Viking, 2012), 228.

8 Bill Bryson, *At Home: A Short History of Private Life* (New York: Doubleday, 2010), 376.

9 United States Department of the Interior, National Park Service, National Register of Historic Places Inventory, nomination form, "Corliss (George H.) House," Providence, R.I. William Slater Allen, 8, "Significance" (Washington, D.C., 1959).

10 *Boston Gazette*, July 27, 1772; Mitchell, *Encyclopedia Brunoniana*, 551.

11 Quoted by Herman Eschenbacher, "When Brown Was Less Than a University but Hope Was More Than a College," *Brown Alumni Magazine*, February 1980, 28.

12 Jury comments, American Institute of Architects press release, "Joukowsky Institute for Archaeology & the Ancient World," March 2012. A fascinating and thorough history of Rhode Island Hall and its restoration can be found on the project website, www.proteus.brown.edu/rihalltransform/6996.

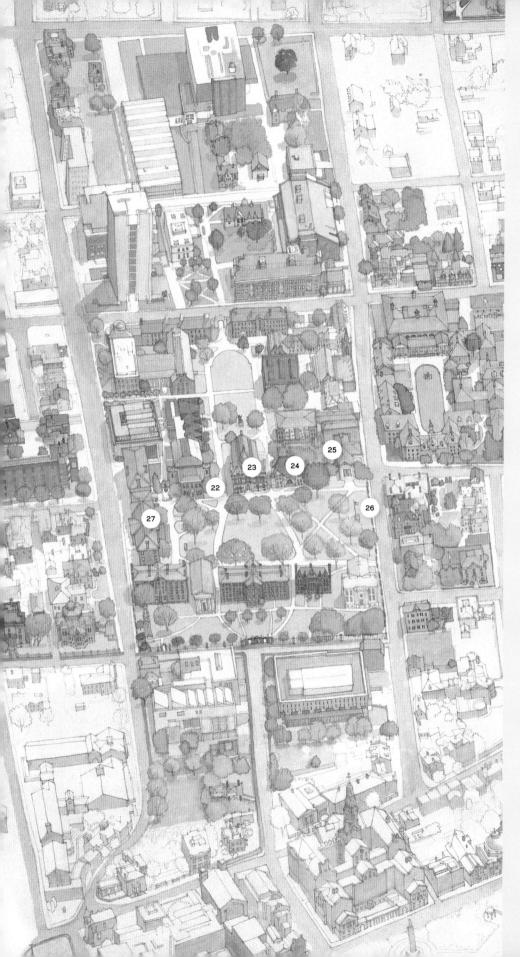

In a city and state so largely devoted to manufacturing as are Providence and
Rhode Island, and to kinds of manufacturing in which competition in every year
calling to its aid the latest results of science, it is evident that the demands on
the one and only University of the state for instruction in applied science must
constantly increase.
—President Ezekiel Gilman Robinson, seventh president of Brown[1]

I have often thought that no student can walk the paths of the College Green for
four years—if he has any sensitivity at all—without learning something from the
appearance, something from the atmosphere that the buildings breathe, something
from the way history looks down upon him.
—Henry M. Wriston, eleventh president of Brown[2]

Until the decade before the Civil War, the row of four buildings, from Hope
College to Rhode Island Hall, was Brown's front door, its face to the community,
a public realm. Towering leafy elms, gravel walks, and a "handsome paling"
(i.e., fence) made the broad lawn that stretched between University Hall and
Prospect Street "one of the loveliest spots in New England."[3] Behind this formal
public face, faculty and students went about more mundane household activities.
This was Brown's backyard, a private realm, muddy with pumps and privies,
the latter not infrequently put to the torch by the students, no doubt terrorizing
the occasional cow that grazed nearby.

The College Green in spring

The College Green in winter

The building of the Chemical Laboratory heralded a transformative evolution of Brown from college to university. It also marked the beginning of the creation of one of Brown's most distinctive features, today's College Green. Two decades on, Sayles Hall rose next door to the Chemical Laboratory; a decade later Wilson Hall became the neighbor of Sayles; and in 1910, the John Carter Brown Library opened next to Wilson. The campus at this point had a second line of predominantly Victorian buildings with a splendid green in between. Brown had turned decisively inward, away from the city. Recognizing the new orientation of the College, Brown added steps (1880) to the rear doors of the original front row.

The historic green space on the west side of University Hall facing downtown Providence, which in earlier years had been something of a shared park between the College and its neighbors, is today a quiet formal lawn. By contrast, the green space behind its oldest building is Brown's Times Square, an ever-changing, tree-shaded park, site of graduation ceremonies, the Campus Dance, pick-up Frisbee, and rallies for the cause of the moment. The layering of history in this one place is extraordinary. More than any other building or space on campus, here is where Brown comes together as a community. A place of respite and restlessness, an outdoor living room where students and faculty, old and young, alumni and visitors meet on equal terms, the College Green is the heart of what defines Brown for students, faculty, and visitors alike.

Students enjoying a spring day on the College Green

Nineteenth-century photo of the Chemical Laboratory, later Rogers Hall

22   Richard and Edna Salomon Center for Teaching (formerly Rogers Hall)
Alpheus C. Morse, 1862; renovation, Goody Clancy, 1989

This first building that began the eastern row, originally called the Chemical Laboratory, was built to support the city's growing textile and jewelry industry. In 1900, an addition was built at the rear and the Chemical Laboratory became known as Rogers Hall in recognition of William Sanford Rogers, donor of $50,000 to endow the Newport Rogers Professorship for Chemistry. A further rechristening occurred after the addition was torn down in 1986. In its place rose a much larger addition designed by Boston-based Goody Clancy to house a 600-seat auditorium and classrooms. Repurposed to support a new program, the expanded facility opened in 1989 as the Richard (Class of 1932) and Edna Salomon Center for Teaching.

Like the row of buildings on the west side of the College Green, those on the east, beginning with Salomon and southward down to the John Carter Brown Library, are chapters in the continuing narrative of America's architectural history at Brown, but with a difference: Those on the west side of the College Green (Slater Hall excepted) reflect a lingering Enlightenment preoccupation with the symmetry and clean, straight lines typical of late Georgian, Neoclassical, and Federal architecture. On the other, east side of the College Green, the narrative moves deeper into the nineteenth century. Rather than brick and stucco, the palette of materials expands and the dominant materials become granite, brownstone, and eventually Indiana limestone. The increasing complexity of the structures on the east side of the Green reflects the impact of new technologies, while the color and bold invention mirror the growing interest in the emerging sciences of chemistry, geometry, and biology. On this side of the College Green, the energetic organic worldview of Charles Darwin replaces the axioms and mathematical proofs of Newton that rule the older row of buildings to the west.

Because Brown did not have the funds to build on a massive scale, and was not dogmatically committed for the first 140 years to any one style, each new building that rose on either side of what became the College Green was different. What they all shared was the determination by the College to build the most up-to-date facility. How Brown and its architects (many of whom were based in Providence) employed the newest technologies can be seen, for example, in the larger panes of glass on the east side of the campus; those of the older buildings to the west were small because small was the only size that was both affordable and available. When the Industrial Revolution made possible large sheets of glass, this allowed the windows of the newer buildings to admit more light, which opened the way for the design of larger and deeper interiors.

Although no two buildings on the College Green are quite alike, there is amity amidst the tumult and it is worth the time to consider why. First, the buildings have enough space between them to command their sites—and, not so incidentally, to reduce the risk of catastrophic fires. Nevertheless, they are not so removed from one another as to seem isolated or adrift. Stand in the middle of the Green and look at the rooflines on either side: With the exception of Salomon, which is the odd man out, there is a procession of triangles, each a variation on a consistent theme. Taken as a whole, the architecture that embraces and defines the College Green reflects the balance of picturesque composition and rational planning characteristic of the best of nineteenth-century architecture.

Like the separate sections of an orchestra, the impression each building makes is distinct yet well tuned to the others to achieve a harmony not unlike a city or village that has grown organically over time. To push the metaphor one more step, the row of buildings on the east side does not fall along a straight line, but like the notes on a musical staff, moves up and down—Salomon back, Sayles forward, Wilson slightly back from Sayles, and the John Carter Brown Library a bit farther back from that. Nor do the buildings on the east side of the Green line up perfectly with those on the west. The resulting asymmetry between and within the two rows (another admired nineteenth-century trait), along with the slight downward slope of the land from the west to east and from north to south, creates a tension that both reflects and reinforces the energy of the College Green, whose size is neither uncomfortably cramped nor so wide that the whole composition falls apart.

Why was the first building on the east side built on this particular spot? Brown owned the lot. Erecting the newest facility here, just across the way from the older buildings, maintained the cohesiveness of the campus. Also, the lot fronted on Brown Street, then a well-traveled thoroughfare, which in the years before the Civil War cut across the campus. It made perfect sense that a second row of buildings would, like the west row, line up along a street. It was not until later in the nineteenth century, when Brown Street was absorbed by the College Green, that the reason behind the siting of the Chemical Laboratory—today's Salomon Center—was erased.

Salomon introduces us to the Victorian affection for variety in the choice of building materials and their color, an affection nurtured by the influential Victorian John Ruskin, who wrote: "The purest and most thoughtful minds are those which love color the most." [4] The roof is covered with Vermont slate laid in bands of purple and green. Windows are gently arched and framed at the top by alternating blocks of olive and brown stone in a manner that at the time was called "Venetian Gothic." However, what might seem to be purely decorative here and in other Victorian buildings on campus was in fact often used to express the different structural functions within a building: stones that bore the weight of the building might be one color, stones that filled a wall, another. Those alternating blocks of olive and brown stone above the windows are a graphic demonstration of how the tension that keeps an arch in place works.

Despite its massiveness, the Goody Clancy addition is very much a background building, which sympathetically echoes the original materials but in a clearly contemporary idiom (the roof is metal). Yes, the older nineteenth-century building is in some ways reduced to a mask, yet because the addition takes advantage of the downward slope of the site away from the Green and the architects avoid grandstanding, the repurposed Salomon Center maintains the symmetry of the College Green. In 2002, the Goody Clancy addition received a New England Regional AIA Award.

Richard and Edna Salomon Center for Teaching

Sayles Hall

23   Sayles Hall

Alpheus C. Morse, 1881; projecting gallery, Stone, Carpenter & Willson, 1903; window replacement, Perry, Shaw & Hepburn, 1944; restoration, Durkee Brown and Carol Sanderson, 2001

Less than two decades after the Civil War, the growing college was in desperate need of additional and better recitation rooms, as well as a hall large enough to hold Commencement dinners and chapel services. The success of the Chemical Laboratory recommended the same architect for a far more ambitious project whose origin was a tragedy. In 1874, William Clark Sayles entered Brown. In his sophomore year, the young Sayles died. Two years later, on what would have been the boy's Commencement day, his father, William Clark Sayles, wrote to President Robinson and pledged $50,000 for a building that would serve the College and honor the memory of his son:

> I have selected this Commencement, when my dear son, if living, would have graduated, for the expression of what I hope will be regarded with favor, in order that when his classmates are conferring credit on their Alma Mater, his brief life may also not be without a beneficial influence on the institution he loved so well.[5]

A portrait of the son hangs on the right side of the vestibule as you enter the hall; a portrait of his father gazes across the space at his son.

The time spent looking at the bold Romanesque pile that is Sayles and then over to the plain geometry of University Hall offers additional clues why the College Green works so well. Note how the two buildings do not quite line up. Not only is the axis a bit askew, the footprint of Sayles is east–west in contrast to the basically north–south orientation of University Hall. Nor are University Hall and Sayles strictly parallel. The older building angles along the southwest to northeast ridge of College Hill; Sayles runs along a straight north–south line. Extend the lines of each row and the green space between is revealed to be neither a rectangle nor a square, but a trapezoid, a bit wider on the south than the north.

Something else: the front of Sayles does not line up with Salomon immediately to the north. Was this the architect's way of asserting the dominance of the new building? In fact Morse had no choice given the size of the edifice he had designed. At the time Brown had not yet acquired the lots to the east of Sayles. To make it fit, Morse had to pull the mass of the building forward almost on to what was then Brown Street. From this necessity emerged an accidental virtue: the absence of perfect symmetry throws the composition of buildings and green space slightly off balance in a way that energizes the space in between. In a subtle way, here again is the tumultuous amity that is the essence of Brown.

If Sayles seems to occupy a commanding position on the College Green reminiscent of those campuses distinguished by a monumental chapel, the resemblance is not totally accidental. The building's dramatic massing, the roughly textured granite, the heavy arches, the massive tower—all suggest the influence of Henry Hobson Richardson's recently completed Trinity Church in Boston (1877). Sayles even sounds like a church, thanks to the massive (more than 3,000 pipes) 25-ton Hutchings-Votey organ given in 1903 by Lucian Sharpe (Class of 1893) in memory of his parents, the largest surviving instrument built by this company. The connection between Sayles and Trinity Church is further underlined by the fact that in the very same year Hutchings-Votey installed a new organ in the chancel of the Boston church.

The three-story tower, large entrance vestibule, wide interior stairways, and high ceilings in the hall and lecture rooms give Sayles a monumental gravitas. As practical as they are decorative, these elements facilitate a natural ventilation of the building, pulling fresh air in and expelling stale air out of the windows at the top of the tower. In a similar practical vein, the thermal mass of the stone here and elsewhere on the row moderated summer heat and winter cold before central heating was widely available. Behind Sayles's central tower, which houses classrooms, the vestibule opens into a two-story assembly room that has hosted a variety of functions from spring training for Brown's baseball team to what for many years was mandatory chapel. Serving as the University's Valhalla, the room contains the impressive collection of large oil paintings of Brown notables, including most of the presidents, that previously had hung in Rhode Island Hall. Equally impressive in its own way is the bold hammer beam construction that supports the wooden roof. The effect is like that of the ribs of a great sailing ship turned upside down and set at rest atop the two-story walls. The original three-color paint scheme discovered behind the organ has been restored.

A side room off the main hall is called the "Little Chapel." It came into being toward the end of World War II. The following year, a stained-glass window designed by Providence artist Robert Barrie was installed. A memorial plaque read: "Erected in tribute to the chaplains in the armed services of the United States." The window, primarily in red, white, and blue, has as its theme "Brave Men of All Races Fighting the Wars of One Nation in One World." After the room was no longer used as a chapel, the window was removed and is today displayed on the third floor of the John Hay Library as part of its special collections.

The completion of Sayles was also the inspiration for the beautification of the College Green. Distressed by the unkempt condition of the site, the donor paid to have the grounds graded and planted. The memorial to his son would be approached not through a wasteland of ashes and weeds, but a landscaped park with winding paths. The Latin quotation carved on the stone band between the second and third stories of the tower—*Filio Pater Posuit*—translates to "the father built this for the son." The inscription comes from the hand of Classics Professor John Larkin Lincoln, whom we will encounter on Walk Three. Prior to the retirement of Brown's highly regarded fifteenth president, Howard Swearer (1977–88), the walks on either side of Sayles were named the Swearer Walkways.

24   Wilson Hall

Gould & Angell, 1891; interior renovation, Robert Hill Architects, 1966

Continuing the Boston theme, several commentators have suggested the red-roofed building designed to house the study of physics and the mechanical arts is reminiscent of Henry Hobson Richardson's Sever Hall at Harvard (1882). Unlike Sever, which is constructed primarily of brick and is relatively restrained, the exuberant random patchwork of rubblestone that animates the front is a veritable quarry of geological delights, rendered especially pleasing by a recent cleaning that has revealed the various colors of the stone. The addition of Wilson to the emerging row of buildings marching down the eastern edge of the College Green was another chapter in the increasing focus on the sciences during the latter half of the nineteenth century. Wilson and its neighbors to the north were Brown's response to developments in German higher education coupled with the close-to-home demands of a great industrial and manufacturing center for graduates trained in the applied sciences, particularly the mechanical arts. The enlightened self-interest the new facility would serve is suggested by the source of the money used to build it, George Francis Wilson. As Martha Mitchell notes in her *Encyclopedia Brunoniana*, "Wilson, in partnership with Professor Eben S. Horsford of Harvard, operated the Rumford Chemical Works....The partnership became a very successful business

Wilson Hall

as Wilson invented the machinery necessary to manufacture Horsford's Acid Phosphates and Rumford Baking Powder."[6] The recipient of an Honorary Master of Arts degree from Brown (1872), Wilson wrote to President Robinson that upon his death, the College would receive funds for scientific instruction. When he died in 1887, Wilson's wishes were carried out and the needs of both Brown and the entrepreneurs of Providence were well served.

Of the many delights of Wilson, consider the subtle play between old and new learning in a building dedicated to science: on the south wall is a sundial, an early "mechanical" way of calculating the passage of time; walk around to the front and you see centered on the roof above the front entrance a modern clock that peers out from beneath its red slate hood. It is the new way of measuring time, freed from nature's cycles. A similar balance exists between the exuberance of the overall shaping of the lively surface played against the architects' invocation of the three-part classical grammar of base, shaft, and capital. It is an agreeable tension between control and release.

The architects who designed Wilson skillfully juggled classical precedents, high Victorian style, and the emerging preoccupation with the handcrafting of utilitarian and decorative objects that came to be known as the Arts and Crafts movement. The intricately carved limestone band above the entrance reflects the influence of the American architect Louis Sullivan (1856–1924), who balanced the seemingly opposing forces of modern architecture and ornament. Like with a musician's cadenza, here as elsewhere nineteenth-century stone carvers were given license by the example and reputation of architects like Sullivan to devise their own ornament based on a close observation of nature. They use their freedom wisely and well.

Two years after its dedication, Wilson and the entire row were connected to the University's new heating and electrical plant. This innovation played a significant role in the construction of the next building, which filled out the southeast margin of the College Green.

25   John Carter Brown Library

George Foster Shepley of Shepley, Rutan & Coolidge, 1904; Casperson addition, Hartman–Cox Architects, 1991

Built for John Carter Brown's world-class collection of nearly 70,000 rare books and maps relating to the European discovery, exploration, settlement, and development of North and South America, the cruciform museum is an unusually florid example of Classical Revival design, which became popular at the beginning of the twentieth century. In other words, it was the very next fashion after Richardsonian Romanesque had exhausted itself. Instead of turning to Roman architecture as their model, which was the more typical choice for civic and public buildings of this period (e.g., the John Hay Library), the architects looked toward Greece. What emerged has been dubbed "German Ionic," though why is hard to say, unless this is an oblique reference to nineteenth-century German concepts of archaeological culture, or still another reference to Greece and Athena without benefit of the owl. Whatever the case, the lush ornamentation that runs across the projecting cornice (carved by the stonecutters John Evans and Company of Boston) is a delight. Palmettes mix it up with scallops (Rhode Island, the Ocean State). The flourishes (acroteria) at the apex

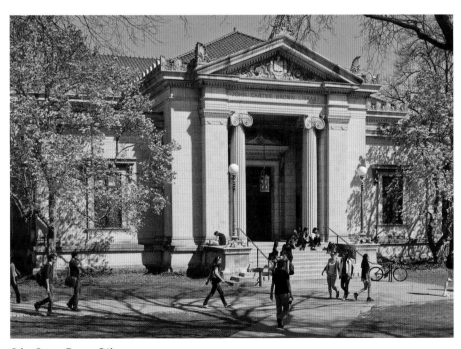

John Carter Brown Library

John Carter Brown Library, detail of lampstand showing scallop motif

and edges of the pediment are stylized Brazilian Indian headdresses (emblematic of the library's exceptional collection of Americana). The seal or insignia of the library (around which are the words "Speak to the past and it shall teach thee") is a reproduction in outline form of the palmette above the entrance, which signifies welcoming.

As you climb the stairs toward the monumental portico (the two supporting Ionic columns are said to be based on the fifth-century BCE temple of Apollo at Bassae), note the finely crafted lamps on either side, yet additional elegant testimonials to the high state of work in base and precious metals that contributed to the prosperity of Providence. They also evidence the way contemporary architects approached a building as a single work of art in which even the most utilitarian elements, from lampposts to sinks, are part of a larger composition.

Once inside, the crisp limestone of the exterior gives way to the softer two-story-high sandstone that embraces one of America's great reading rooms, whose roof is supported by four sandstone monoliths. The softly lit ambience of the polished wooden floors, large Oriental carpets, tapestries, tall curtained windows, and green-shaded Tiffany reading lamps inspire a quality of reverent silence not unlike that felt in a church. Leading off from the central reading room (named in honor of the family of W. Duncan MacMillan, Class of 1953) are four elegantly appointed smaller rooms that serve more focused, scholarly pursuits.

John Carter Brown Library, MacMillan Reading Room

In 1991 Brown dedicated the Casperson Building, a four-story annex, named for the parents of the benefactor and member of the library's Board of Governors, Finn M. W. Casperson (Class of 1963). The twentieth-century architects are deferential to the style and scale of the original building, right down to the ornament that runs along the projecting cornice. The Indian headdresses and palmettes are repeated, but these are appropriately smaller than those on the original building. The difference between the granite used at the base of the original structure and that at Casperson slyly underscores these are two different buildings. Although the addition is subtly designed to look smaller than the library that opened in 1904, it in fact doubled the space. The architects' deference poses the endlessly debated question among preservationists and architects: Should a contemporary addition to a historic structure mask or boldly announce its newness? Should Casperson have reflected "its time" by being an essay in, say, metal and glass? Is what we see today inspired invention within a period style or a more or less literal reproduction? And if so, is that bad?

Throughout its history Brown has tended to take a middle approach: preserving, often restoring the exterior appearance of its older buildings to their original condition, while being increasingly innovative in renovating and repurposing the interiors to accommodate new functions or needs. This was the course pursued at Rhode Island Hall across the Green and, as we will see at the conclusion of this Walk, it was the direction followed in the transformation of Faunce House into the Stephen Robert '62 Campus Center.

The siting of the library was not a foregone conclusion. A number of nearby off-campus locations were considered, and the site that was chosen was not universally approved, because this important building does not, in Beaux-Arts fashion, terminate a long view.[7] According to President Faunce, the argument that most persuaded the Brown family to locate the collection on the College Green had to do with a furnace. If built next to Wilson Hall, the library could be connected to the University's new central heating system. Besides freeing up space in the basement, placing a potential source of fire at some distance from a priceless collection of paper documents was no small advantage.

26 John Nicholas Brown Gate
Hoppin & Ely with Hoppin & Koen, 1904

William Goddard Memorial Gate
Hoppin & Ely, 1910

The John Nicholas Brown Gate at the southeast corner of the College Green was a gift of Brown's widow, Anne. Participating in the laying of the gate's cornerstone was a young boy who later in life would play a major role in the architectural history of Brown, the 3-year-old John Nicholas Brown Jr. One year later, when the gate was opened for the first time to admit the procession at the dedication of

John Nicholas Brown Gate

the John Carter Brown Library, it was the young boy who presented the library's keys to President Faunce. Although his alma mater was Harvard, the son of John Nicholas Brown would come back to Providence and have a powerful influence on the University's architecture.

The palmette capitals of the gate posts, or pillars, echo the dominant decorative motif at the nearby library. Here, as over the door to the library, they are a sign of welcoming. The motif also points to the enduring legacy of the Brown family, stretching back to 1753 to another bibliophile, Nicholas Brown Sr., who headed the city's first library.

On the southwest corner of the College Green, close to Rhode Island Hall, stands the William Goddard Gate. Given by Hope Goddard Iselin in 1911 as a memo-

William Goddard Gate, detail

rial to her father, Brown's tenth chancellor, William Goddard (1888–1907), this is arguably Brown's most beautiful gate, also by Hoppin & Ely. The skilled hand of the welder transforms a base metal into a work of art. Stop to drink it in; the fierce iron menagerie of playful grotesques is well worth the time.

As you walk back toward the Stephen Robert '62 Campus Center, take the path that hugs Brown's old brick row. Note how well the ensemble of buildings holds its side of the Green

College Green, looking south

even though this was not the intent of the original builders, who put the best or ceremonial face on the side looking out to the city of Providence. Note how at either end the temple-like facades of Manning and Rhode Island Halls contribute mightily to the sense of order that delights on every side. (The elephant-headed column at the back of Rhode Island Hall is a replica of one of 142 columns of the Great Temple at Petra, Jordan, site of an important Brown archaeological excavation.)

Now look east across the College Green. Behind you are the brick and stucco buildings that established Brown as a College; in front are the stone buildings that supported research into the sciences that vaulted Brown into the ranks of a university. There is an agreeable rhythm here, but of a different sort from the row of buildings to the west. Overall, the space is wonderfully tied together by the scale of the buildings on both sides that push against and are held back by the Green. The lively conversation between brick to the west and stone to the east is complemented by the ever-changing hand of nature, a hand lovingly assisted by Mary Elizabeth Sharpe (1894–1985), who for three decades guided landscaping at Brown. She had strong support for her efforts: as yet another instance of his stewardship of the campus, John Nicholas Brown Jr. made an anonymous donation in 1970 for the purchase of twenty-five disease-resistant elms and set up a fund for the preservation of all the remaining campus elms.

Lacking a master plan, the architects whose work gave the College Green its shape pulled off something extraordinary: By instinct more than design, they overcame the false dichotomy between architecture and landscape. The dialogue among the buildings and between the architecture and the land became a catalyst for creativity. The gradual evolution of the space that is today the College Green is

Rhode Island Hall

a convincing argument that architecture is less about the making of single objects, however inspired, than the more difficult and ultimately more rewarding task of placemaking.

Just before you reach the Stephen Robert '62 Campus Center, note the bronze pump at the back of Hope College, Brown's oldest residential hall. Given by

Pump behind Hope College

the Class of 1894, it replaced the old cast-iron fixture that for many years stood on top of one of Brown's principal sources of potable water. When it was functioning, the pump filled the pitchers of the students who carried the water inside Hope College. Wastewater was deposited in a large iron bowl in the south end of the building, where the only drainpipe was located. When the pipe froze, the students simply opened their windows and threw the wastewater outside. Central heating was added to Hope in the 1890s; showers, in 1904. These luxuries precipitated an increase in the rent.

27 Stephen Robert '62 Campus Center (Faunce House)

McKim, Mead & White, 1903; east extension, Howe & Church, 1930; renovation, Goody, Clancy & Associates, 1986; interior renovation of west end, Schwartz/Silver Architects, 2010

The controversy that prevented the construction of Slater on the south end of the College Green did not reignite with the building of what was then called Rockefeller Hall, which bore the name of the father of John D. Rockefeller Jr. It certainly helped that Rockefeller Hall was set deep into the landscape so as not to be a visual barrier. The neighbors across George Street could look out into a tree-shaded park that was terminated by the work of the most renowned architecture firm of the day, McKim, Mead & White. The New York firm was at the same time completing one of its most important projects, the magnificent marble Rhode Island State House, on whose dome stands the very symbol of Rhode Island and, one might argue, Brown—the gold-covered bronze statue of the Independent Man.

With the construction of Rockefeller Hall, Brown adopted a modified, open version of a medieval form, the quadrangle. Until that point, the College Green was open on both ends, with a gravel path that continued Brown Street across the eastern edge of the Green. A picket fence at the north and south ends of the Green defined the space. Narrow gates gave access to George and Waterman Streets. The change brought about by the siting of the desperately needed student union was applauded by Olmsted. The new building became something of a hinge, tying together the east and west rows. This gave the College Green a true focus, a cherished axiom of Beaux-Arts planning.

Faunce Arch

Stephen Robert '62 Campus Center in Faunce House

Besides a commitment to rational planning, Rockefeller Hall represented a return to what President Faunce and the Corporation felt was the University's design brand—Georgian or Colonial Revival. Like Princeton and Yale, Brown consciously embarked on image- or myth-making at the opening of the twentieth century to project a distinct identity. But this is getting ahead of a story that will be told in Walk Three. Among the highest items on Faunce's wish list shortly after he became Brown's ninth president was "a building in some central location devoted to the social and moral welfare of the student body."[8] It was only the third student union building to be constructed on an American college campus, and both the sure hand of the architects in designing a handsome Colonial Revival building and the student services it housed were widely applauded. However, the demands of a growing student population forced a constant repurposing of the interior to accommodate a variety of functions, from dining and billiards to the delivery of mail and the cutting of hair. Ultimately the spaces could be chopped and diced in just

so many ways. In 1930, Rockefeller again came forward with funds to enlarge the building to the east along Waterman Street. The donor's sole stipulation was that the enlarged complex of what were now two buildings, both separated and connected by an arch, should be renamed as a memorial to the man who during his thirty years as president presided over the greatest spurt of growth in the University's history.

The addition to the east is essentially a background building, complementing rather than overshadowing the work of McKim, Mead & White. Perhaps the two most enduring contributions of the addition were space for a 360-seat theater (enthusiastically welcomed by Brown's growing drama department) and the arch, which became the formal entrance to the College Green. Like the aperture of a camera, the arch frames and focuses the scene on either side. Of the many entrances into the older campus, this is by far the most dramatic. The central role it plays is confirmed by the city's taxi drivers who make Faunce Arch their destination of choice when they drop off visitors to the campus. It is Brown's front door.

Despite the doubling of space made possible by the 1930 addition and periodic attempts to meet changing student needs, an increasing number of functions collided with form. Before long, the interior declined into a collection of rooms with closed doors. (One lasting improvement was the broad flight of stairs built in 1977 that spill out from the building. It is the most popular seating and meeting place on the College Green. Prior to this innovation by the Boston firm of Goody, Clancy & Associates, the south-facing space immediately outside of Faunce was a fenced-in terrace.) A 2009 renovation by Boston's Schwartz / Silver Architects finally came to grips with the most vexing issues of the chopped-up interior of the original, west building.

Perhaps the single feature of the renovation that best captures the new sense of openness and flexibility can be found in the inspired treatment of the

Stephen Robert '62 Campus Center, interior

arch. One side of the masonry has been penetrated and a new glass wall and entrance inserted. With the information desk clearly in view and a large map on the other side of the arch, visitors for the first time have a coherent and welcoming introduction to the heart of the Brown campus. By imaginatively rethinking how the building could work, the architects have successfully brought new life to the northern end of the College Green. Named after former chancellor Stephen Robert (Class of 1962), Brown today has a first-class campus center that serves contemporary needs.

Several features deserve comment. First, the three-piece bronze sculpture in front of the terrace, *Bridge Prop* (1963), by English sculptor Henry Moore. If the sculptor is to be trusted, it represents a reclining female. Moore explained his choice of name thus: at eye level with the base, one discerns a series of arches; the "Prop" is the arm that holds up the shoulder and head against the middle part. The sculpture also accommodates the occasional reclining student. *Bridge Prop* was given by Laura and David Finn, whose intent was to encourage a commitment to make encounters with outdoor sculpture and art installations a part of a student's experience.

Between the Robert Campus Center and Salomon rears a life-size bronze sculpture of *Ursus arctos middendorffi*, i.e., a Kodiak brown bear, the University's mascot. Sculpted in 1923 by Eli Harvey, the bear was moved to this site from its previous lair in front of the now-demolished Marvel Gymnasium. At the rear of the pedestal on which the bear glowers is an inscribed piece of the slate rock on which Roger Williams disembarked as a refugee when he arrived from Massachusetts in 1636. The stairs behind the bear lead to a quiet below-grade terrace at the back of the Faunce annex. Named in memory of Casey V. Shearer (Class of 2000), the sculpture and fountain were designed by Howard Ben Tre in 2003. If the College Green is Brown's very public living room, outdoor spaces like this are intimate warm-weather nooks in which to pause to read a book, have a quiet conversation, or simply chill.

This Walk around the College Green has been taken during daylight hours. However, the Green (indeed, much of the campus) should also be experienced by night. Enjoy the effect of the up-lighting on the rusticated stone side walls of Sayles. At night these seem to drip luminescence from scattered small pools of light. An argument can be made that architecture's geometry is more pronounced

Brown Bear Statue

(if properly lit) after the sun sets. The effect is not unlike the sharp outlines of a black-and-white photograph versus a photo shot in color.

Although it is heavily planted, the green (thankfully) is not lit up like a shopping mall. The circles of light beneath the period street lamps (which are in fact newly installed), the softly lit facades of the buildings in which shadows highlight details not often obvious in the light of day—the triangular outline of University Hall's central pediment, the curves of Sayles's entry tower—these and more are magical and the Green no less safe for those walking than had this wonderful space been saturated by the blinding glare of klieg lights.

1 R. M. Kliment and Frances Halsband, *Campus Heritage at Brown University: Preservation Priorities* (Providence: 2006), 58.

2 Martha Mitchell, *Encyclopedia Brunoniana* (Providence: Brown University Library, 1993), 594.

3 President Wayland, quoted in Mitchell, *Encyclopedia Brunoniana*, 111.

4 John Ruskin, *The Stones of Venice*, ed. J. G. Links, vol. 2 (New York: Farrar, Straus & Giroux, 1960), 53.

5 Walter C. Bronson, *The History of Brown University 1764–1914* (Providence: Brown University, 1914), 393–94.

6 Martha Mitchell, *Encyclopedia Brunoniana*, 579.

7 Kliment and Halsband, *Campus Heritage*, 85. The criticism was leveled by the contemporary architect (and Brown graduate) Norman M. Isham.

8 Kliment and Halsband, *Campus Heritage*, 80.

The Lower Green and Its Monuments

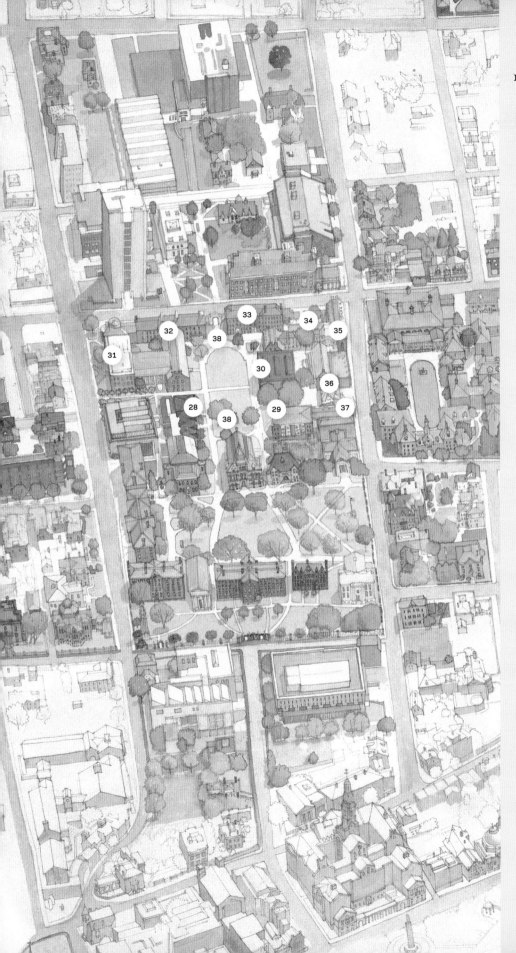

> We thank you for your report and may have occasion to consult you a little later.[1]
> —President Faunce

A page-turning event in the history of American architecture and urban design was Chicago's World's Columbian Exposition (1893), or the "White City," as it is often known. The Exposition was held to commemorate the landing of Christopher Columbus in the Americas and, more to the point, to promote the emergence of Chicago as a world-class city. What the project architect Daniel Burnham (1846–1912) achieved on 633 acres bordering Lake Michigan was nothing short of a revolution in the perception of what the nation's crowded and dirty cities could be *if* shaped rationally. The revolution was not simply or even primarily about the appearance of urban centers, as the memorable but misleading label "City Beautiful" implies. Instead, architects took a comprehensive approach to the design of cities, from sanitation and parks to patterns of circulation and law enforcement. This was the progressive era in which progress was America's manifest destiny. The latest technologies and integrative thinking could be employed to achieve supreme functionality and delight. Never before and perhaps never since has the design expertise of America's architects been so highly regarded by the public and sought after by influential clients.

The lessons of the Columbian Exposition, including the use of physical form to communicate an institution's image of itself and its values, were not lost on administrators who were transforming their colleges into research-oriented universities. A college could exist casually in a park; a great university, however, was organized and planned. A cohesive organization of the campus would more powerfully express the larger idea of a university's mission and its ideals. At Princeton, the transformation of what had been a Victorian campus into Oxbridge Collegiate Gothic was led by University President Woodrow Wilson. Wilson's vision bought Princeton four hundred years of history. At Brown, it was William Herbert Perry Faunce, who looked back to a history of a different sort. Shortly after becoming President in 1899, he contacted Frederick Law Olmsted Jr. to bring his vision to light.

What subsequently emerged from six years of letters and meetings between Faunce and Olmsted was not a radical physical transformation of Brown. Olmsted could and did give advice; Faunce could and often did disregard what he heard. Also, unlike Princeton and Yale, Brown lacked the funds to initiate a comprehensive reworking of the campus. Nevertheless, the very fact that President Faunce initiated the conversation with America's leading landscape architect (who with his father had worked on the Columbian Exposition) shows he was thinking about the campus in a big-picture way. Having in hand a planning document would organize and direct future growth. And the style of architecture would communicate a compelling message about the University's values.

The message or brand advanced by President Faunce and the Brown Corporation was pointedly different from that pursued by Princeton. While both institutions were committed to a program of orderly, rational growth, the roots being cultivated on College Hill reached not to English Gothic precedents but rather to the eighteenth-century and Colonial architecture: "We decided that our architecture must henceforth conform in general to the Georgian or Colonial style, which not only reminds us of the age in which the University was founded, but is far better adapted than the Gothic to give the generous lighting needed in modern libraries and laboratories."[2] To the aristocratic carved stone, stained glass, and gargoyles of Princeton and Yale, which evoked late medieval England, Brown responded with the straight lines, clear glass, and plain Jeffersonian brick of a democratic American tradition. Without questioning the sincerity of Faunce's affection for Colonial architecture, it is perhaps relevant to suggest that faced with limited financial resources, brick rather than hand-carved limestone was a more prudent way to build.

The first canvas on which the new way of comprehensive planning would be sketched out lay directly east and perpendicular to the College Green. What today is a parklike setting for residential dorms and a wide range of Brown's academic disciplines was, until 1880, a swamp "partly covered by water, inhabited by a numerous colony of bull-frogs."[3] The initial transformation of "a tropical growth of shrubbery and tall grass" 10 feet below the grade of Thayer Street was driven by the increasing popularity of baseball and college athletics in general.[4] Under the supervision of Professor Samuel S. "Betsey" Greene (Class of 1837), two of whose sons were on the baseball team, the site was cleared, drained, and graded for a baseball diamond and a track. Professor Greene seems to have been able to field an extraordinary range of disciplines, including didactics, mathematics, natural history, astronomy, and logic, when, in his spare time, he was not busy guiding a landscaping project for his sons and their friends. The new athletic green was named after a much-beloved professor of Latin, John Larkin Lincoln, and in 2012 renamed the Ruth J. Simmons Quadrangle by the Corporation to honor Brown's eighteenth president.

Lincoln Field, looking toward the back of Rogers Hall, c. 1890

28 Lyman Hall and the Catherine Bryan Dill Center for the Performing Arts

Stone, Carpenter & Willson, 1891; Colgate Hoyt Pool addition, 1903; interior renovation and reconstruction, Armstrong Childs Associates, 1978

Francis Wayland had advocated the construction of a gymnasium the very year he became Brown's fourth president (1827–55). But as with a number of Wayland's far-reaching insights, decades were to pass before they were put into practice. When Brown at last welcomed the concept of sound mind *and* sound body, the embrace was total. The two-and-a-half-story brick and stone Richardsonian Romanesque gymnasium that rose on the northwest corner of the newly graded Lincoln Field was a stunner. The larger of the building's two elements, distinguished by an ample off-center arched entry and an adjacent tower, housed a bowling alley, batting cages, running track, and wrestling room. For more than a decade after Lyman first opened its doors, the space immediately to the east was merely a deep hole in the ground, until a donor, Colgate Hoyt, provided the funds for a swimming pool. (The first meet, a water polo game between Brown and Yale, took place in 1903. Yale emerged the victor, 3–0.)

In its style, masonry, and detailing, Lyman is among the last of Brown's distinguished Victorian buildings. However, the lowering of the curtain of this particular moment in Brown's history is done in spectacular fashion. From the march of the dormers across the roof to the decorative corbel arches that radiate around the entrance (see especially the band of small stone faces), there are many fine instances of craftsmanship to delight the eye. The stairs, for instance, seem to flow in an ever-broadening series of stone ripples from the main entrance. Utilitarian, yes, especially as they anticipate the energy of the students pouring

Lyman Hall

Lyman Hall, entrance and University seal

Lyman Hall, detail

out of the building, but also aesthetically satisfying in their proportions. Or take the oxeye / porthole-like window by the handicap entrance at the southeast corner. Here the line between function and beauty is completely erased. Consider the inspired handling of the materials that make up the building's surfaces. If nearby Sayles is a study on the theme of the color brown, Lyman explores the various permutations of red. The rusticated pink granite of the foundation—which inclines out to deflect water from the basement—sparkles in the sunlight like rock candy. The horizontal belt courses that run along the facade are another variation on a theme that culminates in the brilliant red of the slate roof.

Of the many images of the University's logo that appear on campus, the fiery terra-cotta anthropomorphic orb to the left of the arch and under the stone plaque that reads "Lyman Hall" is the most wonderful. A jolly sun beneath his double rows of twisting rays, he promises a burst of laughter once his face is completely visible. A larger and equally sure detail is the clever way the tower and the adjacent loggia (which offers a fine elevated view of the quad) serve as a hinge that provides a visual transition between the gym and the pool. There is nothing at Brown more surely and cleverly wrought.

The brilliance of Lyman Hall is more than skin deep. The beefy masonry acts as a thermal buffer, maintaining an even temperature inside. It was also designed to stand up to the punishment inevitably inflicted by young athletes. Besides identifying the way in, the tower, together with the windows of the dormers, enables a convection current that allows a quick exchange of fresh air to dissipate the heat and sweat inside. If the building has something of the air of a turn-of-the-century gentleman's club that would fit comfortably into downtown Boston, Chicago, or San Francisco, the resemblance is surely not accidental.

After Marvel Gymnasium opened in 1928, most of the men's athletic programs moved out of Lyman to the larger, more modern facilities a mile away at Aldrich Field (basketball and handball remained). When these sports made the leap to Marvel in 1946, Lyman Gym became Lyman Hall.

In 1978, Lyman experienced another transformation. The architecture firm of Sasaki, Dawson, DeMay Associates recommended that Lyman, together with the east building of Faunce Hall, be repurposed as an experimental theater complex (today's Catherine Bryan Dill Center for the Performing Arts), and that the adjoining Colgate Hoyt pool be decked over to support a dance studio. The work was carried out by Armstrong Childs Associates (Leslie Armstrong, Class of 1962). Perhaps the single most transformational gesture visible to passersby on Lincoln Field was opening up the blank faces of the original decorative brick arches around the exterior perimeter of the Colgate Hoyt Pool, and the substitution of clear glass for brick. The addition of windows brought the activity inside the dance studio out to the green, an effect especially memorable at night when the dancers practicing their moves are a colorful, ever-changing billboard for the most kinetic of the arts. As the architect intended, this transparency expands our performance experience beyond the brief moment of formal presentations. While the pool and Lyman were being repurposed (into the Ashamu Dance Studio and the Isabelle Russek Leeds Theatre, respectively) the architects were also engaged to repurpose a suite of existing buildings on Brown's newly acquired East Campus into a home for the Music Department. Repurposing rather than tearing down its older buildings would become a cornerstone of the University's commitment to sustainability.

29   Maxcy Hall
Hoppin, Read & Hoppin, 1895; interior renovation,
Brewster Thornton Group Architects, 2011

Named after the College's second president, Jonathan Maxcy (1792–1802), the next facility on the Field was, like University Hall, designed to serve a number of purposes. The five-story brick building housed students on the third, fourth, and fifth floors; provided classrooms on the second floor; and accommodated a botany laboratory on the ground floor. The hope that Maxcy would eventually be devoted entirely to dormitory space was finally realized in the late 1930s. For the next two decades, Maxcy remained a residence hall before becoming the home of the Department of Sociology in 1959. The most prominent change to an all-residential interior (besides the addition of bathrooms on every floor) was the replacement of the common stair in the center of the building as the sole means of egress. New fire-safety codes explain the addition of a fire stair and fire escapes on the north and south sides. This concern for fire safety was no doubt prompted by memories of a blaze that seriously damaged the interior thirty years earlier and the emergence of life-safety codes that would increasingly drive how Brown renovated its older buildings.

A somewhat ungainly composition that uneasily mixes Colonial Revival and Italianate elements, Maxcy is nevertheless an intelligent design, especially in the way the exterior clearly articulates the separate functions inside—laboratory, classroom, and dorm. Note how the row of tall, round-arched windows at the second floor are appropriate for the classrooms into which they open, appropriate because they admit a lot of light for students taking notes without glare since they are on the north side of the building. Those above convey a residential message. The light-colored paired three-story bays on either side that begin a bit below the level of the third floor break up both the color and mass of the brick. (Compare these to the much more shallow bays at Gregorian Quad, Walk Seven.) They also admit additional natural light into the interior and give the square layout of the typical dorm room a nice outward bump. The stack of large, tripartite windows at the center do not line up with the floors, because they are meant to illuminate the landings of the building's central staircase. Not only practical, these windows, along with the bays, choreograph a sense of rhythm to help soften what otherwise would seem to be an oppressive pile of brick. However, all those portico-like elements standing on each other's shoulders seem to overwhelm the rather modest entry door.

The siting of Maxcy created problems for the next generation of planners, who struggled to impose a more rational, symmetrical design on Lincoln Field. In a strictly Beaux-Arts scheme, there ought to have been a clear alignment between the east ends of Maxcy and Lyman. There was not. The implications will be discussed on our next stop.

30   Lincoln Field Building
Clarke & Howe, 1903

Built more in sync with what had become the *de rigueur* Brown Colonial Revival brand (symmetry, a central portico that steps forward from the facade, dentil molding along the cornice, etc.), the third building constructed on Lincoln Field was built to be a workhorse, a facility for mechanical and civil engineering. What was studied inside its walls was another contribution to the city's need for an educated workforce to deliver the innovation that would keep Providence vibrant economically. Supporting this mission, both figuratively and literally, was the muscularity of a structure required to support the heavy machinery the engineering students worked with.

The building's most outstanding design feature is the large windows. Indeed, the facility appears to be constructed of almost equal parts brick and glass. To prevent students from physical harm given the heavy equipment, the windows, together with the north-facing sawtooth skylights on the roof, bring the light of the outside indoors, which was especially important for the drawing classes on the top floor. No doubt this amenity was particularly appreciated since the University's future chancellor, Buffom Chace (1907–1932), who oversaw the construction, favored kerosene lamps over "newfangled" electric lighting.[5] A prejudice that might have discouraged liberal arts students was for the engineers an interesting challenge they quickly met. They simply "appropriated" a generator and wired the building themselves.

The handling of what is the spine of the composition—the central stairway—is carried out in a manner that is simultaneously more monumental yet more subtle

Lincoln Field Building

than Maxcy next door. The door is not much larger, but it is surrounded by a limestone frame and Doric columns that add grandeur to pure utility. The effect is magnified by the balustrade immediately above and the one-and-a-half-story arched window, which echoes the shape of the windows on the first floor. The strongest geometric form, the triangle, is repeated across the facade: the three windows on either side of the first and second floors; the three elements of the entry and the large window above; the keystones above the second-story windows; the three horizontal belt courses; the three parts of the facade itself; and so forth. Whether by accident or design, the strict yet playful geometry suits a facility that houses students pursuing careers in mechanical and civil engineering. It also contributed to the success of the building as a pleasing addition to the growing campus.

Up to this point, Lincoln Field was growing more by instinct and the constraints of the site than by design. This changed when Faunce became president. As noted earlier, Faunce sought out the advice of Frederick Law Olmsted Jr. Nowhere was this advice more earnestly solicited than in the ongoing expansion of the University east on Lincoln Field. How should the University proceed? Lyman Gymnasium and Maxcy Hall were facts that could not be ignored. Also, there was the problem of a 10-foot difference in grade between the west and east ends of Lincoln Field. How would all these disparate elements be wrestled into a plan whose logic would be clear and coherent? Olmsted proposed a new facility between Maxcy and the Lincoln Field Building. The eastern edge of the new building would line up with the eastern edge of the Colgate Hoyt pool. As for the difference in grade, this would be handled by moving the earth of the Field to create two distinct levels, an upper and a lower green, negotiated on either side by a set of stairs. In between the stairs, the bank of earth would be sculpted to form an amphitheater with a flat presentation area to the east, no doubt for the staging of pageants, concerts, and the classics of the Greek and Roman stage as performed by Sock and Buskin, Brown's drama club founded in 1901.

The excavation proceeded as Olmsted recommended and the stairs were constructed. However, the amphitheater never came to pass. Nor was the building Olmsted proposed built, leaving what one commentator describes as a "hole" or gap on the south edge of Lincoln Field that exists to this day.[6] Somewhat buried in Olmsted's recommendations was an intriguing proposal to physically link the Brown campus with the new Women's College emerging a few blocks to the east. Although buried, the idea was not dead and would emerge with new vigor during the tenure of President Simmons.

31   Arnold Laboratory

Clarke & Howe, 1915; penthouse, Conrad Green, 1949;
addition, William Warner, 1963; entry plaza, David Presbrey Architects

Made possible by the bequest of Dr. Oliver H. Arnold (Class of 1865), this new
facility, also by the firm of Clarke & Howe, addressed the University's urgent need
for an up-to-date biology laboratory. Technically part of Simmons Quad, Arnold Lab
turns its back on the green and faces out to Waterman Street. An argument can be
made that Arnold is less successful than the firm's earlier Lincoln Field Building. In
part, it is the difference of site: the earlier building is set on the green; Arnold faces
a busy thoroughfare and is partially screened from Waterman Street by dense
planting. More significantly, Arnold is longer, and individual elements, such as the
window frames, are heavier. The result is a more horizontal squat structure.

Like the Lincoln Field Building, Arnold Lab is a house of many windows.
The glazing addressed the need for natural light to avoid unintended dissections in
the dark. The glass is so extensive, especially above the first floor, that the brick
in between is treated like pilasters rather than walls, an effect underscored by the
capitals and bases that bracket each "column." Perhaps one of the most attractive
features is the 50-foot-deep landscaped grounds. Viewed from the street, Arnold
sits serenely in a pleasant park. Currently it is used for administrative offices and
for the University's collection of preserved plant specimens.

Arnold Laboratory is not likely to make anyone's top ten list. Taken on its
own terms, it is an example of a well-crafted background building that admirably
served its original intent as a modern research facility. Like a good neighbor, it
complements rather than intrudes upon its surroundings.

Arnold Laboratory, Waterman Street entrance

Metcalf Chemical Laboratory
Day & Klauder, 1923

Metcalf Research Laboratory
*Day & Klauder, 1938; addition, William Warner, 1965; renovation,
Leers Weinzapfel Associates, 2011; landscaping, Steve Stimson, 2011*

Two recent and very different stops on the Brown campus illustrate the
creative relationship that, at its best, exists between the architect and the educator.
In the opening decades of the twenty-first century, this has meant using architecture to dismantle the rigid boundaries that used to separate various disciplines. One
project is a new facility built in the first decade of this century, the Perry and Marty
Granoff Center for the Creative Arts (Walk Five). The other is the radical repurposing of two interconnected buildings designed by one of the most influential and
prolific twentieth-century architects of academic buildings and campus designs.
This part of our narrative takes up the story of the older buildings first. In June
1904, a position was created for superintendent of grounds and buildings. Nearly
two decades later, in 1920, the Brown Corporation took an additional step toward
a more deliberate approach to the development of the campus of "Greater Brown"
(the words of President Faunce) by creating a committee whose charge was the
comprehensive planning and development of University property. At the same time,
the Corporation established the office of supervising architect. Both would ensure
that Brown would no longer "live from hand to mouth, purchasing a piece of ground
because it is in the market," and both would see to it that Brown would no longer
select "a style of architecture because of the wishes of friends or donors." [7]

Instead, there would be a common Colonial Revival style "not indeed as a
straitjacket, but as a pattern in the mount." [8] This qualification indicates Faunce did
not intend Brown's architects to merely copy or reproduce facsimiles of eighteenth-
century buildings. It would be enough to evoke or be inspired by the period, not to
attempt to re-create it. The well-regarded Philadelphian Charles Klauder was hired
as the University's first supervising architect. His assignment was to carry forward
an update of Olmsted's recommendations made by Klauder's Philadelphia colleague,
architect Paul Cret. With Olmsted and Cret as his guides, Klauder would complete
the shaping of Lincoln Field by filling in the remaining empty spaces with buildings
that he himself designed.

At first glance, Klauder seems an odd choice. After all, the firm of Day &
Klauder had made its reputation as masters of Collegiate Gothic architecture,
which was transforming older campuses, including Princeton and Yale. However,
Klauder had more than one string in his bow. Before he set pencil to paper, he
carefully researched what was special about the location, climate, history, tradition,
and curricula of whatever college had retained him—and many did. This was
the starting point. What emerged would speak therefore to the unique genius of
a particular place. What was not negotiable in any project was his deep commitment

Metcalf Research Laboratory (left) and Metcalf Chemical Laboratory (right)

to a core Beaux-Arts principle—order: "That the group of buildings shall not be a motley jumble of discordant styles, erected at haphazard, confusing to beholders and irritating to occupants, but rather that it should be homogeneous, clearly to be apprehended scheme."[9] Whatever the style, it had to serve a larger legible concept. This is the spirit that complemented Olmsted's own Beaux-Arts vision and completed Lincoln Field.

The first of Klauder's four buildings, Metcalf Chemical Laboratory, set the pattern. Like Klauder's other work at Brown, Metcalf Chemical Lab does not jump out as a "look-at-me!" architectural prima donna; rather, it defers to the larger vision of a unified constellation of structures tied together by a landscaped green. The key to the architect's skill is the way he sites this and the other buildings he designed for Brown—their scale and orientation—and the care that went into everything from the rhythm of doors and windows down to the very brick. "[He] went back to University Hall…studied the original 1770 wall, the brick patterns, the mortar joints, the rhythm of openings, the size and shape of the windows, with their slightly arched masonry tops, and recreated the wall in his new buildings."[10] Note in particular the return to small-paned windows, a deliberate echo of Hope College and a nostalgic turning away from the large-paned glass so eagerly adopted by Victorian architects. Brown could not return to the world that gave it birth, but its architecture could look back across the generations to recall its origins as a child of the Enlightenment.

Built fifteen years later, Metcalf Research Laboratory showed no lessening of the architect's skill; nevertheless, there is clearly a more austere or leaner spirit at work. The difference most likely stems from a change in Brown's and the country's fortunes. The earlier of the two research facilities was designed during the Roaring

Twenties; Metcalf Research Lab was built in the tense twilight between the worst years of the Depression and World War II. The architect had to pay even more attention to budget than usual.

In 2001, the University realized the emerging field of brain sciences required a new facility if it was to maintain a leadership position in teaching and research. Understanding that scientific research would over time pursue new paths, Klauder designed both Metcalf Chemical and Metcalf Research Laboratories to be adaptable. His foresight paved the way in 2010 for a repurposing of the complex to house the newly formed Department of Cognitive, Linguistic, and Psychological Sciences.

Repurposing meant gutting both buildings, whose interiors had been compromised by a series of uncoordinated interventions; recovering wasted basement and attic space; and installing new energy-efficient HVAC and fire-safety systems. Repurposing also meant opening up the buildings internally and externally, thus intentionally blurring the boundary between public and private space, while creating an environment where information collaborations can thrive. As originally designed, the Metcalf Research Complex was something of a wall between Lincoln Field and Waterman Street. Today, one can see straight through. Like Klauder, Leers Weinzapfel was guided by what the firm believed defines Brown—not the colonial past, but Brown's position as a vital, evolving part of the larger urban fabric of College Hill and Providence.

Metcalf Research Laboratory, first-floor lounge

Susan P. and Richard A. Friedman Auditorium

In the same vein as the reworking of Faunce Arch, which removed the brick on the west wall and replaced it with glass, transparency and permeability became the order of the day. Inside, natural light is brought into the building by uncovering windows and skylights that had been hidden for years. The third-floor faculty colloquium and reception room (under the white dome seen from Waterman Street) and the intimate, two-story MacDougald Family Library are small jewels among the many pleasures of the newly configured interior of the L-shaped complex, which has been reorganized into a faculty office wing and a research lab wing. The 225-seat Susan P. (Class of 1977) and Richard A. Friedman (Class of 1979) Auditorium on the first floor easily takes the prize for the most dramatic interior space. Auditoriums can feel claustrophobic, but not here. The gentle lift of the curved ceiling and the celebration of natural light allow the space to breathe.

Interior walls were removed in both buildings to encourage interaction both formal and conversational among different disciplines. This is most apparent where the two wings of the complex meet at a pivotal gathering and circulation core of open lounges and conference rooms. The numerous kitchen areas invite the pleasures of spontaneous kaffeeklatsches. Instead of blind, opaque surfaces, the wood doors frame large areas of frosted glass, which admit soft diffused natural light into the halls. Showers and changing rooms have been designed into the building to encourage faculty and students to bike, a telling amenity that affirms the University's commitment to environmental stewardship and health by design.

The reworking of the Metcalf complex and the craftsmanship that distinguished this project are no less dramatic on the outside. The brick walls and fieldstone foundation have been cleaned and repointed. Three or more decades earlier, cleaning old brick usually meant sandblasting and the use of rough solvents, which causes brick to exfoliate. And if new mortar is allowed to set harder than the brick, problems are inevitable when expansion takes place. The excellent condition of the postrestoration walls is a measure of the care that was taken. Bringing back the bones of Metcalf to a new life also meant the installation of energy-efficient double-hung mahogany multipaned windows and a new slate roof.

Entry into the Metcalf complex from the north or Waterman Street side through what had been a previously closed main entrance includes the experience of *P-131317*, a glass installation by Sarah Oppenheimer (Class of 1995). By removing sections of the floor and installing slanted mirrored glass at the courtyard entrance, views are opened between the basement and the outdoors. Depending on the time of day, students experience the space up, down, and through the building and see their own reflections as they walk across the short bridge that leads into the

Simmons Quad

building. The theory behind Oppenheimer's installation is to show how perceptions of the world can differ—an appropriate metaphor for those working in the field of brain sciences.

Directly across from the entrance, in the connector that links both wings, is an intimate, light-filled first-floor common lounge whose glass wall affords views out to the Simmons Quad. Close to and framed by the glass is a memorial designed by Richard Fleischner dedicated in 1997, a granite and lattice sculpture that honors those Brown men and women who died in World War II, Korea, and Vietnam. Each spring and summer, the rose that climbs over the lattice affirms in the midst of death the hope that comes with the annual renewal of life. Once a seeming afterthought positioned in a shaded corner, this quietly respectful tribute has found a voice it lacked before.

The view out to the landscaped green is another variation on the theme of connections. Here, it is war and peace, life and death, learning and service. At the Metcalf complex and elsewhere around the Brown campus, the confining walls and gates erected by the University at the beginning of the twentieth century are being literally and metaphorically flung open to welcome not only interdisciplinary study, but also a fluid interaction between town and gown, thus carrying forward Brown's growing engagement with the world beyond its campus. The controversy that might have been ignited by a new research facility elbowing its way into the historic fabric of the College Hill neighborhood has been preempted by the familiar bottle into which new wine has been poured. By saving the energy that would have been needed for the construction of an entirely new building (not to mention the hauling away of debris to landfills), and by rendering the existing building more energy-efficient, the University and its architects have put into practice Brown's commitment to sustainability. In an age of relentless novelty, the remodeling of a familiar landmark is a reassuring reminder that existing buildings can be given new life and in so doing offer comfort in continuity.

Before walking over to Caswell Hall, step directly across Thayer Street and look back at this side of the Metcalf complex. Notice how within the confines of limited space (the building pushes up close to the sidewalk) Klauder subtly breaks up the three-story brick facade into wings and a projecting central bay with two smaller windows on either side of the door. Between the second and third stories there is the suggestion of flanking brick pilasters. (Klauder manipulates the brick in a similar fashion over the entry to Metcalf Research Lab.) The four parallel stacks of brick chimneys at the top of Metcalf Chemical Lab are both practical and decorative: the vertical thrusts convey a sense of energy. The two rows of chimneys at the center that bracket a parapet further accent the entrance by making the central bay seem taller than the rest of the building. This is an architect whose confidence does not require a brass band. It is as brilliant as a Chopin étude.

33 Caswell Hall
Hoppin & Ely, 1904

As noted earlier, President Faunce drew up a long list of projects when he became president. Both he and the Corporation were eager for a physical plant that would position Brown to catch up with its growing reputation, and position the University for future growth. Although Faunce did not identify which projects should come first, new dorms were clearly high on his list: "A strong element in our Brown life has been the democracy and solidarity induced by our campus dormitories. Students scattered in residences easily become divided in feeling. Unity and loyalty are nourished by dormitory residence." [11] Unity and loyalty were served two years later when Caswell Hall, named after Brown's sixth president, Alexis Caswell (1868-1872), opened its doors. The newest building followed roughly—but only roughly—Olmsted's plan for Lincoln Field. Had Olmsted's advice been followed, Caswell would have faced north and lined up with a proposed building on the opposite side of Lincoln Field. Instead, the brick Colonial Revival dorm was situated at a southeast site at the bottom of the Field, parallel to Thayer Street.

By consciously echoing elements of the First Baptist Meeting House (the Vermont marble porches imitate the doorway on the south side of the Meeting House) and Brown's first residential dorm ("externally resembling our venerable Hope College"), Hoppin & Ely created what was regarded as Brown's finest residential house. [12] Indeed, apart from the pedimented entryways, the resemblance between Hope College and Caswell is uncanny, although it requires a second glance, since a later residence hall, Hegeman, partially blocks the view. The new dormitory had furnished suites (an innovation) and single rooms to house

Caswell Hall from Thayer Street

seventy-two students. This amenity, together with individual fireplaces and electricity, merited a higher rent—$425 annually, compared to $260 at Slater.

Divided into three separate residential spaces—north, middle, and south—Caswell is an example of a pattern of dormitory design that existed in England: student rooms arranged around stairways with direct access to the outside. More residential, yes, than the institutional double-loaded corridors of the top residential floors of University Hall when it was first built; however, the design was eventually deemed a fire hazard, since the only means of egress were those single stairwells. Brown addressed the issue by installing the fire escapes as well as at Maxcy and Hegeman Halls.

34   Hegeman Hall
Day & Klauder, 1926

Two decades after Caswell opened, President Faunce reported the University had rented over one hundred rooms throughout the city to house students. The time had come to build yet another new dormitory to honor Brown's commitment to be a residential college.

Once again Klauder's genius as an architect and urban planner is clear. He deftly manipulates the buildings of the complex as if they were plastic, bending the mass now this way, now that to create a footprint that resembles the letter Z. That is, the complex reads as three separate parts, which are in turn subdivided into five entries or, as the University calls them, "towers." Beginning on the south side of the

Simmons Quad, Hegeman is initially encountered as a smallish one-story Colonial Revival house that originally had a reading room in a two-room suite. The structure then makes a sharp 90-degree turn south and slides past St. Stephen's Church as it responds to a change in grade, which allows Hegeman to expand to a height of four stories; then the building once again reverses course to head east toward Thayer Street. The south wall of Caswell and the east- and north-facing walls of Hegeman form a leafy courtyard entered either from Thayer Street or on the north side through a small arched paved court down a flight of shaded stairs.

Applauded at the time for embodying the most up-to-date thinking about the comfort and convenience of dormitory life, Hegeman as seen from the street comes off as a well-liked resident of long-standing. How is this achieved? Breaking up the mass and juggling the elevations are a pair of obvious tactics. But take the time to look more closely. Note the slight variations of the windows from floor to floor. These and any number of countless subtle details read "residential," rather than institutional.

35   St. Stephen's Church

Richard Upjohn, 1862; chancel, Henry Vaughan, 1882; tower and steeple, Hoppin & Ely, 1900; vestry alterations, Cram and Ferguson, 1933; interior renovations, Robert and Toby Robbins, 1964

If the Corporation wanted to show the newly appointed supervising architect what style of architecture was unsuitable for Brown, they needed only walk a few yards south to the granite Gothic Revival, High Church edifice on George Street. Affectionately known as "smoky Steve's" (for the blue haze of incense that robes the sanctuary every Sunday and on saints' days—of which there are many), the church exhibits everything Brown at that moment in time deliberately strove not to be—medieval English versus colonial American, hierarchical rather than egalitarian, spiritual and mysterious rather than rational. Yet how much poorer the unique tapestry that is Brown and College Hill would be without this gorgeous pointed Anglo-Catholic hosanna in the midst of the Corporation's invocation of the sober straight lines of the Enlightenment.

Had St. Stephen's been designed and built a century earlier, the church, both inside and out, would most likely have looked like the First Baptist Meeting House. Trinity Episcopal Church in nearby Newport (1725–26), with its light-filled interior and classical detailing, is the obvious contemporary example that makes the point. With an emphasis on preaching the Word (which Episcopalians shared with other Protestant denominations in the eighteenth century), the raised pulpit in Trinity rather than the altar occupies the central place.

In the opening decades of the nineteenth century, Enlightenment clarity gradually began to be replaced by a renewed emphasis on liturgy and the rituals of the medieval Church. The shift was in reaction to what many felt was a spiritually deadening emphasis on passionless reason at the expense of the claims made

St. Stephen's Church

by the spirit. This drift toward what might be called a more emotional, romantic approach to worship was soon reflected in everything from the design of churches to the clothes worn by the ministers. The plain white surplices of the eighteenth-century Episcopal clergy were replaced by rich vestments. The somewhat worldly hard-charging parsons who populated the novels of Henry Fielding and Jane Austen (herself a daughter of a poor parish minister) gave way to the piety of bowed heads and hands folded in prayer. The clear glass windows of the typical eighteenth-century Episcopal sanctuary were replaced by figurative stained glass. The beautiful twilight space pierced during the day by shafts of colored light, and at night, by the flicker of candlelight, was an introduction to the beauty of Heaven.

Although a number of eighteenth-century sanctuaries (including the First Baptist Meeting House) were "modernized" in the following century by the addition of memorial windows, often beautifully wrought, St. Stephen's never had to be updated to conform to this new / old understanding of communal worship. It emerged full-blown in all its shadowy splendor in the hands of several High Church architects who, inspired by the work of the English architect Augustus Welby Pugin (1812–1852), brought the resurgent Gothic aesthetic of romantic Victorian English church architecture to these shores.

The English-born Richard Upjohn (1802–1878), in his day the leading practitioner of Gothic Revival architecture, was the first in a line of preeminent architects and artisans who over the years lent their talent to shape a house of worship whose form, both inside and out, harkens back to rural pre-Reformation English parish churches. Instead of the dazzling white clapboard of the First Baptist Meeting House, the exterior of St. Stephen's is gray stone with brownstone trim. Initially Upjohn had designed a steeple that would have soared 180 feet above George Street. The tower that was built with its rather understated copper-clad steeple is half the size, 93 feet high. The oxidation of the copper is an unexpected verdigris exclamation point on top of all the dark stone.

A visit to the interior is a must. Marvel at the finely wrought stained glass windows and the delicate wooden tracery of the rood screen that veils the ritual function of the service from the congregation. No element of the interior, from candlesticks and baptismal font to the rood screen, is without iconographic or historic significance. The richness of the décor should not, however, be construed as a dry academic exercise, nor as a purely aesthetic piling on of ornament. Instead, men like Upjohn and his predecessor, Pugin, believed that architecture could and should exercise an uplifting moral force. President Faunce would not have disagreed. However, at St. Stephen's the moral force would be felt by the senses rather than the intellect.

Students and visitors not inclined to attend a service should by all means use the frequent excellent musical offerings as an excuse to step inside. As McKenzie Woodward writes in his *Guide to Providence Architecture*, the experience will be a feast for all the senses.[13] In 1973, St. Stephen's was listed on the National Register of Historic Places.

36   Gardner House

Joseph Hale, builder, 1806; restoration, Dr. and Mrs. George Warren Gardner, 1930s; interior renovation, Irving B. Haynes and Pauline C. Metcalf, 1978

The building immediately west of St. Stephen's is a persuasive illustration that architectural beauty comes in many forms, plain and fancy. The language may be different, but the poetry is ultimately the same. The mason Joseph Hale is associated with the house not because he designed it, which cannot be proved one way or the other, but rather because of the fine craftsmanship that went into the brickwork. The elegant three-story Federal townhouse would have served as an advertisement for his trade. After the Gothic interlude of St. Stephen's, Gardner takes us back to a type of high-end residential architecture perfected by Providence carpenter-architect John Holden Greene (1777–1850)—a cube generously penetrated by well-proportioned windows topped with flush lintels in a stepped shape. Although positive proof is lacking, the house may in fact have been designed by Greene.

The portico deserves special attention. Grand and welcoming, decorative and functional, an allusion to an aristocratic colonial past yet a celebration of the success of the new republic, it subtly choreographs the expectations of the visitor: here lives a citizen of some importance who nonetheless is open and hospitable. The back and forth play of control and release, light and shadow, is especially obvious in the treatment of the front door at the top of a double flight of stone steps: a

Gardner House

solid barrier to the street is softened by the delicacy of the elliptical fan light whose leaded arrangement of alternating oval and flared diamond motifs is repeated somewhat more formally—though with no less wit—in the glass of the sidelights beside the door. This is an entrance equally welcoming to visitors and light. Yet the porch is not original: it is either a skillful copy or salvaged by the property's subsequent owners, the Gardners, from a period house.

Acquired by Brown in 1932, the house was then leased to George and Jessie Gardner, who gave their existing home on Orchard Avenue to the University. It was a clever arrangement that accomplished three worthy goals: Brown gained the Orchard Avenue property; the Gardners invested their own money in restoring

106 George Street, which the University maintained ownership of; and the Gardners' superb collection of period antique furnishings (from William and Mary to Sheraton and Empire) was moved from Orchard Avenue to its present location in the house. The Gardners then set about remodeling the house to mirror their impression of what a Federal dwelling should look like, right down to reworking the cellar as a colonial pub. It is not authentic, but it is done very well. Everything they touched was first-rate, including the fireplace treatments on the first and second floors, which they rescued from local wrecking companies. The owners were seized by the same spirit that during the same period conjured an idealized replica of the nation's formative years most famously realized in Colonial Williamsburg.

From the entrance porch to the dividing wall the Gardners removed on the west side of the first floor to create one large library-living room, the house we see today is clearly not the house that Hale built. But who would want to remove these additions, including the fine interior woodwork, to bring the house back to something more closely approximating what might have existed in 1806? The changes are part of the property's rich history.

Upon the death of Mrs. Gardner in 1948, the property became a historic house museum and a well-appointed inn for visiting dignitaries and guests of the University's president. Today Gardner House bears the plaque for the Donald Saunders '57 Family Inn. Wearing quite comfortably its various changes and alterations over the years, Gardner House is listed on the National Register of Historic Places.

37   Littlefield Hall
Day & Klauder, 1926

At the same time Hegeman was rising on the southeast corner of Lincoln Field, Littlefield Hall was built on the lot immediately up the street from Gardner House. Set perpendicular to George Street and running north behind the John Carter Brown Library, Littlefield Hall, like Day & Klauder's other work, remembers elements of Brown's first building—University Hall. The rows of brick belt courses set at the floor level of each story are an eighteenth-century touch both decorative (the flat planes of the facade are subtly broken up) and functional (deflecting rainwater from the walls). The steep pitch of the roof and the paired chimneys at the gable ends provide a pleasing vertical thrust, which adds interest on George Street, even though we are not looking at the front of the building but the side. If a tall brick wall can be a thing of beauty, this is surely it. As in his other work on campus, Klauder does not limit his best shot to the primary facade but instead designs architecture in the round.

Littlefield Hall appears uncomfortably squeezed into a narrow site and married in the architectural version of a shotgun wedding to Maxcy Hall. However, at the time Littlefield Hall welcomed its first residents, John Carter Brown's Casperson Building (1990) had not been built and the residence hall opened onto a pleasant courtyard not unlike that at Hegeman.

World War II, Korean, and Vietnam War Memorials

38   Marcus Aurelius
Soldiers Arch
World War II, Korean, and Vietnam War Memorial

This third Walk ends where it began, within sight of Lyman Gymnasium. Nearly a half century in the shaping, Lincoln Field is different from the formality of the University's front lawn and the Times Square that is the College Green. It has its own intimate vibe that resonates with students. In winter, the difference between the elevation at the top and bottom of the Field (site of Olmsted's proposed amphitheater that has yet to come to pass) invites sledding and spontaneous snowball fights. In spring, Simmons Quad is framed by a pink froth of cherry trees and saucer magnolias. During the annual Commencement / Reunion Weekend in May, this is where the seniors come at Campus Dance, not "upstairs" on the College Green. The verdant heart of Simmons Quad is a less formal outdoor space, most evocative of student memories. It reminds us that architecture is about more than buildings; it embraces everything else.

With its trinity of arched windows, the rear of Sayles Hall at the western edge of the Field looks like the chapel President Faunce wanted but never saw built. How many buildings have that kind of presence or contribute to the aesthetic pleasure of a site when viewed from the back?

In its shadow stands the equestrian statue of Marcus Aurelius, a bronze copy of the original (c. 175 CE) on Rome's Capitoline Hill. The base was designed by Frederick Field, a Providence architect. Exceptionally well done, the University's

An equestrian statue of Marcus Aurelius

Soldiers Arch

statue was used as a model when the Roman original was taken down in 1981 for restoration.

A few notes on the iconography: That the emperor is clothed in a tunic, rather than armor, indicates he has been victorious in battle. His right arm is outstretched in a gesture of clemency; his left hand is believed to have held a globe. He is proportionately larger than the horse on which he rides (after all, he *is* the emperor). Presented to the University in 1908 by Colonel Robert Hale Ives Goddard, Marcus Aurelius seems to gesture toward the world, linking Brown to the concepts of service and duty associated with Rome's philosopher king. A mere decade later this Stoic philosophy was put to the test by those students and alumni who entered the Great War. Before moving on, do not overlook the shaded seating area behind the statue. Here is yet another of the intimate landscaped grace notes that are a recurring delight.

Tucked between Caswell Hall and Metcalf stands the Soldiers Arch, designed by Charles A. Coolidge of the Boston firm Shepley, Rutan & Coolidge. Dedicated on April 6, 1921, the limestone triumphal arch commemorates the forty-two students, alumni, and faculty who died in World War I. Carved sprays of laurel and the wreaths of oak leaves at the top of the walls refer in the first instance to victory, in the second, to steadfastness, strength, and honor. The bond between the American and English allies is reflected in the choice of poems on either side of the Arch: "Sacrifice" by Ralph Waldo Emerson on one side and "The Spires of Oxford" by the Anglo-Irish poet Winifred Mary Letts on the other. Soldiers Arch is best seen by night, accented by a new lighting installation that gives it a compelling presence that is somewhat lacking in the unforgiving light of day.

The dialogue between the stern philosophy of sacrifice advanced by the last of Rome's "good emperors" and, on the eastern end of the green, the solemn celebration of the "triumph" that we know sowed the seeds for the greatest horrors of the twentieth century is in subtle but profound counterpoint to the quiet beauty of the fields on which those who gave their lives once played.

1 Letter to Frederick Law Olmsted Jr., December 14, 1906; Frederick Law Olmsted Papers. Manuscript Division, Library of Congress, Washington, D.C. Quoted in Jacob Reidel, "Unbuilt Brown" (senior thesis, Brown University, 2002), 39.

2 President Faunce to the Brown Corporation, 1920. R. M. Kliment and Frances Halsband, *Campus Heritage at Brown University: Preservation Priorities* (Providence: 2006), 14–16.

3 Anthony McCabe, *Memories of Brown: Traditions and Recollections Gathered from Many Sources*, ed. Robert Perkins Brown, Henry Robinson Palmer, Harry Lyman Koopman, and Charles Saunders Brigham (Providence: Brown Alumni Magazine Co.: 1909), 366–67.

4 Ibid.

5 Martha Mitchell, *Encyclopedia Brunoniana* (Providence: Brown University Library, 1993), 346.

6 Reidel, "Unbuilt Brown," 48.

7 President Faunce to the Corporation, 1920. Kliment and Halsband, *Campus Heritage*, 14.

8 Ibid.

9 Frances Halsband, "Charles Klauder's Brilliant Invisible Hand," *Chronicle of Higher Education* (March 25, 2005), B24.

10 Ibid, B25.

11 President Faunce to the Corporation, 1903. Kliment and Halsband, *Campus Heritage*, 88.

12 For a bird's-eye view of how cleverly Caswell and Hegeman dorms relate to one another, go to www.wikimapia.org/11702/Hegeman-Hall.

13 William McKenzie Woodward, *PPS/AIAri Guide to Providence Architecture* (Providence, Providence Preservation Society, 2003), 73.

The summer of 1890 I spent in Europe and returned with a desire to attend Oxford University. The following winter at a dinner in Providence my Father, sitting next to President Andrews of Brown, spoke of that ambition, a remark which President Andrews answered by the inquiry, "Why does she not come to Brown?"[1]

The issue of emancipation in mid-nineteenth-century America was not confined to race; it also embraced gender. The hero of this chapter of Brown's history is Elisha Benjamin Andrews, the University's eighth president (1889–98). If Faunce was the builder-president, Andrews was the architect who drew the blueprints for the transformation of Brown from a regional college to an international university. During his tenure, research and graduate study flourished, under-graduate enrollment increased 140 percent in his first eight years, and women were admitted in 1891, in large part through his efforts. This fourth Walk is the story of the campus that grew to welcome the education of women at Brown.

In its first years, the "Women's College" did not have a name, a faculty, a building of its own, or, for that matter, a master plan to guide its future growth. Gradually these omissions were corrected. In 1897, Brown's female students pursued their studies in a facility designed by the city's top architecture firm and paid for by the women themselves; in 1903, the Women's College was given a faculty; and in 1928, a name—Pembroke College in Brown University. (The first alumnae made it known they would have preferred "The Elisha Benjamin Andrews College in Brown University," in recognition and appreciation of the role President Andrews played in admitting women to Brown.)

Pembroke Green

In hindsight, the seemingly piecemeal purchase of lots in the area north of the main campus was in fact carefully calculated to assemble a larger parcel on which not a few buildings but a whole new campus would arise. Although the Women's College and Brown merged into a fully coeducational institution in 1971, the Pembroke campus maintains a distinct physical identity. The open-ended quad that emerged in the course of the twentieth century is an attractive urban park, combining features of the three historic greens at the men's College—an outward-facing front lawn, a public space that invites interaction between students and the neighborhood, and intimate green spaces that foster a special sense of belonging for the men and women who now live there. This Walk begins with what is arguably the most architecturally significant building on the Pembroke campus. It is an imposing red-brick and terra-cotta structure whose exuberant design is a deliberate evocation of the type of sixteenth-century academic building Roger Williams would have seen as a student in England.

Pembroke Hall

39 Pembroke Hall
Alfred Stone of Stone, Carpenter & Willson Architects, 1897;
renovation and restoration, Toshiko Mori, 2007

Like University Hall, the first building on the emerging campus supported many
functions: academic, social, religious, and (unlike University Hall) athletic needs of
the students. An undergraduate writing with tongue-in-cheek described the
multipurposefulness of Pembroke Hall thus:

> The gymnasium of the Women's College is a long, wide room, well lighted by many
> windows. The walls are delicately tinted, and at each end of the hall stands a fine old
> fire-place. A handsome reproduction of Raphael's Madonna hangs upon the south wall,
> and forms a most appropriate decoration….The chapel of the Women's College is a
> long, wide room well lighted by many windows. The walls are delicately tinted, and at
> each end of the hall stands a fine old fire-place. Cases of dumb-bells and Indian clubs
> accentuate the contrast between the strenuous world without and this quiet spot,
> and form a most appropriate decoration….The reception hall of the Women's College
> is a long, wide room well lighted by many windows. The walls are delicately tinted,
> and at each end of the hall stands a fine old fire-place. A handsomely carved reading-
> desk stands at one side of the hall, and forms a most appropriate decoration.[2]

Also like University Hall, Pembroke's first building is urban, oriented to the life of the street. However, if University Hall is proper and respectful, even sober, Brown's first building for women is a dynamic arrangement of overscaled elements, from the gables to the cavernous entrance surmounted by a three-story bay. The architecture skips and dances. The architects well understood the spiritual exhilaration of the vertical line and the pointed arch. The steep pitch of the roof and the wonderfully crafted sunflower-embossed tapered chimneys that rise from the ground level and thrust through the gabled ends are a lesson in how a sure-handed design can relieve a heavy mass of masonry by providing ample delight. Wherever one looks, every element boldly announces that something of consequence has arrived in the neighborhood.

Another significant difference between the two buildings is the manner in which they were funded. Whereas the fledgling College solicited funds from this country and abroad, including donations from Benjamin Franklin and Thomas Penn, Pembroke Hall was made possible by a fund-raising effort spearheaded by the women themselves, under the inspired leadership of the prominent educator and women's rights activist, Providence resident Sarah E. Doyle (1830–1922). After the Corporation refused Doyle's request for funds to build a permanent facility for women's education at Brown, it was the women cheered on by Doyle who in thirteen months raised the $37,601 needed for construction. At the dedication ceremonies on November 22, 1897, Doyle spoke for all future Pembroke students when she said: "The women's sphere is one of infinite and indeterminate radius." In 1894 Doyle was the first woman to receive an honorary degree from Brown.

Since its $9 million renovation in 2007, Pembroke Hall now houses the Pembroke Center for Teaching and Research on Women as well as the Cogut Center for the Humanities. The renovation, which exposes long-covered portions of the original building, provides fully fitted seminar and lecture rooms, performance and gallery spaces, and an interactive humanities lab. Two new entrances have been created, one on Meeting Street, the other facing the historic Pembroke Campus. In architect Toshiko Mori's own words, the pursuit of light dominated her approach to this project: "By introducing an exceptional quality of light, we hope that this renovation will create a serene atmosphere essential to fostering intellectual activities within the hall."

If there is a single element of the renovation that defines Mori's aesthetic, it is the room at the top floor that once served as Pembroke's library. The two-story space is crowned by the tracery of an open timbered ceiling whose exposed wood trusses support the pitch of the gabled roof. In renovating the library to serve a new purpose and bring it up to code (e.g., accessibility, bathrooms, fire safety, etc.), a lesser architect might have divided the room into separate floor-to-ceiling spaces, thus compromising the visual impact of the splendid ceiling, which, along with the fireplaces, is one of the room's most striking features. Instead, new amenities, such as a catering kitchen for receptions and lectures, are handled like furniture that can be pulled into the space as needed. Nothing is allowed to overpower or intrude

Pembroke Hall, detail of Hubert frieze

on what is the exclamation point of the building's interior architecture. If you have access to the library, spend some time looking closely at the fireplaces, beginning with the floral terra-cotta capitals that support either side of the mantel. Victorian architects and builders, when given the opportunity, time and again transform the mundane into the marvelous, whether it is a fireplace for heat or the supports that hold up the roof.

Mori's research-based approach to historic architecture is in evidence throughout. Some of the more outstanding elements of the original interior that have been preserved and carefully restored include the fireplaces and the bronze plaster frieze on the second floor in what had been Pembroke's first library. The frieze, executed by local sculptor Hippolyte L. Hubert, portrays the theme of education from a distinctly female point of view, beginning with a mother surrounded by her children. Succeeding figures around the room depict Genius, Sculpture, Architecture, Agriculture, Engineering, Navigation, Crafts, and Commerce, all dressed in flowing gowns.

The first facility constructed for women's education at Brown was a welcome ornament in a neighborhood not lacking architectural treasures. It is a building that anyone with a talent for sketching could sit in front of for hours, enjoying the play of light and shadow conjured by the curves and deeply etched surfaces of the architecture. Those challenged by freehand sketching would be better served and far less challenged by walking down Meeting Street to the straightforward grid of Emery Hall.

40   Smith-Buonanno Hall (formerly Sayles Gymnasium)
Edward B. Willson of Stone, Carpenter & Willson, 1907;
renovation, William Kite Architects, 2001

The firm that designed Pembroke Hall was commissioned for the women's second building, Sayles Gymnasium, named after its benefactor, Frank A. Sayles, the surviving son of the Providence businessman who contributed the funds to build Sayles Hall on the College Green. Once again firm principal Edward B. Willson produced a light-filled, red-brick composition very much in the English Renaissance mode of Pembroke Hall, right down to the impressive, functional yet decorative chimney that distinguishes the west wing of the building, which was devoted to offices and classrooms. Even though both facilities were designed to house very different functions, it is worth a second glance (beyond the common use of brick) to see how well the architect ties the two together as complementary elements

Smith–Buonanno Hall, from Pembroke Green

of a unified ensemble. The belt courses of the two buildings are a good place to begin; also, of course, the vertical thrusts of the gables in both. As for the brick, it is handled as if it were molded by hand. (Compare the relative flatness of the material at the next two stops, Miller and Metcalf). The entrances into Sayles and Pembroke Hall are equally bold, yet welcoming.

The functionality and, in contemporary terms, sustainability of Sayles is apparent in the many windows, some quite large. Look closely at their sizes and the rhythm of how they are placed. There is a rich language of windows that would profit any student of architecture to learn. The large central stairway, along with the operable windows, stokes natural convection currents to ventilate the interior, a not inconsiderate detail in a building dedicated to physical exertion. However, once the exercising young women had developed a bit of a glow, there was a resting room on the upper floor of the west wing "reserved for tea service and quiet contemplation."

Unlike Pembroke Hall, the L-shaped mass of Sayles is not oriented toward the neighboring street. Instead, the entrance to the gym faces east. With this gesture, Brown signals its intent to turn the Women's College away from the city to face what in time would become a landscaped park. As Brown assembled adjacent properties, "a true campus, with walks and shrubs and shade trees" began to emerge.[3] Before that vision could be fully realized, the University would have to close Cushing Street, which continued to bisect the Pembroke campus until the building of Morriss and Champlin Halls in 1960.

In 2001, Sayles was renovated for classroom use. Renamed Smith-Buonanno Hall in honor of Vincent Buonanno (Class of 1966) and his wife Linda Anne Smith (Class of 1967), the historic shell of the building has been painstakingly restored and the interior completely renovated to house its new functions. The present interior configuration includes two lecture halls, eight classrooms, and a media center office. In their choice of industrial materials and fixtures, the architects have preserved the muscularity of the original, a feature deftly expressed in the soaring main lecture room (the repurposed gym) and central hall. Additional classroom and seminar space were added above the lecture area and common room, giving the illusion of a suspended structure. Even more natural light is admitted into the building, thanks to a skylight above the main lecture hall vestibule. That vestibule slices deep into the building, allowing daylight to pass through the second floor and continue down to the first. The new chunky wood spindles of the staircases suggest rather than duplicate how this feature would have been handled in the first decade of the twentieth century.

Radical surgery has given the building renewed life and advanced the University's growing commitment to freedom of movement and transparency. The success of this feat has earned the architects numerous accolades, including a 2002 National AIA Honor Award for Interiors.

Smith–Buonanno Hall, lecture hall

Miller Hall (right) and Andrews Hall (background)

41   Miller Hall
Andrews, Jacques & Rantoul, 1910

Metcalf Hall
Andrews, Jacques & Rantoul, 1919; interior renovation, CBT *Architects, 2013*

After the close of the firm that designed Pembroke Hall and Sayles Gymnasium, Brown looked north to a Boston firm to design its first buildings specifically intended to house the growing number of students. First Miller then, nearly a decade later, Metcalf are evidence of a new direction at Brown. Pembroke moved from Victorian eclecticism to the increasingly dominant Colonial Revival narrative. Unlike Pembroke Hall and Smith-Buonanno Hall, which look institutional in the best sense of that term, the new dorms are overscaled versions of the Colonial Revival houses then being built on College Hill. The new direction of Pembroke's architecture was meant to read "community" and "home," an appropriate message for residence halls.

In form and function, each four-story residence hall (counting the dormers) is the mirror of the other. The brick facades are similarly broken by projecting and pedimented monumental entry porticos; both have wings that step out at either end from the plane of the facade; both increase the illusion of verticality by decreasing the size and shape of the windows from the ground floor to the floor above, continuing up to the dormers; and both have entrances that open on to broad patios that become pleasant outdoor rooms when the weather is fair.

The most important feature that distinguishes one hall from the other is that, unlike Miller, Metcalf was constructed with fireproof concrete. This eliminated the need for the fire escapes that cling to the sides of Miller. Although the buildings are obviously larger than the surrounding private residences, the detailing—gable roof, dormers, brick—and the canopy of trees, as well as the slope of the land down from Brown Street, allow these dorms to fit relatively well into the neighborhood.

Old postcards show a rusticated stepped stone wall that ran along the north side of Cushing Street, when Cushing still cut through the Pembroke campus. Midway stood a pair of formal gates that opened into the north end of the Pembroke campus—the Josephine Martha Scholfield Gates, erected in 1913 by the Class of 1900. Gone are the gates, the wall, and most of Cushing Street, save for a landscaped rump on the west side of the campus that terminates in a clump of trees and space for parking. Preferring to recycle rather than destroy, Brown simply reinstalled Ms. Scholfield's gates at the back of Andrews Hall, providing a grand wrought-iron fanfare to what in effect is a service entrance.

The extensive renovations undertaken in 2013 include converting single-occupancy bedrooms to doubles, the removal and replacement of all finishes and systems, and the restoration of the building exteriors. In addition, existing connections to the large residential block that is Andrews Hall are to be severed, resulting in Miller and Metcalf being restored as independent residential halls. To counter the overwhelming sense of isolation that can beset first-year students far away from home, architecture is being used to nurture more intimate and supportive communities.

Metcalf Hall

Alumnae Hall

42   Alumnae Hall
Andrews, Jones, Briscoe & Whitmore, 1927

In the thirty-five years that had passed since women were first admitted to Brown, Pembroke acquired classroom and office space, a gym, and residence halls. What it lacked was a student center "for the natural cultivation and expression of social aspiration and activity."[4] This need was met by a new building across the Green from Sayles Gymnasium (now Smith-Buonanno Hall).

Continuing the Colonial Revival idiom, Alumnae Hall was Pembroke's answer to Brown's Faunce House. The same firm (with different partners) that had designed Miller and Metcalf Halls gave students an impressive facility that both confirms and works against the Green. Whereas the north and south wings more or less hold the eastern edge, the center of the building breaks the edge by stepping back to form a court or vestibule. This opening serves as a transition space between the Green and Alumnae Hall. The entrance from here opens into an ample two-story auditorium entered by crossing a balustraded stone terrace. The procession of large arched windows on the east and west sides of the room fill the space with light throughout the day. It is a place well suited for large assemblies, entertainment, or religious services, an option furthered by the gift of an organ shortly after the building opened. The large polished-brass chandeliers and the detailing of the plaster molding above the windows and along the ceiling suggest an eighteenth-century reception room or a sparely decorated New England church sanctuary.

The south end of the auditorium opens into what appears to be an almost separate three-story structure that makes a 90-degree turn in the direction of Pembroke Hall. This part of the building houses offices, a sitting room, and a snack bar, The Gate, which opened in 1947. The Gate was Pembroke's answer to the Blue Room at Faunce House, which at the time was available to the women—but only if escorted by a Brown man. The Gate reciprocated the courtesy by allowing inside only those Brown men escorted by a Pembroker. Perhaps the most attractive interior element of Alumnae Hall is the central flying spiral staircase that runs from the basement to the top floor. Whether or not the equiangular spiral was modeled, as some have suggested, after a chambered nautilus, the description fits.

A bird's-eye view of the site reveals something else: Unlike at Brown's College Green, it was not possible to complete a row of buildings on the east side that roughly paralleled those to the west. Given the large sprawling footprint of Alumnae Hall, no structure of any consequence could have been placed directly south that would have lined up with Miller and at least the northern two-thirds of Alumnae Hall. The lot was too cramped and, in any case, occupied at the time by two small properties. Today, the site remains an open green space bisected by a diagonal path that runs from Meeting Street to the Pembroke Tribute, a brick-and-stone memorial dedicated in 2008 to honor the legacy of women at Brown. (Note the bronze model of the Pembroke campus as it existed before the Women's College was fully integrated with Brown.) The monument, walls, and garden were designed by landscape architect Todd Rader and mark the northern terminus of "The Walk," which will be the subject of Walk Five. The concrete sculpture between Alumnae and Miller Halls is *Art* by Brown Professor Emeritus of Art Hugh Townley (1923–2008).

43   Andrews Hall

Perry, Shaw & Hepburn, 1947; landscape design, Todd Rader + Amy Crews, 2013; renovation and restoration, CBT *Architects, 2013*

With two pairs of buildings in place at the east and west ends of the Pembroke Green, the obvious location for a new building was to the north on a site bordering Bowen Street. Like the addition of the Stephen Robert '62 Campus Center in Faunce House on the College Green, the construction of this new residence hall transformed the Pembroke campus from a park into an open quadrangle. Named after the president who embraced the idea of higher education for women, Andrews Hall nearly doubled the number of women who could be housed at Pembroke.

At a distance, Andrews appears to be of the same scale and period as Miller and Metcalf Halls. But on a second and closer look, the differences jump out. Perry, Shaw & Hepburn use Colonial Revival detailing like a skim coat over the post–World War II megastructure that has much in common with the later Keeney Quad for men (Walk Seven). The projecting central gabled bay and the row of arched windows at the level of the terrace are attempts to soften the building's massiveness. A building this large allowed the University to admit more women, and resident students give the rooms high marks.

Andrews Hall

Sixty-six years following the completion of Andrews Hall, the University retained the landscape firm Todd Rader + Amy Crews to radically rework the landscape at the front: Andrews Hall visually blocks off the Pembroke Green in a way that becomes something of a cul-de-sac. The goal for a renewed Andrews Hall is a student commons for first-year students, with spaces for studying, socializing, and dining that will function like the Stephen Robert '62 Campus Center on the College Green. The repurposing of this space and the larger manner in which it is approached from the Pembroke Green will be transformational. Equally transformational is the work underway as part of the larger project involving the adjacent Miller and Metcalf Halls. Again like Keeney Quad, Andrews Hall will be broken into smaller pieces. It will no longer be connected to the older residential halls. Paired single bedrooms will be converted to doubles, and lounges will be created on each floor. Architecture is being used not simply to house students, but, more importantly, to facilitate community and closer relationships. In keeping with the University's commitment to sustainability, the goal at Andrews, as well as at Miller and Metcalf, is to achieve a much-coveted LEED Gold rating from the U.S. Green Building Council.

44 **Morriss Hall**
     Champlin Hall
     Robert C. Dean of Perry, Shaw, Hepburn & Dean, 1960

     Emery Hall
     Woolley Hall
     Perry, Shaw, Hepburn & Dean, 1963

     Verney-Woolley Dining Halls
     Perry, Shaw, Hepburn & Dean, 1966; interior remodeling,
     Moser Pilon Nelson Architects, 2002

The leisurely pace at which the Pembroke campus grew was impossible to maintain in the years after World War II. Brown faced the challenge of welcoming the rising tide of returning veterans, and then the even greater challenge of the baby boom. Facilities had to be built and built fast, especially residence halls. Andrews Hall was an early outcome. The approach of the University's bicentennial in 1964 provided the spark to embark on a building boom on both campuses.

 Since the University no longer had the leisure to gradually assemble individual plots of land as they came on the market, Brown built on the property it already owned. This had major consequences for what was built and the overall design of the Pembroke campus. The fairly formal Beaux-Arts layout that existed before 1960, with its focus on Andrews Hall, broke down in the space of five years as new residence and dining halls were squeezed into the available space. What emerged was a second quad whose western edge is defined by the back of the first, but with greatly constricted open space. Depending on one's point of view, the irregular new quad is either intimate or shadowy and cramped. Intimate or cramped, there is no focus. The spaces in between can hardly be called a *green* as the term is traditionally understood.

 As for the buildings themselves, the architects jettisoned Colonial Revival and turned their hand to a pared-to-the-bone modernist style. In place of a sure-footed (if predictable) arrangement of pediments, pilasters, and quoins, they

designed boxy, unadorned buildings that used the construction techniques and mass-produced products developed during World War II. What has since come to be called the "Miesian grid" (named after the Modernist architect Ludwig Mies van der Rohe), which can be replicated ad infinitum, allowed the construction team to assemble in short order large, functional facilities using modular construction and

Emery Hall

inexpensive prefabricated materials. Like wartime efforts, construction was quick, standardized, economic, and impersonal.

However well the buildings may work inside, the exteriors come off as skinned and vacant. The exterior cladding of choice is Pembroke's ubiquitous brick, though the dusty rose color is wan and appears to be of a lesser quality than the brick found on Pembroke's older, historic buildings. The industrial windows are operable but sullenly repetitious from one floor to the next. The flatness of the facades allows for no play of light and shadow. The few attempts at what might be called decorative touches—the limestone bands or belt courses at each floor level—are feeble gestures that do little to alleviate the visual weight of all that brick. The straight lines only reinforce the relentless horizontality. Capping the building with a flat rather than a gable or pitched roof does yield the maximum amount of square footage on the top floor, no small consideration when trying to find room for the first wave of baby boomers. But at a price: The new dorms no longer reference the residential scale of College Hill. Individualism is replaced by the impersonal. Little on this site reminds us that architecture is built with light no less than brick and stone.

The architectural equivalent of the '50s organizational man was bound to provoke a backlash. However, before moving on to see how this played out, look in on the 2002 remodeling of the Verney-Woolley Dining Halls (the "V-Dub"). What had been ho-hum as originally designed has been transformed into a skylit space with an open kitchen and multiple options for seating. Innovative surgical intervention into outmoded or even poorly designed interior spaces has yielded amazing results. Plans are afoot to carry this new, light-filled aesthetic throughout the midcentury buildings of the Pembroke campus to revive and reinforce the unique personality of this special place.

The nearby sculpture, *Group of Three* (1969), is by Hugh Townley, Brown's first professor of sculpture.

45   New Pembroke Dorms
Donlyn Lyndon of Moore, Lyndon & Turnbull, 1974

The complex of buildings at the corner of Bowen and Thayer Streets is arguably some of the boldest architecture at Brown. Nothing like it exists on the men's campus. This radical break seems to have been championed by the chairman of the University's Planning and Building Committee, John Nicholas Brown Jr. If University Hall and Manning Hall exemplified the best of their era, he believed the University should pursue a similar commitment to quality, not by invoking the past, but by speaking in a language that reflected the most creative thinking of the day.

The site chosen for a new direction posed a host of challenges, beginning with the very different personalities of the abutting streets: Bowen, quiet and residential; Thayer, a busy commercial artery. Rejecting the timid, almost barracks-like dorms built in the previous decade, the architect travels a far more innovative route, creating the kind of intricate composition one might develop by piecing together

New Pembroke Dorms

children's blocks. The separate entries and varying elevations of the four buildings that comprise the New Pembroke Dorms embrace an inner court that is open on the southwest. On the side facing Bowen, the architect, Donlyn Lyndon, pulls a three-story building back from the street and tucks it behind a wall and green space. In this way, Lyndon acknowledges the residential nature of this part of the neighborhood. On Thayer, the commercial activity of the street dictated a different, more urban approach. The dorms rise an additional floor to four stories. The first floor is placed directly at the edge of the property line, a common commercial tactic. This is appropriate since the ground floor is reserved not for landscaping but business. The upper stories step back, ensuring a measure of privacy for the students, away from the noise and activity on the street. Lyndon is responding to a traditional inner-city pattern of shops on the ground floor and residents on the floors above.

The fairly straightforward approach of the facades on Bowen and Thayer gives way on the rear or courtyard side to a three-dimensional pile-up of terraces, balconies, bay windows, and towers that visually have the liveliness of an Italian

hill village. It is as if the architect had called a recess and sent the architecture out to play. Here individuality and personal space are emphasized. For example, each of the entries has a distinct personality. The organization of the rooms and hallways, few of which are quite the same, is calculated to achieve a residential rather than an institutional effect. In a welcome departure from earlier practice, and clearly responsive to the tenor of those rebellious times, the design encouraged students to take ownership of and shape their own living spaces.

How well do the New Pembroke Dorms meet the opposing demands of a complex site? Well enough to have been awarded first place from among 670 entries in an annual nationwide competition sponsored by the magazine *Progressive Architecture*. However, there were constraints on the architect that raised issues then and now.

Building within the strict limits of financing sponsored by the U.S. Department of Housing and Urban Development, with a designated dollar limit per student, the architect had to make difficult decisions regarding the choice of materials. Creative as Lyndon undoubtedly was, even design ingenuity cannot entirely overcome the off-the-shelf manufactured elements with which the dorms were built. Had the windows been recessed more deeply or allowed to jut out from the plane of the facade, the walls would not have seemed as flat as they do. The different colors of glazed brick on the walls are an inexpensive way to suggest ornament, but the suggestion seems forced. For instance, the pop-graphic band of blue tile above the stores on the Thayer Street side is the ghost of a traditional cornice. As for the commercial spaces, too often they are small, dark, and undistinguished. An archway that would have led directly from Thayer to the interior courtyard and invited movement was unfortunately walled off years ago in response to a perceived need for greater security. That single nervous act subverts one of the architect's primary intentions, which was to open Pembroke to the neighborhood and the neighborhood to Pembroke.

The whimsical, Tinkertoy-like sculpture that sits on brick piers in the court-yard behind Thayer Street was designed by the architect's wife, Alice Wingwall, a noted sculptor and photographer. In place of a traditional campus green space, it is meant to provide a focus or center for the overall composition, but to some eyes the sculpture might seem flimsy and fussy. A related issue is the open space of the courtyard that cries out for a heavy dose of landscaping and is a future opportunity for trees and grass.

Few buildings, if any on the Brown campus, offer more food for thought about the challenges that face an architect when designing a building that must engage town and gown in a positive dialogue. If Lyndon does not always get it right, he certainly asks the right questions.

Before turning west, look across the street to 315 Thayer. It is an early project by Providence architect Frederick Ellis Jackson (1879–1950), who seems to have approached this commission as if it were a master's thesis. There is a youthful restlessness and exuberance as Jackson attempts to corral—not always successfully—a host of gestures to break into a more human scale what is a fairly large composition. One has to admire if not necessarily approve of the effort. The brick-faced and wood frame Colonial Revival four-story U-shaped building opened in 1902 as the Cushing Apartments. Major interior renovations carried out in 2012–13 by Lerner | Ladds + Bartels Architects improved accessibility and fire safety. Perhaps most challenging was the steeply sloping roof that had prevented students from living on the top floor. This challenge was cleverly met, yielding two suites and eight stand-alone singles. Hardly a treasured landmark, this new / old residence hall is a reminder that an important trait of effective architecture and urban planning is a quality of creative resourcefulness under tight constraints.

The renovation of 315 Thayer is one of the outcomes of the University's *Strategic Framework for Physical Planning* (2003), which committed Brown to consolidate its core rather than to continue to encroach on the College Hill neighborhood. The renovation also firmly anchors the north entry to what is Brown's agora or marketplace. Not always appreciated as such, because they are perceived by some as untidy, the commercial blocks of Thayer Street are a great asset for the city of Providence and for Brown. This is where townies and students rub elbows on equal terms. Thayer Street is a template for the energy Brown wants to help create in the downtown Jewelry District (Walk Nine). Maintaining a tumultuous amity over the raucous and edgy diversity of these five blocks without stifling what gives it a welcome vibe is an ongoing challenge.

While on Thayer, walk down to the Brown Office Building (Kent, Cruise Associates). Erected in 1970, the four-story commercial building is assembled from off-the-shelf parts rather than a designed structure. At the time, this kind of anonymous building appeared like a rash across America: blocky, quickly and inexpensively thrown up, dutifully functional, out of scale with anything around it, and frankly not caring. The building does offer two amenities: It is set back farther from the curb than the rest of the buildings on that side of the street, which allows

Thayer Street at night

vendors to set up shop. This provides something of a movable feast, with curbside peddlers hawking everything from umbrellas to popcorn. Also, the building's large plate-glass windows are a definite plus. These give pedestrians visual access to the interior. Although hardly utilized at the time it was built, that feature has since been seized on by one of the Ivy League's two remaining independent bookstores. A major 2009 renovation of the three floors occupied by the Brown Bookstore has yielded a coffee shop, nooks for reading (some of which are close to the windows), a community room for book clubs, and bright red awnings that flare out over the sidewalk on Thayer and Angell Streets. These give some bright visual punctuation to an otherwise blank face. Like a coconut, however, this commercial building has its most appealing features on the inside.

At this point, turn west and head up Meeting Street past some of the splendid residential architecture the Hill is known for. The next stop is Prospect Street.

46 First Church of Christ Scientist
Hoppin & Field, 1913

No single building in this neighborhood is more distinctive as a way-finder than the church whose copper-clad dome floats above the neighborhood's leafy canopy on one of the highest spots on College Hill. Christian Science was not formally organized until 1879, and it is remarkable that such a major edifice was commissioned and built for a Protestant sect that was less than four decades old.

The architectural precedent is clearly the classical Mother Church in Boston designed by Brigham & Beman (1906). However, the dome atop the Providence church may have more in common with what Brunelleschi designed for Santa Maria del Fiore in Florence. Whatever the precedent, the classical language of the building makes two important statements. First, by referencing the Italian Renaissance, the church stakes a claim to the intellectual tradition associated with the rebirth of science and knowledge in sixteenth-century Italy. No medieval mysticism here. Second, and perhaps just as important, the imposing size and

First Church of Christ Scientist

quality of the design is a statement that although the sect is new, it is a player of consequence. Then again, the architecture is perhaps conveying an even more subtle message.

The composition of the building is, in essence, a dome set on top of a square. The symbolism of such a configuration is a staple of many religious and philosophic traditions stretching back to prehistoric times: The dome is the arch of heaven and points to transcendence and timelessness, since in a circle there is neither beginning nor end. Depending on the tradition, the cube or square is the heart or the earth. Mediating the space between cube and dome are the classic stone urns, their flames shooting skyward, material to transcendent. The square itself outlines the shape of a Greek cross, which carries the implied symbolism of the entire architectural composition one step further in perfect harmony with Christian Science beliefs.

Did the architects of the church on Prospect Street consciously tap into this tradition? Perhaps, perhaps not. Whatever its origins or message, the First Church of Christ Scientist is certainly one of the brightest threads in the architectural fabric of College Hill. In the early morning, the dome with its bracelet of Ionic columns is painted by the first rays of the rising sun, while the surrounding streets are still in shadow. In the evening, the dome captures the last golden light as the sun slips below the western horizon.

47 Antonio Machado House (Ellen Dexter Sharpe House)
Parker, Thomas & Rice, 1912; dormitory wing, Stephen L. Lerner, 1975

Rochambeau House (Henry Dexter Sharpe House)
Parker, Thomas & Rice, 1928; renovation, R. E. Dinneen Architects and Planners, 1987

Continuing north on Prospect Street, we come to a pair of related (literally) houses. Designed for two women related by marriage, each residence is a skillful exercise in the revivalist styles favored by wealthy clients in the first decades of the twentieth century.

The earlier of the two, the Antonio Machado House, is Elizabethan Revival with its sharply pitched gables, elaborate brickwork, and of course the bold paired chimneys. Like its companion across the way, it is an example of an *hôtel particulier*, that is, a grand free-standing house located between an entry court on the front and a garden out back. Purchased from the Rhode Island School of Design in 1955, the building was renamed the Antonio Machado House in 1989 to honor the early twentieth-century Spanish poet. The contemporary addition at the rear shows how with the right sense of taste and design skill an architect can make an intervention into an existing structure, giving it new purpose and extending its life.

Rochambeau House

Across the street, the Departments of French and Hispanic Studies reside in Rochambeau House. Strongly influenced by the aesthetic of the writer Edith Wharton and her friend Ogden Codman, the 20,000-square-foot house is a transatlantic version of an eighteenth-century French chateau. The decorative accents here are classical. Mrs. Henry Dexter Sharpe—Mary Elizabeth Sharpe—had a love for all manner of things French, reflected in the striking interior, much of which is intact on the ground floor, save for the furnishings, which have been removed. Many of the cornices and all of the paneling in the southeast room were imported from France. Upon her death in 1985, the house was deeded to Brown University as a gift in memory of her husband (Class of 1894), a former chancellor, and her son (Class of 1945).

Among her many gifts to the University, Sharpe's greatest may well be the decades she spent pursuing her life's passion, gardening. For approximately three decades she supervised the landscaping of the University's grounds. To gain some insight into the skill and taste of this self-taught landscape architect, visit the garden at the rear of the house. It is another reminder of the essential role women have played as enlightened stewards of the built and natural environments of College Hill, Providence, and indeed the nation. The garden benches, by the way, are copies of those Napoleon sat on while he was calculating his next moves at his enforced retreat on the island of Elba.

If you have the time and energy, walk east to Hope Street and then north, gradually ascending to a hidden jewel of the Brown campus, Ladd Observatory.

Ladd Observatory

48   Ladd Observatory

Stone, Carpenter & Willson, 1891; tower addition, Perry Dean Rogers & Partners, 1997; landscape design, Halvorson Design Partnership; Transit Room restoration, Ed Wojcik, 2010

Although the Ladd Observatory is not part of the Pembroke campus, Walk Four is the closest jumping-off point to experience a building well worth the hike. If further excuse is needed, the Observatory was designed by the architects responsible for the first building of the women's College, Pembroke Hall. It is a nice way to conclude a Walk that began with the work of this firm.

Inside the 43-by-27-foot brick and stone building named for Rhode Island Governor Herbert W. Ladd, there is a masonry pier that is independent of the structure around it. The pier supports a telescope, a refractor of 12 inches aperture and 15 feet focal length. Since 2004, the historic instruments inside the Observatory have been gradually restored and carefully preserved. This includes the two transit instruments in the ell at the rear of the building, which were designed for the precise observation of star positions. The windows slide cleverly into pockets in the floor to afford an unobstructed view of the sky through shutters that are opened in the ceiling. Enclosed by a railing both decorative and practical, the flat roof of the main building was designed to be accessible from the tower and was used for observations by large classes. Sadly, what those first students were able to see has been compromised by modern light pollution.

When Ladd Observatory opened in the summer of 1891, it served three purposes: instruction in astronomy, astronomical research, and providing the official standard time for all of Providence. If any one building on the Brown campus demonstrates that the revivalist styles employed by Victorian architects veiled the latest construction techniques and welcomed the newest technologies, this brick and brownstone diamond on Tin-top Hill is it. (An oft-told tale behind the nickname identifies the site as the former dumping site for old tin cans.)

Weather permitting, Ladd Observatory is open to the public free of charge, 8 PM – 11 PM each Tuesday evening. In 2000, the building was added to the National Register of Historic Places. The way back from Ladd Observatory to the south entrance of the Pembroke campus takes us to the starting point of the next Walk.

1   Martha Mitchell, *Encyclopedia Brunoniana*, 583. Mary Emma Woolley (Pembroke, Class of 1894), who went on to become president of Mt. Holyoke College.

2   Mitchell, *Encyclopedia Brunoniana*, 426; quoted from the 1903 Ivy Day issue of Pembroke's newspaper, the *Sepiad*.

3   President Faunce, report to the Corporation, 1907, quoted in R. M. Kliment and Frances Halsband, *Campus Heritage at Brown University: Preservation Priorities* (Providence: 2006), 92.

4   President Faunce, report to the Corporation, 1923, quoted in Kliment and Halsband, *Campus Heritage*, 110.

"The Walk":
Consolidating the Core

"The Walk": Consolidating the Core

> Brown is a place of beauty and charm....As chairman of the Planning and
> Building Committee, I started with the idea that it was just as wrong for Brown
> to have bad architecture as it was to accept an illiterate thesis.
> —John Nicholas Brown Jr.[1]

At the beginning of the twenty-first century, students walking south from the
Pembroke campus could choose one of two routes: turn right at Meeting Street
and proceed along Brown Street, which led to Faunce Arch, or turn left at
Meeting Street and walk along Thayer Street to the Sciences Library and Metcalf
Chemical Laboratory, where Thayer meets Waterman Street. There was, however,
an unofficial third route: a more or less straight path through a patchwork of
parking lots, a gas station, and trash bins. This was Dumpster Way. Nearly one
hundred years earlier, Frederick Law Olmsted Jr. anticipated this third way. In his
correspondence with President Faunce about the still largely unbuilt Lincoln
Field, Olmsted drew a straight north-south line across the east-west axis of the
Lincoln Field green, clearly suggesting a path in the direction of what was to
become the Pembroke Campus.[2] Olmsted's proposal was a classic Beaux-Arts
strategy, which emphasized symmetrical avenues that led to a destination
of some distinction.

What brought Olmsted's suggestion back into play is a classic phoenix-
rising-from-the-ashes narrative. Brown's decision in the late 1990s to locate a
major new facility, its Life Sciences building, on Meeting Street provoked a
strong pushback from people in the neighborhood, who felt a building of this
size was inappropriate. Ultimately, Life Sciences was built, but at a price of delays,
several redesigns, and community ill will that precipitated an environmental
impact study. To avoid future costly and time-consuming confrontations,
the Brown Corporation and incoming President Simmons recognized the need
for a framework to guide the University's future growth. In meeting the
growing needs of a growing university, did Brown have to continue to nibble
at the surrounding neighborhood? If not, where were the new facilities for
expanding programs to go? How would Brown maintain its standing with its
peers? Clearly, the University needed to return to the kind of big-picture
thinking that prompted President Faunce to contact Olmsted a century earlier.

In 2003 the *Strategic Framework for Physical Planning* was presented to
the Corporation for approval. Developed by AIA Firm Award recipient Kliment
Halsband Architects, the plan articulated three principles:

1. Develop circulation infrastructure to foster community,
   unify, and enhance the campus and its surroundings,
2. Consolidate the core, and,
3. Move beyond College Hill[3]

A year after the *Strategic Framework* was adopted, the architects unveiled a bold proposal that implemented the first two principles. That proposal, simply called "The Walk," expanded on Olmsted's suggestion by laying out the outlines for a circulation spine of interconnected green spaces between Pembroke and Lincoln Field. Kliment Halsband Architects also discovered close to one million square feet of buildable space on land the University already owned, and half a million square feet primed for major renovations that would improve how Brown was using its existing facilities. Deploying more wisely the resources Brown already had and filling in existing gaps would be the course for future growth.

Still a work in progress, The Walk has begun to pull into a coherent scheme a previously disjointed stretch of the campus between what today is Simmons Quad and the Pembroke campus. We begin on the south side of Meeting Street with the project that revealed the urgent need for a comprehensive plan.

49   Sidney E. Frank Hall for Life Sciences
Ballinger Architects, 2006

One of Brown's largest buildings at 173,000 square feet, the Sidney E. Frank Hall for Life Sciences met a critical need. Together with the existing Bio-Medical Center and Grimshaw-Gudewicz, the Sidney E. Frank Hall accelerated the University's commitment to build a first-class medical school. Named for the late New York businessman Sidney E. Frank (Class of 1942), the Life Sciences building celebrates contemporary materials and contemporary ideas about the best way to open a student's mind to inquiry. The glass and brick structure weaves around existing buildings, accommodating 62 offices, 30 laboratories, 10 conference rooms, and a 98-seat seminar room. Connected to the neighboring Bio-Medical Center, the Life Sciences building fosters collaboration among neuroscience, molecular biology, cell biology, and biochemistry, making this neighborhood a hub of life science research.

Compared to its near neighbors, the Life Sciences building has a welcome transparency, although there is little effort to bring this transparency down to the street level on the Meeting Street side. The expansive series of glazed bays begin only above the second floor. Still, the rhythm of those bays, which dramatically break up a massive building, along with the glass entryway, sheds a welcoming warm glow at night as one walks by. The tall, two-story lobby that runs behind the glass offers pleasant seating areas that invite informal interaction. Also, the view out to the Pembroke campus is smashing. The abundance of glazing throughout the Life Sciences complex gives those inside direct views to the exterior in 90 percent of the regularly occupied spaces. In the daylight, the intense blood-red brick plays nicely against the glass.

Sidney E. Frank Hall for Life Sciences

Sidney E. Frank Hall for Life Sciences, interior

The complex is in fact two buildings or wings set at right angles to one another. Connecting both wings is the two-story glass Greenspan Ruben pedestrian bridge. Serving what appears to be a purely utilitarian function, the bridge was the first public artwork commissioned by Brown in its Percent-for-Art program, which designates a percentage of the construction costs for public art. Designed by Diane Samuels, *Lines of Sight* is made from 140 custom-manufactured, double-pane windows. Each window is completely and painstakingly filled with free-floating glass elements, including magnifying lenses, beads, prisms, and disks. Interspersed throughout are 7,500 small glass rectangles, hand-engraved by the artist, with excerpts of poetry or prose submitted by Brown students, faculty, administration, staff, friends, and alumni, as well as by the artist herself. The installation speaks to the theme of closely observing the world, an activity associated with artists and scientists alike. On each side of the bridge, sandblasted into the outer surface of the glass panes and stretching the entire length, is the faint image of a hand. Rumor has it the handprint belongs to one of Brown's most beloved former chancellors, Artemis A. W. Joukowsky (Class of 1955).

If transparency and interdisciplinary pursuits are core values, so is a commitment to sustainability. A number of the design tactics pursued by the architect and Brown's Department of Facilities Management include: 80 percent day lighting in work areas; occupancy lighting sensors in each room; a white reflective roof membrane to deflect solar gain; terrazzo flooring in the main halls composed of recycled glass; the use of minimal off-gassing materials; recycling and use of regional materials; a rainwater collection system that provides water for landscaping irrigation; and bicycle storage, showers, and changing rooms that meet the needs of alternative transportation. In 2009, the Life Sciences building received a LEED Silver rating from the U.S. Green Building Council.

Two additional details before moving on. First is the secret pocket garden between the west wing of Sidney E. Frank Hall and Grimshaw-Gudewicz. Donated by the building's contractor and designed by Todd Rader, the Gilbane Garden adds to Brown's growing necklace of vest pocket oases amid the hard edges of metal, stone, and glass. The stairs leading from the garden fan out onto The Walk like a cascading stream when it reaches the bottom of its run. The second feature worth noting is the way the two wings of the Life Sciences building define the opening to The Walk. Like the neck of an hourglass, the walls on either side restrict what we can see behind and in front of us. The passageway separates two precincts one from the other, yet connects both in a manner similar to Faunce Arch. Movement through is speeded up, only to slow down as one emerges into the relaxed, open space on either side.

Also, note the differences between the way the Sidney E. Frank and Grimshaw-Gudewicz buildings meet The Walk. The margin of the former is defined by a long low marble bench that invites seating; behind this, plantings; and behind these is a row of ground-level windows that allow views into and out of the building. By contrast, Grimshaw-Gudewicz has no ground floor windows, no landscaping, and is entered through a low one-story arcade, which at least provides a sheltered space for bike racks. In fairness, at the time Grimshaw-Gudewicz was built, the east side of the building faced a maze of dumpsters and parking lots. The rather austere, do-not-stop-to-linger design no doubt seemed an appropriate response.

50   Bio-Medical Center
Shepley, Bulfinch, Richardson & Abbott, 1969; southwest two-story addition, Shepley, Bulfinch, Richardson & Abbott, 1982

The liberal arts can be fit in relatively small quarters. A desk and a chair will do. The sciences, especially the experimental sciences, require much more elbow room. In 1963, when Brown inaugurated a six-year program leading to the degree of Master of Medical Science, a large modern facility to serve the new program was an urgent need. For Brown, this meant picking up the thread that had been cut in 1827 by President Wayland, who closed the University's first medical program, which had begun in 1811. Brown chose one of America's oldest and most respected

Bio–Medical Center

architecture firms. Yet however much the new facility enriched the pursuits of those inside, the overblown scale, relentlessly repetitive elements, and brutish street presence made it an unwelcome neighbor. It is easy to imagine the outcry when plans for this building were first made public. But the neighborhood's complaints had little legal standing. Despite concerns voiced about the possibility of hazardous materials, environmental impact assessments were not required at the time of construction, and the Bio-Medical Center was built pretty much as designed. However, that was not the last word. The neighborhood backlash was fuel for those who wanted and eventually succeeded in having College Hill designated a National Historic District. This would raise the stakes for future conflict whenever Brown attempted to build into the neighborhood.

Like many buildings of the period, the Bio-Medical Center offered what was believed to be an amenity—an open plaza or terrace. The one on the north side of Meeting Street was to be known as Founders' Court. It would have been a dubious honor. Like many of these period amenities, the plaza is windswept and desolate. At some point a landscape proposal was developed that would have softened the hard edges with plantings and brightly colored chairs that could have been moved into informal seating arrangements, like in a Parisian park. But no Parisian park has to make room for two giant, boxy vents.

In 1982, what had been an open plaza at the south end of the Bio-Medical Center was occupied by a 30,000-square-foot structure to house Brown's Center for Health Care Studies. The two-story brick addition with its pitched standing-seam, lead-coated copper roof appears to be an attempt to reintroduce a residential scale to a corner whose residential character had disappeared. Each element of this addition has a large expanse of fixed glazing with mullions at the second-story level, but these are opaque, at least from the outside. The side of the addition facing Brown Street is windowless. If the addition was in fact an effort to humanize this corner of the Bio-Medical Center with something approaching a human scale, it is difficult to imagine the result pleased either the students or the neighborhood.

51   Grimshaw-Gudewicz Building
Shepley, Bulfinch, Richardson & Abbott, 1989

This research facility tied together the existing classrooms and laboratories of the older Bio-Medical Center to become what is now referred to as the Bio-Med Pavilion. Today, it serves the downtown Alpert Medical School with additional offices, labs, and classroom facilities. Named after George Grimshaw and Irene Gudewicz, the facility poses a familiar challenge: How do you evaluate a building that lacks curb appeal but may in fact do everything it was programmed to do and do it quite well? Architecture is of course more than skin deep. Yet for the pedestrian, that is often the only thing you see. And for a neighbor living close by, it is a fact that has to be looked at every day.

Although the address is Brown Street, the orientation of Grimshaw-Gudewicz is largely along the north side of Olive Street. The five-story brick wall that crowds the length of the narrow sidewalk leading to The Walk is oppressive. Red oaks

Grimshaw–Gudewicz Building (left) and Sidney E. Frank Hall for Life Sciences (right)

and American hornbeam have been planted part way down the south side of Olive Street. One hopes they will flourish and the building will be at least partially planted out. The third element of the complex along Olive Street introduces an additional floor distinguished by bands of flat inoperable windows that march around the upper stories. There is the suggestion of a cornice. Also the band of windows at the very top is set back to soften the impression of the kind of research warehouses that proliferated at Brown and other college campuses during the 1960s. The tower at the southeast corner is a vertical flourish intended, it would appear, to relieve the boxiness of the building to which it is somewhat unconvincingly attached. However, the tower does serve as a destination landmark for students traveling north from the Simmons Quad toward the Pembroke campus. The role of way-finder is enhanced after the sun goes down when the top is illuminated from within and glows on the night sky.

52   Peter B. Green House (formerly Lippitt-Guild House)

1868; restoration and relocation, Lerner | Ladds + Bartels Architects and H. V. Collins Company, General Contractors, 2007

In the summer of 2007, this classic Second Empire–style house (the steeply pitched slope of the mansard roof is the giveaway) was carefully wrapped, pried loose from its site, put on a flatbed, and in the course of three days moved intact approximately 450 feet from 142 Angell Street (via Olive Street) to the corner of Brown and Angell Streets. For a few days at least, the house was a mobile home.

Relocating this 300-ton structure achieved three positive outcomes: it created green space for future development; the new location more clearly defined the boundary between the residential neighborhood and the campus; and saving the house from the wrecking ball along with a painstaking restoration (down to the historically appropriate color scheme on the exterior) was a major act of steward-ship. Recycling one's design heritage is also easy on the eyes and good for the planet. Bringing up the building to the latest ADA-accessible and fire codes had advantages both inside and out, including the removal of all but one of the intrusive fire escapes that had marred the exterior at its original site.

Acquired by Brown in 1966, the house is named for Peter B. Green (Class of 1980), who funded the restoration to honor his late wife. Today, it provides space

for the Department of History. One final note: New England may have lost many of its magnificent elms, but not (so far) its stately beeches. The copper beech immediately to the east of the house is nature's gift to the beauty of the Brown campus. The architecture of this specimen is well worth closer observation.

Peter B. Green House

Sharpe House

53 Sharpe House
Alpheus C. Morse, 1873

A formidable four-story double residential pile, Sharpe House (much like Green, which had been its neighbor) was built in the Second Empire style by the same architect who designed Sayles Hall. Lucian Sharpe (whose family managed Rhode Island's internationally regarded tool-making business) lived in one side; Brown Professor John Larkin Lincoln (of Lincoln Field fame) lived in the other. It is another postcard from Angell Street as it appeared in the latter half of the nineteenth century, when most of the University's faculty lived within easy walking distance of the campus. The porch on the east side of the house speaks to a lost style of relaxed living after classes let out, and to quiet summer days. Brown acquired the house in 1921. Until 1960, it was used as a dormitory for Pembroke students. Today, it houses faculty members of the University's Department of History.

54 The Glenn and Darcy Weiner Hillel Center (formerly Rapaporte House, previously Froebel Hall)
Stone, Carpenter & Willson, 1878; addition, Fred Babcock (Babcock Design Group) and Cornelis de Boer (Haynes / de Boer Associates), 2003

Established in 1947, the Hillel Foundation moved to its first permanent home in 1963. Not owned by Brown, this building is nevertheless an important part of the architectural and intellectual fabric of both the University and the neighborhood. The original structure—Froebel Hall—illustrates the impact and the legacy in America of important nineteenth-century developments in Germany. These include the rise of great research universities and the introduction of kindergartens. Named after the German educator Friedrich Froebel (1782–1852), who recognized that children have unique capabilities, Froebel Hall was built as a school to train kindergarten teachers. It was the second such facility in America—Boston had the first. (The wooden blocks Froebel developed for children to learn the elements of solid geometry would have a profound impact on the architect Frank Lloyd Wright.) The picturesque, chalet-like style of the original building is a nice nod to the residential architecture of Thuringia, the "green heart of Germany," where Froebel was born. It is additional evidence, as if additional evidence were needed, that even minus Willson, the firm of Stone, Carpenter & Willson was capable of conjuring with great skill whatever architectural style was called for.

As Hillel's Brown and RISD membership increased, more room was needed to meet the cultural and social needs of the community. This was met by reworking the existing building and integrating it with two adjacent late eighteenth-century brick Federal houses on Angell Street, acquired in 1996 and 1998, respectively. The result is a complex encompassing more than 25,000 square feet that includes assembly, student activity, and administrative spaces. The new two-story entrance at the corner of Angell and Brown Streets functions like a hinge, nicely mediating the aesthetic distance between the Federal houses and the original nineteenth-century Froebel building. It is deferential to both in materials and massing. Also the roof provides welcome space for outdoor functions. As the design strategies at Hillel make clear, modesty is sometimes the most becoming trait of an architect.

As clever as the integration of the interior spaces of all three buildings is, there are some admittedly minor issues. The exteriors of the Angell Street houses seem overly restored. Two centuries of patina have been meticulously cleaned, leaving the pristine brick somewhat Botoxed. Time and urban pollution will take care of this. Less easily remedied are the front doors of the two properties on Angell Street. These are clearly no longer intended for pedestrians to enter; they have been demoted to emergency exits or fire doors. This perhaps drains some of the life from Angell Street. These are small points considering the quality of the facility that has emerged, and the fact that two important Federal houses on Angell Street were preserved and restored, gaining for the architects and client a 2005 AIA Rhode Island Merit Award.

The Glenn and Darcy Weiner Hillel Center

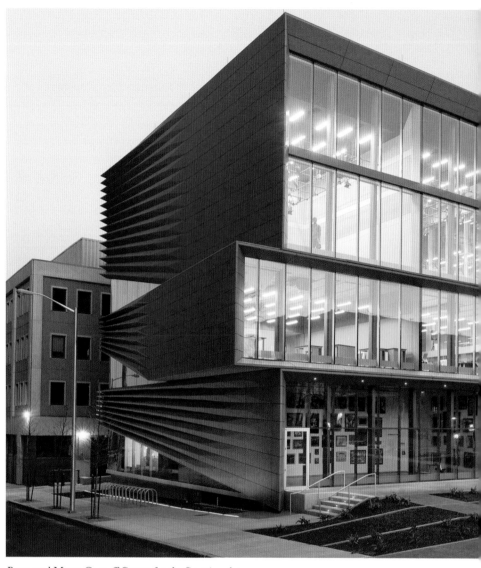

Perry and Marty Granoff Center for the Creative Arts

55   Perry and Marty Granoff Center for the Creative Arts
Diller Scofidio + Renfro, 2011; lighting design, Tillotson Design Associates

Into a sciences precinct, whose energy is focused internally on research and teaching, comes what is in effect a zinc and glass hand grenade tossed with giddy abandon by the unruly tribe of the creative arts. At the time it opened, there were few students—and faculty—who did not feel something seismic and unprecedented had happened architecturally on the Brown campus. The Granoff Center is in fact the culmination or convergence of a number of forces that began to grow in strength from the beginning of the twenty-first century, if not earlier: Brown's

commitment to interdisciplinary study, transparency, and sustainability. Succeeding on all counts, the architects score a triple play.

First, they blur the boundary between in and out, creating a lively public space. The creative arts are taken off an elitist pedestal and made accessible to everyone. As for sustainability, innovations in glass and glazing technologies ensure that openness to natural light is not an invitation to heat loss or gain. The automated shading system on the west facade tracks the sun by automatically adjusting the angle of the blinds to deflect the maximum amount of solar heat; even with the shading deployed, those inside can see out and enjoy natural daylight. These and other gestures, including the first green roof in Providence, earned the Granoff Center a LEED Gold rating.

Because the building is sliced in the middle and the floors deliberately misaligned, dancers on the first floor can see actors on the second, who can watch musicians and painters on the third, and so on. Glass walls facilitate the visual interchange without the distractions of sound. If the visual activity is too distracting or the sunlight too strong, there are blackout and scrim shades. The suspended steel staircase at the back is intercepted at the landings by informal spaces or living rooms complete with sofas and chairs where students and faculty can simply hang out. Think of these as green rooms where performers relax, converse with one another, and prepare for their public performances. How often is a staircase more than utilitarian or, at the most, a well-designed aesthetic footnote? At the Granoff Center, it is the biological equivalent of a spine that connects and communicates energy to the studios and performance spaces out front.

Another way to think about the building is to see it as a stage or series of stages with rehearsal halls whose opaque walls have been stripped away so the

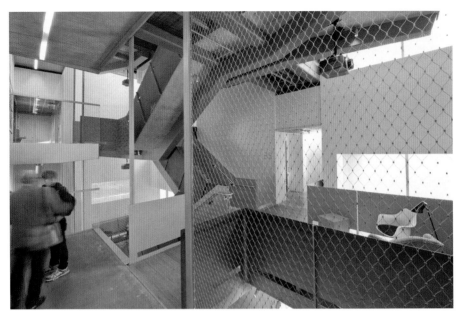

Perry and Marty Granoff Center for the Creative Arts, interior staircase

audience can see everything from the catwalks to the dressing rooms. The Granoff Center is a performance, or perhaps more accurately a series of rehearsals and ongoing experiments. Approaching the building from Thayer Street, one has a tantalizing view of an interior gallery space, since the CNC-milled zinc composite cladding is pulled up at the corners into a three-dimensional pleat rather like a curtain. The lights embedded in the sidewalk that parallel the north and south sides are, in a manner of speaking, footlights. At night the light they cast onto the folds of the building's skin is magical. Hard metal assumes the soft texture of drapery.

Like the architects of the John D. Rockefeller Jr. Library (Walk One), Diller Scofidio + Renfro are not reluctant to flaunt the industrial technology that made the design and construction of the Granoff Center possible. But there is a big difference between what happens here and on Prospect Street, and it is not just a matter of the metal cladding versus concrete panels. At the Granoff Center, we have arrived at the next phase of the Industrial Revolution, mass customization, made possible by the development of new materials, laser technology, and especially computer-aided design. Whereas Rockefeller Library looks assembled from standardized parts, the Granoff Center is made up of products individually tailored to realize the architects' unique vision. That pleated zinc wall, for example, was not pulled off a factory shelf. The freedom to innovate made possible by the Industrial Revolution has made an evolutionary leap in the twenty-first century, opening up possibilities in the design of everything from arts centers to the perfect fit of the latest prosthetic device.

The land opened up by the relocation of the Peter B. Green House invites passersby to stretch out on the grass and watch the ever-changing rehearsal and production spaces whose energy splashes out to and past The Walk. What might have simply been a convenient path from Pembroke to the Simmons Quad has been transformed into a precinct for discovery and interaction for those who pause, sit down, and watch. Using a totally modern design vocabulary, new computer-aided technologies, and contemporary materials, the architects have captured the expressive dimension of architecture as forcefully in its way as the old Robinson Hall or Pembroke Hall. A small building with a remarkable sense of expansiveness, the Granoff Center is the brilliant buckle on the belt of The Walk.

In 2012, brothers Jan and Tim Edler installed 2x5, a pair of 14-by-5-foot light boxes at the Granoff Center's Angell Street entrance. At night, these wash the surrounding space with a changing palette of white, rose, blue, mustard, and red light. After a project at the newly renovated Metcalf Building (Walk Three), 2x5 is the University's second light installation. It is a singularly creative way to allude to the luminosity of the rising sun in the University's crest and to make the point that a building can itself be a stage for artistic expression.

As you cross Angell Street heading south it becomes clear The Walk is not an exercise in rigid geometry, but a chain or sequence of three open spaces in varying stages of being fully realized as the buildings and landscaping settle in. There is even a pleasant west-to-east jog as the spaces or voids subtly expand and contract from one to the next. Olmsted may have been the first to suggest the straight line to connect the Pembroke and Brown campuses, but on this Walk, getting there can indeed be half the fun. The challenge for the architects developing the master plan was to bring some sense of order out of confusion and to enhance functionality and aesthetics. Just how great a challenge is revealed by three buildings on the south side of Angell Street.

56   Hemisphere Building
1989

This is a curious building. It appears to be a joke, a knowing postmodern wink at what in the twentieth century had been Brown's official architectural brand. Is the architect, who has not stepped forward, trying to have it both ways—"I know my classical orders but, as you see, do not really believe in them"? Whatever the case and however well the building may serve those who use it, the Hemisphere Building is worth a second glance, if only to sharpen an appreciation of the Colonial and Federal originals that are the glory of Brown and College Hill. A far more adult interpretation of how to do a period style is seen immediately next door.

57   Churchill House
Thornton & Thornton, 1907

Built for the Rhode Island Women's Club, Churchill House was integrated into the Brown campus in 1970. Named for the Club's founder, Elizabeth Kittredge Churchill, the building is a respectable if undistinguished example of Colonial Revival architecture by a firm that did little work in Providence. (Compare the competent Palladian window over the entrance to Churchill House with that pasted on the facade of the Hemisphere Building.) Currently, it houses the Rites and Reason Theatre and the Africana Studies Department. With the Granoff Center directly across the street, the two make this part of The Walk a gathering place for the performing arts. The potential of this alignment is only beginning to be realized.

58   The Urban Environmental Lab
Alpheus C. Morse, 1884; interior renovations, c. 1980

The backstory behind this next building designed by the busy Alpheus C. Morse begins in 1963 with the arrival on campus of Harold Ward, a young chemistry professor. Ward's arrival coincided with the first stirrings of what would become the environmental movement, which Ward and his students soon found themselves leading. By 1978, a full-blown program of study had emerged. The only thing lacking for the intended "living laboratory" was a home. Thanks in part to a generous $221,000 grant from the Richard King Mellon Foundation, what became the Center for Environmental Studies was able in 1981 to move into this two-and-a-half-story Gothic Revival carriage house. Supplementing the grant were the countless hours of sweat equity put in by the students themselves to renovate the property before moving in. They stripped off rotting wood, put on a new roof, installed new windows and water-conserving plumbing, and built a greenhouse that provided much of the building's heat. With commendable energy and a sense of mission, Brown students ingeniously transformed a Victorian carriage house into what is arguably one of the nation's first "green" buildings or, if you will, the first institutional commune. In short, the building itself became a major part of the curriculum, demonstrating that older structures could be made more energy-efficient using traditional and new technologies. The garden at the rear of the building was itself a teaching resource, reminding students and passersby of our connection to the Earth.

A historical footnote illustrates the difficulty of maintaining ideological purity. Next to the new Urban Environmental Lab stood a large maple tree well loved for its age and shade. No one treasured it more than the faculty of Brown's American Civilization program, next door in Norwood House. Fearing the maple's shade would compromise the effectiveness of their solar collectors, the environmentalists were prepared to chop it down. A vigorous "Save the Tree" campaign was launched by Norwood's residents. In a spirit of compromise, the maple was given a one-year reprieve, time enough to crunch the numbers regarding the ratio of sunlight to shade. Fortunately for all concerned, especially the tree, it was determined the impact on the solar collectors was minimal. The maple continued to cast its cooling shade.

The future of the Center with its lovingly tended vegetable and flower garden is a matter of debate. The carriage house is in the way of plans for a new academic

The Urban Environmental Lab and Garden

building on the west side of The Walk. Ongoing discussions are not about abolishing the Center, but where best to relocate it. What is being offered to its residents are modern facilities that will better support the teaching and research of what now is a global movement. A far less contentious story is told by the building on the next block. Strictly speaking, it is not part of The Walk, but close enough and of a quality well worth the time to cross Brown Street.

59 Samuel B. Wheaton House
1850

68 ½ and 70 Brown Street addition
Lerner | Ladds + Bartels Architects, 2001

Built for a prominent Providence banker, the original 9,000-square-foot building on the corner of Angell and Brown Streets has lived three lives: first, as a single-family residence; then, beginning in 1914, a popular business (Carr's Restaurant

68½ and 70 Brown Street

and Catering); today, an attractive piece of the architectural mosaic that is Brown. To make this transition both seamless and yet boldly new, the architects drew on many years of experience in residential and institutional design along with a modern commitment to sustainability. The lucky beneficiaries of their work are the faculty and students of the University's English and Creative Writing Departments.

The 29,000-square-foot addition attached to the south—three times the size of the original brick Italianate residence—does several things skillfully: it provides a contemporary facility that satisfies the needs of faculty and students, and it reinforces the residential character of College Hill on the west side of Brown Street. Taking their cue from the older building right down to dormers (squared off

instead of peaked), the deep eaves, and the relatively flat profile of the roof, the architects perform an inspired variation on a Victorian theme. The setback hyphen, or connector, between the old and the new makes it clear the architects are not trying to fool you. There is no question what is old and what is new. Yet there is a clear family resemblance, and both generations sit comfortably next to one another.

By breaking up what is a fairly large complex into a collection of brick cubes, the architects suggest if not a village, at least an inviting neighborhood. There is a push and pull of volumes as the building moves toward and from the sidewalk; instead of flat planes, there is a nice play of light and shadow. Even Fones Alley is part of the game: rather than being walled off, as it is on the other side of the street,

Samuel B. Wheaton House

the alley becomes a way through, providing a depth of vision, a tactic to further break up—but not fragment—the mass of the addition. As the architects describe it: "The two halves are conceptually bridged across the alley by mirroring entry arcades and window bays."

By giving new life to the older building and using it to develop their larger concept, the architects provide the key to the initially curious Gertrude Stein quotation that appears on the building: "And then there is using everything." The use of "everything" is no doubt the most fundamental strategy of sustainable design and yet another marker in Brown's commitment to be a leader in sustainability. In 2002, the Samuel B. Wheaton House received an Institutional Rehab / Restoration Award from the Providence Preservation Society.

60   Third World Center / Partridge Hall
Alpheus C. Morse, 1885

Here is yet another project from the prolific shop of Alpheus C. Morse. You could not achieve a more colorful and complex pattern by shaking up the pieces of glass in a kaleidoscope. Brick on the first floor, slate shingle on the second, and clapboard on the third-story dormers and gable end add up to the classic more-is-better Queen Anne parfait style. There are also elements of the Stick style, or Carpenter Gothic— for example, the boards on the surface of the gables that, in Carpenter Gothic fashion, are meant to suggest the structural skeleton. Other details follow suit: roofs are gabled or hipped, often with second-story projections; the upper sash of the double-hung dormer windows is treated decoratively; the chimneys are as ornamental as they are functional, bold exclamation points on the building below.

The porch with its projecting and sheltering pedimented entry is another Queen Anne gift to posterity first popularized by the influential writer and

Third World Center / Partridge Hall

landscape designer Andrew Jackson Downing (1815–1852), who believed that interacting with nature would have a positive moral effect. Having a porch opens a house to the world outside, allowing residents to enjoy cool summer breezes, while maintaining a zone of privacy. Georgian, Federal, and even early Italianate houses offer little in the way of porches. In these homes, porches were not really an option because in the city, houses were typically built right up to the property line. Once owners and architects started to pull houses back from the sidewalk, outdoor living became a possibility only to be lost again in the twentieth century when air-conditioning and television drew people back inside to the detriment, one might argue, of a nurturing sense of community.

One Victorian innovation that has shaped interiors ever since is the way the living spaces are organized. The size and location of rooms began to be dictated by function rather than the classical symmetry we associate with Colonial and Federal homes—two rooms on this side, two equal rooms on that. From the Victorian era on, interiors tend to be shaped to serve not how the residents should live but how they actually use the spaces.

The many delights of Partridge Hall do not stop at the front porch. Walk around the corner to Waterman Street. Just as he had on the College Green, the architect of Sayles Hall designed this building in the round. That is, the facade facing Waterman is no less interesting architecturally when viewed from the sidewalk than the facade that faces Brown Street. Note how a number of the elements on the front (gables, windows, and bays) are adroitly reshuffled on the side facing Waterman Street. The seeming randomness of the overall composition is revealed to be tightly choreographed.

The Third World Center began in 1969 at the Afro House, at 227 Bowen Street. When this building was razed to make way for the New Pembroke residential complex, Afro House moved into the basement of Churchill House. This was an opportunity to rethink the mission. The result was a new Center organized in 1976 to serve all students of color. The purpose was and remains to provide an environment that celebrates the variety of cultural heritages that make up the American experience and to promote racial and ethnic pluralism in the Brown community. The Center moved to its present location in 1986.

Crossing over to the south side of Brown Street brings us back to the precinct directly defined by The Walk.

J. Walter Wilson

61   J. Walter Wilson

Robinson Green Beretta, 1961; Sol Koffler Wing addition, 1983; renovation, LLB *Architects, 2008*

J. Walter Wilson represented a major leap forward in bringing to pass Brown's decision to create a program in medical education. Aesthetically, it was, unfortunately, a backward step. Gone was the intimacy or human scale of what had been built before World War II. To be sure, flexible, larger, and fireproof spaces were required for modern laboratories. Faced with the onslaught of the postwar baby boom and the launch of a new program, the need to fast-track research facilities often trumped more complex questions of site and context.

Brown has since tried to put something like a smile on Wilson's face. After the Sidney E. Frank Hall for Life Sciences opened two blocks north, the University could move research activities out of a facility that had become obsolete. The University seized the opportunity of the Kliment / Halsband *Strategic Framework* to rethink the building's purpose and function. Brown opted for more office space and the creation of a student-services satellite to complement the new Stephen Robert '62 Campus Center across Waterman Street. After the mechanical systems on the ground floor were moved to the roof, possibilities emerged that would bring some life to the building and the street. Most welcome was the addition of ground-floor windows on the Brown Street side and sensitive landscaping that somewhat softened the corners on the north end. The most dramatic transformation occurs where the 10,000-square-foot Sol Koffler addition meets Waterman Street. This part of Wilson has been reprogrammed as a student services center (mail room on the ground floor, and upstairs, the registrar, financial aid, office of the chaplain, and seminar rooms). Totally new is a glass hinge that links the original twin Koffler towers. By day, the glass harvests light; by night, the interior glows like an enormous porch lamp affixed to the older building.

Moving south, we come to three nineteenth-century houses repurposed by Brown to support a number of University programs. Together they offer a snapshot of a time when this stretch of Waterman was one of College Hill's most desirable residential addresses. Side by side they also reveal at a single glance the salient differences among three nineteenth-century period styles—Italianate, Second Empire, and Colonial Revival—that contribute to the architectural mosaic that is College Hill. The chronology is progressive, beginning with Walter Hall.

62   Walter Hall
1857; renovation, c. 1950

Built for John F. Chapin, a Providence merchant, the rather austere three-story brick Italianate-style house (grouped double-hung windows, projecting eaves, and bold entry porch) is named after Brown Professor Herbert E. Walter (1867–1945). Perhaps the most distinctive design feature apart from the expected Italianate cube shape of the house is the Palladian window directly above the porch and the smaller, arched windows of the third floor. These are like the flourish of a handkerchief in the top pocket of an otherwise formal businessman's suit. The property was acquired by Brown in 1937 and served as the Delta Upsilon fraternity house, until all fraternities were corralled in Wriston Quad two decades later. Renovated in the 1950s with the aid of a grant from the National Institute of Health, Walter Hall is currently the home of Brown's program in Ecology and Evolutionary Biology.

Walter Hall

Norwood House

63 Norwood House
1865

The building began life as a boarding house, which perhaps explains its size, especially at the back. Named in 1982 for V. Lee Norwood (Class of 1953), the building is currently used by the University's American Studies program. This Second Empire house, with its characteristic mansard roof (double-pitched with a steep lower slope), has all the charm the rather buttoned-down Walter Hall avoids. Sited on an elevated lot, the house lifts its skirts above the noise and dust of Waterman Street. The off-center entrance is formal, yet welcoming in a way that is different from the somber approach of its next-door neighbor.

The boarders who first lived in the house no doubt enjoyed the spacious porch that runs along the front half of the east facade. Oriented away from the traffic of Waterman Street, the porch achieves a degree of privacy that nevertheless allows those who sit in its shade to engage passersby.

Placed at the center of The Walk near Waterman Street between Norwood House and the next stop stands one of the most recent additions to Brown's growing collection of public art, American artist Tom Friedman's *Circle Dance*. A gift from an anonymous donor, the slightly larger than life-size stainless-steel sculpture is modeled after Henri Matisse's painting *La Danse*. Known for creating contemporary sculptures out of everyday materials, Friedman crafted the manquette out of aluminum turkey roasting pans. As described in the press release that accompanied the November 2012 installation: "Hints of the original material can be spotted throughout the final version…with imprints of the words 'bottom' and the pans' manufacturer remaining visible." *Circle Dance* is precisely the right joyous note to strike in mediating the rigid geometry of The Walk.

64   Frederick Lippitt and Mary Ann Lippitt House

1900

The brother and sister Brown alumni who owned this house compiled an extraordinary list of contributions to the University, including an endowment in 2002, which transferred the house to Brown as the new home of the Harriet W. Sheridan Center for Teaching and Learning. The roof is mansard, which delivers extra square footage on the top floor. But the rest of the house reads Colonial Revival, a style that became increasingly popular for residential architecture and for the architecture at Brown in the first half of the twentieth century.

Before crossing Waterman Street, note the parallel rows of elm trees planted on either side. When mature, the trees will not only soften the hard edges of a major west-to-east artery, they will also form a tunnel of green, absorbing sound and auto emissions. The planting is another chapter in the University's continuing campaign to bring back a tree that, along with the bear, is an iconic emblem of Brown.

Frederick Lippitt and Mary Ann Lippitt House

Architectural rendering of Hunter Laboratory renovation and redesign

65   Hunter Laboratory
Perry, Shaw, Hepburn & Dean, 1958; renovation, Toshiko Mori, 2013

Exactly 106-by-106-feet square when it was built, this brick box marked the
petering out of Brown's twentieth-century affair with Colonial Revival architecture.
Described at the time as "modified Georgian," Hunter Laboratory of Psychology
(named for Walter S. Hunter, the chairman of the Department of Psychology from
1936 to 1954) was the architectural equivalent of a Skinner box writ large: a tight
chamber in which human behavior was dissected and studied. Although Hunter
Laboratory opens onto a main thoroughfare, the lack of any windows on the first
floor effectively discounted the pedestrian. In fairness (perhaps) to the architects,
the building that opened in 1958 was not the architects' initial proposal. Drawings
of a scheme developed in 1955 show a far larger building distinguished by a
windowless center flanked by two five-story wings. Whether it was a matter of
budget or second thoughts, that building was never constructed. Succeeding
generations may count themselves lucky.

Increasingly obsolescent, increasingly at odds with the University's growing
commitment to promote collaboration and engagement, and too big to tear down,
Hunter was a candidate for corrective surgery. As part of the Kliment / Halsband
Strategic Framework, Brown undertook a complete renovation beginning in 2012 to
provide modern facilities for engineering and environmental studies. Toshiko Mori,
the architect responsible for remodeling Pembroke Hall, was given the commission
to fashion a silken purse out of the brick box that was Hunter Laboratory. What
the architect and the University saw went beyond repurposing this particular
building. It was an opportunity to complete the southern end of The Walk at

Simmons Quad. What stood in the way was Brown's outdated greenhouse wedged in between Hunter and Arnold Laboratory.

This part of the larger project is perhaps the boldest initiative. The greenhouse is to be torn down and a new one built in a place that complements the University's environmental studies program—the roof of the reconfigured Hunter Laboratory. In a new, sun-filled environment, students and faculty will be better able to pursue genetic experiments in plant culture. In addition to wearing an attractive, multifaceted glass hat that looks like an abstract crystal sculpture, Hunter will have a new entrance on the east side that opens into something the building lacked in its previous life—a light-filled lobby with seating and research displays. The building is thus reoriented from the entrance on Waterman to the green plaza that will echo the Pembroke Tribute at the northern end of The Walk. In the bargain, the project is designed to achieve a LEED Gold rating. More than one hundred years after it was first proposed by Olmsted, the thin line connecting the Pembroke campus and Lincoln Field, today's Ruth J. Simmons Quadrangle, will at last be fleshed out and completely drawn.

Hunter Laboratory was the last academic building designed for the University by Perry, Shaw, Hepburn & Dean. It was the end of an era and the beginning of an uncertain one for architecture and urban planning at Brown. Perhaps no other firm has left such a mark on the campus in the design as well as the planning of new facilities and the restoration of old. Its legacy was, and continues to this day to be, an important part of the image that is Brown.

1 *Brown Alumni Monthly*, November 1979, 39.

2 R. M. Kliment and Frances Halsband, *Strategic Framework for Physical Planning* (Providence: Brown University, 2003), 56.

3 Ibid, 61. The discussion of the evolution of The Walk owes much to the *Strategic Framework* and a separate document, "The Walk: A Proposed Design for the Extension of the Brown University Campus Joining Lincoln Field and Pembroke Green," 2004, produced by Kliment Halsband Architects and Todd Rader + Amy Crews Architecture Landscape Architecture. Readers interested in the background of this major planning initiative and recommendations for future growth will find these invaluable sources of planning principles guiding the growth of the University in the first two decades of the twenty-first century.

Manning Walk and the Sciences Precinct

Manning Walk and the Sciences Precinct

> With Brown University eastward the course of empire takes its way....[W]hen the land we already own on Manning Street shall be filled with dormitories for our students, then we shall discover that Marcus Aurelius has really been placed upon our front campus and is facing the line of future growth.[1]
> —President Faunce, 1908

> The issue is essentially whether Brown goes up in the air, spreads out more, or stands still. We are prepared to operate under City policies that will permit us to go up or spread out. If the pressure on the University is to stand still, we shall have to resist.[2]
> —President Keeney in a letter to the City of Providence, 1962

Unlike Horace Greeley, who famously advised America's youth to seek their fortunes by going west, President Faunce set the University's course toward the rising sun. Here would rise a future quad ringed by residence halls to house a growing student population. A block or so of Manning Street would be absorbed, just as the College Green had absorbed Brown Street. The new residential quad would face west across Thayer to Lincoln Field, which would ultimately replace the upper or College Green as the heart of Brown. That was Faunce's vision.

It did not turn out that way. For one thing, over the years the program or purpose of the site had changed. By the time the University assembled a superblock that embraced Manning Street, both the Wriston and Keeney residential quads had been built a few blocks south. These residential projects, the largest in Brown's history, eliminated the need for additional student housing—at least for the time being. By the late 1950s when Barnaby Keeney was president, Brown had a more pressing need: modern facilities to carry on the work of a great university—research. And there were matching federal funds to get the job done.

As you look east down Manning Walk, what is immediately apparent is the incoherence of it all, both the individual buildings and their relationship to each other. It comes as no surprise to learn the University lacked a comprehensive plan or vision of how the area around Manning Street would be shaped. Say what you will about Brown's six-decade-long affair with Beaux-Arts planning and Colonial Revival architecture, at least it was a coherent point of view. The only large idea that seems to have guided most of what was built was the need for a radical break with the past. Modern architecture, many argued, was more "honest." In practice honesty meant the triumph of technology over nature, abstraction over a figurative language, the conceptual over the sensuous, bare bones over ornament.

It is hard to imagine the shock verging on panic when in 1957 the Soviet Union succeeded in kenneling a dog in space. Sputnik jolted America's self-image as preeminent in science. In addition to the inevitable congressional hearings and political posturing, there suddenly were federal and corporate dollars available for research. This did not go unnoticed by college administrators who were enlisted or volunteered in the academic version of the Cold War arms race. If Brown were to attract new science faculty to do its part in service to the nation, the University needed to embark on an unprecedented campaign to build new and modernize existing research facilities. President Keeney's letter seeking zoning exemptions from the city is up-front about the millions of government dollars Brown was at risk of losing. Indeed, the very reputation of Brown among its peers was at stake. When America's involvement in Vietnam became an issue on college campuses, Brown would find itself increasingly uncomfortable with its dependence on government funds and the conditions that were attached. But that was in the future. For the moment, the creation of facilities that supported modern research was a driver in Brown's bicentennial planning and fund-raising campaign.

At the formal conclusion of this Walk, two additional destinations are included. Although not technically part of the sciences precinct, they are added because of their intrinsic interest as architecture, and also because they are, if not a chapter, at least footnotes well worth the time to explore.

A map of the site from Soldiers' Memorial Gate east to Hope Street reveals what might be described as an exploded quad. At the Thayer Street entrance to Manning Walk, the Sciences Library to the north and W. Duncan MacMillan

Manning Walk

Hall on the south frame a pleasant tree-shaded court. The next paired buildings, Thomas J. Watson Sr. Center for Information Technology alongside Waterman Street and the Geo-Chem Building by George Street, continue a fairly orderly march east. The landscaped green is still ample and imposes some coherence. But farther along, Marston Hall and the Barus Building break ranks and pinch the open space, reducing it to little more than a broad brick walk that continues east.

Once you cross Brook Street, the second stage of the science quad is crowded by large buildings and a number of smaller houses to the south that predate the closing of Manning Street. Capping the vista is the curved glass face of the Charles H. Giancarlo (Class of 1979) Engineering Laboratories.

Warner, Burns, Toan & Lunde, 1971

Susan P. and Richard A. Friedman Study Center
*Architecture Research Office (*ARO*), 2006; landscaping, Michael Van Valkenburgh*

In the 1950s, the University built two large residential quads a few blocks south of Manning Street. The ensuing controversy focused on the large, destabilizing bites the University took out of the neighborhood, and the many buildings (some of undoubted historic significance) that were either razed or moved. An argument could be made that the decision two decades later to build a high-rise science library atop a low-rise podium was Brown's attempt to forestall renewed controversy by standing tall on a smaller footprint of land the University already owned. While this no doubt figured into what was built, the background story is more complex.

The architect Danforth Toan (of the same firm that designed the John D. Rockefeller Jr. Library) first proposed what might be called a research shopping center: three eight-story towers, one three-story pavilion, one two-story pavilion, and a single one-story pavilion, a total of six buildings all in brick. Had that design been built, the resulting facility would have stretched most of the distance between Thayer and Brook Streets. A much larger footprint, true, but the differing elevations and the breaking up of the mass in smaller pieces would have been more in keeping with the scale of the neighborhood. As Jacob Reidel discovered in his

research, there are a number of clues that point to the intervention of the University's Planning and Building Committee chair, John Nicholas Brown Jr., who argued for, and eventually got, a tower.[3] Over time—and not much time—the limitations of a tower's tight, uncompromising floor plan became apparent and has resulted in an ongoing reprogramming of the building. But first, a few words about the Sciences Library as built.

One can be forgiven for regretting Brown's flirtation with the architectural fad of the moment, Brutalism—the repetitive angular geometries; the bands of stock, off-the-shelf windows strung like lines of laundry from the four corner monumental piers; the "honesty" (and low cost) of poured concrete;

Sciences Library

the inhuman scale; and the stand-alone, context-be-damned arrogance of the whole thing. Yet, like with a disagreeable uncle, time and some skillful intervention have encouraged genuine affection, at least among the students. To see why, alumni can ask permission from the front desk to tour the three levels of the award-winning Susan P. (Class of 1977) and Richard A. (Class of 1979) Friedman Study Center, which opened in 2006. The lower level is dedicated to collaborative and individual study. Even though the space is below grade, the ceiling is high and the study area is bathed by filtered natural light, which enters glass walls that open to views of intimate, well-kept gardens designed by Michael van Valkenberg as part of ARO's creation of the Friedman Center. The plantings of each garden are carefully designed around the solar exposure of that particular site. Vertical blind-like fabric sculptures that hang from the ceiling gently break up the large floor area into barrier-free "rooms." This softens the hard geometry of the space, a feat augmented by the carpet, whose colorful patterning creates islands and renders a pleasing acoustic. The artificial light, which is directed at the ceiling (thus eliminating glare and hot spots), is designed by Tillotson Design Associates, the same firm that created Brown's outdoor lighting design. Students can find places to work quietly alone or noisily in groups. The space has been allowed to heal itself (with a lot of help from ARO) because as originally designed, it is column-free.

Something as utilitarian as the wiring to operate computers is handled with imagination, carried down from the ceiling in channels that are decorative as well as functional. By all means check out the art on the piers that run along the center or interior of the study area. Even that cliché of Brutalist architecture—revealing the texture of the wooden forms used for the casting of the concrete—contributes to what is perhaps one of the most surprisingly pleasant and thoughtfully designed spaces on campus. You forget you are at the bottom of the building. Upstairs on the lobby level there is a cafe. In fair weather, it opens to the south terrace. The mezzanine level is an additional quiet study space that looks over the activity on the lobby floor and out through the two-story glazing to the south terrace. In 2011, the fourth floor was reconfigured into a quiet study area.

These and other steps transforming the Sciences Library are yet another consequence of the conceptual framework of the Kliment / Halsband plan, which calls for recapturing existing space within all the University's libraries to create collaborative study opportunities. Digital Technologies staff, now housed on the top or fourteenth floor, enjoy an up-to-the-minute work space and a view that reveals the original source of the city's wealth—the water that surrounds College Hill on three sides. Over time, the books on the other floors will be stored elsewhere and the vacated spaces throughout the building opened up for classes, conference rooms, and study areas, giving further energy to what has emerged as a vibrant community center, a 24/7 focus for student life.

Two additional footnotes before moving on: 1½, the 7,000-plus-pound bronze and stainless-steel sculpture between the library and the Geo-Chem Building, was commissioned by Artemis A. W. Joukowsky (Class of 1955) and his wife, Martha Sharp Joukowsky (Class of 1958). At the dedication during the 1985 Commencement Weekend, Joukowsky said: "Brown needs more areas of comfort and peace and contemplation. It's wonderful for kids to see these kinds of things around them, rather than just see them in museums." Commenting on her work, the sculptor Carla Lavatelli wrote: "I have continued to struggle to make beautiful forms and beautiful places, places where my work and my sculptures could continue to be alive and one could stop awhile and be inspired." An inspired work of a different sort appeared in 2000 on the south face of the library. Enterprising students from Brown's Technology House spent five months planning and then installing what at the time was the world's largest Tetris game or, if you will, art installation, which was called La Bastille. The results can be seen on YouTube and earned a well-deserved place in the *Guinness Book of Records*.

67   Thomas J. Watson Sr. Center for Information Technology
Cambridge Seven Associates, 1988

By turning to Cambridge Seven Associates to design a major building for a rapidly developing field of research, Brown commissioned one of the most respected twentieth-century American firms. Celebrated for the quality of cutting-edge contemporary design, the work of the firm, founded in 1962, is guided by a commitment to collaboration, that is, the belief that working together a varied group of designers with complementary skills will achieve a better result than a single individual, however talented. This has generated a legacy of outstanding work, a distinction recognized in 1993 when the Cambridge Seven Associates received a prestigious American Institute of Architects (AIA) Firm Award, the highest honor the Institute can bestow for a distinguished record of excellence. How does the firm's work measure up at Brown?

Unfortunately, the word *bunker* comes to mind. Having designed what is in essence a large five-story brick box (underwritten in part by a $10 million appropriation from the U.S. Department of Energy), the architects try to soften the impression of a fortress. The most conspicuous gesture is an incision into the southwest corner, which marks the building's entrance. The common criticism leveled at post–World War II buildings—that it is often difficult to find the front door—is addressed here in dramatic fashion. It is the equivalent of delivering a hammer blow to a desert rock. Instead of water flowing out from the resulting crack, a cascade of glass boxes tumbles down this corner of the Thomas J. Watson Sr. Center for Information Technology (CIT), pooling at ground level in a two-story glass lobby, whose panes are subdivided into perfect one-story squares. There is no mistaking this is the way in.

The side facing the campus is, relatively speaking, by far the most successful. The failure of the other three sides results from the architects' failure to engage the College Hill neighborhood. Why is the building so buttoned-up? In part, that may be the function of erecting a big building on a tight site. However,

Thomas J. Watson Sr. Center for Information Technology and America One

the CIT's function, or program, is the likely driver: The University's primary data center is located here. Security had to be assured. In this sense, the design does succeed in conveying the message that this building is impregnable—like a vault.

The sculpture outside the CIT, *America One* by Dušan Džamonja, was dedicated in 1990. Much of the sculptor's work is based on circles and spheres signifying unity.

Marston Hall

68   Marston Hall
William Welles Bosworth, 1926

The cool aristocratic Indiana limestone of Marston Hall seems to turn its back with studied indifference on the CIT's brick box of sharp elbows. It is not a calculated snub. When it was built, Marston fronted Manning Street, which was still open to traffic. Unlike the CIT, which is an isolated object, Marston had a real urban presence, both in its relation to the other buildings that then stood on the street and its engagement with the street itself. When this block of Manning was absorbed by Brown, the logic of how and why Marston was placed was lost.

In carving out a new presence in what had been a residential neighborhood, Brown gained a building of some distinction. By commissioning an architect who in his day was recognized as a leading light (a favorite of Brown alumnus John D. Rockefeller Jr. and the architect of MIT's new campus), President Faunce and the

Corporation entered a prestigious residential neighborhood with a somewhat modest yet sure step. Marston Hall was more of an ornament than an intrusion. In style and impact, it belongs in the same league as the John Hay and John Carter Brown Libraries. That is to say, Marston Hall is a child of the 1892 Columbian Exposition and the so-called classically inspired American Renaissance. In addition to offering the prestige of a style of building that could easily be mistaken for a small fine arts museum, Marston Hall reflects a vision of higher education different from the grind of the lecture hall and the solitary pursuit in library stacks. The large fireplace in the central hall gathers, in the words of President Faunce, "groups of teachers and students for those informal contacts which often bring larger educational results than the scheduled lecture of the curriculum."

Although built at the height of the University's stated commitment to Colonial Revival and brick, Marston Hall is neither. Why this deviation from the official style? Why choose an architect whose work reflected the classical aesthetic he learned during his student days at the École des Beaux-Arts? Perhaps Rockefeller put forward Bosworth's name. Perhaps the choice was dictated by the donor himself, Edgar L. Marston, a successful lawyer whose son, Hunter (Class of 1908), was manager of Brown's track team. Whatever the case, the design Bosworth produced for Brown was inspired by Charles McKim's design for New York's Pierpont Morgan Library, developed two decades earlier.

One final detail easily overlooked is the manner in which the Brown seal or coat of arms is displayed. To the left of the entrance is the original seal of the College adopted in 1764. It shows King George III facing Charlotte, his queen. On the right is a representation of the seal as adopted in 1834. In each instance, the accompanying prose is in Latin. Political systems rose and fell, texts changed, but well into the twentieth century, the passport to being considered educated continued to be written in the language of Virgil and Ovid.

69   Barus Hall (Henry Pearce Carriage House)
Angell & Swift, 1898

Directly across from Marston sits what looks like an architectural folly—that is, a highly decorated object set in a garden whose only purpose is to delight. However, the confection of caramel-colored granite with chocolate trim was the carriage house for a grand residence across the way at 182 George Street. The horses and liverymen have been replaced by teachers and students who investigate a different sort of energy, that is, child development. Little of the original interior remains save the main staircase that twists and turns like a snake. Stalls and tack rooms have morphed into offices and activity rooms.

Barus Hall is a late example of Richardsonian Romanesque, a style distinguished by rounded arches, window and door frames picked out in blocks of stone in contrasting colors, deeply recessed windows often grouped three or more and flanked by decorative columns, cavernous door openings, roughly cut masonry, and

Barus Hall

of course crowning the whole thing like a pennant or flag, a tower with a conical roof. Giddy in a somewhat lumpish way, Barus Hall is a welcome holiday from the uptight architecture around much of Manning Walk. This is a miniature fairy castle of caramel and chocolate with pistachio-colored copper trimmings and a cherry-red roof, all eminently suitable in scale and whimsy for the program's clients—children.

70 Geology-Chemistry Research Building
Davis, Brody & Associates and Russo & Sonder, 1982

In choosing a firm to design sorely needed classroom and laboratory space for both departments, Brown once again reached for an acknowledged leader of the profession. In 1975, Davis, Brody & Associates received a coveted Firm Award from the AIA. Both the Geology-Chemistry Research Building and MacMillan Hall immediately west on Thayer Street are part of a larger story whose subtext includes a renewed appreciation of the human scale, urbanity, and a growing commitment to sustainability.

The Geo-Chem Building is the first gust of something new on the superblock that swallowed up a piece of Manning Street. Delivering 128,000 square feet of laboratory space, the architecture of the four-and-a-half-story building makes a tentative step away from the severely rigid International Style. Gone is the flat roof; in its place is the slope of an exaggerated teal-green copper gable with what appears at first glance to be large chimneys on either end. Gone is the gray of poured concrete; red brick regains the field. The rigid symmetry of a building like the Science Library and, farther to the east, Barus and Holley, relaxes here as the architects clearly make an effort to acknowledge the neighboring residential scale.

Although the Geo-Chem Building anchors the south side of the Manning Walk, there is a real front door on George Street set behind a small but pleasant

Geology–Chemistry Research Building

tree-shaded courtyard. This renewed sensitivity to context is evidence that Brown was turning away from the inward focus of the architecture of the '60s and '70s. The large expanse of glass at the tower-like entry, which gives a view into the interior and a sculpture-like staircase leading to the upper floors, is additional evidence of a new direction. Glances into a science building are no longer discouraged by blank walls or yards of reflective glass.

The neighboring building, which followed sixteen years later, completed the southwest corner of the Manning Walk science precinct and carried the new spirit of contextualism even further. But before we move on, the sculpture in the lobby of the Geo-Chem Building is by Robert Scofield, who was the chair of the Arts Department at the nearby Moses Brown School. It was dedicated by the Chemistry Department to the memory of Professor William T. King.

71   W. Duncan MacMillan Hall
Koetter, Kim & Associates, 1998

The marriage of the 75,000-square-foot W. Duncan MacMillan Hall (named for W. Duncan MacMillan, Class of 1953) with the Geo-Chem Building created a shared teaching space for chemistry, geology, and environmental studies. If the older building sticks a tentative toe into contextualism and transparency, MacMillan Hall jumps in with both feet. For example, the facade uses 150,000 specially darkened bricks to approximate the neighboring older buildings; and the green slate gable roof, with its muscular brick structures that appear to be chimneys but in fact house large ventilation fans, likewise mirrors the roofs of buildings across Thayer Street. Like Geo-Chem, but even more dramatically, the mass of this large facility is carved into various pieces of varying sizes, even stepping down at the corner of Thayer and George Streets to become a two-and-a-half-story overscaled, ironic postmodern nod to the brick Federal townhouses common in the neighborhood. That said, no Federal house would have notched the gable end and inserted a skylight penthouse along the ridge of the roof. On the other hand, the architects do not intend to give the illusion of a Colonial streetscape, but to creatively allude to what in the neighborhood has disappeared.

Before continuing down Manning Walk, look across Thayer Street north to the earlier Metcalf research complex. There appears to be a deliberate effort by Koetter, Kim & Associates to echo in contemporary terms the earlier building designed by Charles Klauder. It is a nice way to bridge both sides of the street, from the three-story massing along the length of Thayer Street and the choice of brick, right up to the paired chimneys on the gable ends. On the side facing the Manning Walk, the entrance references a classic monumental portico complete with columns. (Compare the treatment of the entry to the Science Library, which is typical of the "honest," undecorated, and at times hard to spot front doors of the International Style.) A one-story glass corridor that gently angles into the green runs along the eastern face of the building, harvesting daylight into the first-floor corridor, a nice grace note where fluorescent lamps usually prevail. This is among MacMillan's many energy-conscious gestures to solve an issue that dogged the neighboring Geo-Chem Building almost from the day it opened its doors.

The construction of Geo-Chem occurred at a time of unusually and unanticipated high inflation, which in the twelve months between 1979 and 1980 jumped from 9 to nearly 15 percent. To try to get a handle on spiraling costs, the University accelerated planning and construction, both of which occurred almost simultaneously. One casualty was building performance. Geo-Chem quickly gained a reputation as one of the biggest energy hogs on campus. Besides the expense of operation (the cost of energy had dramatically shot up as well), Geo-Chem was

W. Duncan MacMillan Hall

increasingly seen as a black eye in the University's growing commitment to reduce its carbon footprint. The Talloires Declaration, an international voluntary agreement hammered out in 1990 to which Brown was a signatory, had as a goal not only more energy-efficient physical plants, but environmentally literate graduates who would be advocates for sustainable development.[4] This was a modern interpretation of Brown's historic mission to populate the community with alumni who would discharge "the Office of Life with usefulness and reputation." If for no other reason, these words made it imperative that Brown translate words into deeds. The Geo-Chem Building was a highly visible candidate for a positive step forward.

However, instead of simply retrofitting the building to make it more efficient, the University took a more creative approach. By marrying Geo-Chem and MacMillan, Brown was able to transfuse the new wine of MacMillan into the bottle of the older building. For example, MacMillan's chilling system was connected to the existing system in Geo-Chem for a saving in space and energy use. The science and art of architecture were thus yoked to transform a liability into a winning strategy that advanced Brown's commitment to environmental stewardship.[5] Having circumnavigated the first half of the precinct defined by Manning Walk, it is time to head east, cross Brook Street, and pause in front of a curious two-story building.

72 Prince Engineering Laboratory
Sherwood, Mills & Smith, 1962

In 1957, the "modern classical" architect Minoru Yamasaki (1912–1986) won a prestigious *Progressive Architecture* Award for a project that featured a folded-plate roof atop a long, low structure whose interior was organized around a skylit circulation spine defined by concrete load-bearing walls. It was a demonstration project for the client, the American Concrete Institute. As if to show that awards do have an impact as tastemakers, a rather similar facility appeared on the Brown campus in the space of a few years.

Although fashions come and go—Victorian architecture was once roundly despised—it is difficult to imagine a day when Prince Engineering Laboratory will inspire wonder, much less affection. An isolated stand-alone shed with no urban aspirations, it is representative of an era when architecture, like much of what was created in the postwar consumer society, was considered disposable. The baggage of the all-too-common institutional buildings constructed in the 1960s has already been unpacked at J. Walter Wilson on Brown Street. Though not as tall as J. Walter Wilson, Prince has a surprisingly larger footprint. A bird's-eye view reveals a facility that looks as if it could comfortably swallow three, perhaps even four Marston Halls. Since there are few visual clues as to what goes on inside—certainly not from the 163 tiny windows on the north and south sides—what was the 273-foot-long, 94-foot-wide, two-story shed with the curious roof designed to do?

The short answer is to house a heavy engineering laboratory; that is, machine shops, metalworking, welding, turbines, and a wind tunnel. Inside, running along

Charles H. Giancarlo Engineering Laboratories

the entire length of the south side of the building, is an elevated walkway. Students and faculty use it to reach stairways that provide access to each major area on the main floor. The passageway also serves as a gallery from which visitors can observe work in progress. All eminently practical, as is the folded construction of the roof. Those folds are not a decorative flourish; instead, they are meant to reduce vibration. The thickness of the building envelope muffles sound. Glass fills up the folds at the roofline to admit light without sacrificing wall space. Again, all of this is admirably functional.

Among the aspects of Prince that disappoint is the lack of a single gesture to appeal to the eye, if not the soul. If the building were merely sullen, that would be bad enough. But Prince Laboratory seems aggressively hostile, a stance underscored by the rough razor-sharp stucco that covers like whipped cake frosting the exterior of the windowless first story. Even ivy would not risk attacking these walls. If architecture is the marriage of science and art, then art perhaps gets the worst of the bargain here.

It has to be said that Prince Laboratory did not start out quite that bad. Sketches of the yet-unbuilt facility that appeared in the October 1960 issue of the *Brown Alumni Monthly* do not show the white heat of design genius at work, but we do see a more interesting building.[6] For example, the wall parallel to Manning Walk folded out in shallow Vs separated by tapered columns. Also these earlier drawings indicate many more small apertures. The roof is quite different too. In the architect's initial renderings, the folds do not run all the way across; rather, they seem to flair out on the north and south sides in the manner of gables. Prince Laboratory demonstrates once again that the distance between the architect's original concept and what is eventually built is seldom short and hardly straight.

73　Barus and Holley Building
Sherwood, Mills & Smith, 1965

The building is named in honor of faculty member and physicist Carl Barus, and alumnus and engineer Alexander Lyman Holley (Class of 1853), who was the first to be graduated from Brown with a degree in engineering. Part of the $4.2 million construction cost was paid by the Advanced Research Projects Agency of the Department of Defense and the National Science Foundation.

Initially, Brown wanted to build a long seven- or even fourteen-story slab of offices and laboratories that would have run parallel to Hope Street. Not surprisingly the neighbors did not embrace the idea of waking up each morning to be confronted by a high wall punctuated by repetitious rows of windows that looked for all the world like a giant's waffle iron. They did their best to derail what they saw as an out-of-scale intrusion into the residential neighborhood. President Keeney pushed back hard and played on Cold War angst when he made the following case to the mayor of Providence:

> It is well known to all but the cloistered [this would be the neighbors and the preservation community] that the United States is in a life-or-death struggle with the Communist bloc. This struggle will be won or lost depending on the quality and numbers of our scientists and engineers. Brown wishes to contribute to this effort more than we have already done.[7]

In other words, not to build this new research facility would provide aid and comfort to the enemy. Moving forward was also a financial matter. The U.S.

Department of Defense had pledged $3.5 million for the first four years after the building opened. After that, the University was promised an additional $1.25 million annually for the next ten years. The only stipulation the government made was that 40,000 square feet or the equivalent of two floors would be devoted to government research into the basic nature of materials. No building, no government money.

After a year of heated and costly protest, Brown compromised: the building was rotated 90 degrees. The largely windowless short end now fronted Hope Street, and the bulk of the seven stories of brick and precast

Barus and Holley Building

panels was designed considerably smaller than what was first proposed. Although Sherwood, Mills & Smith had developed a positive reputation as a firm that produced handsome contemporary homes, here at Brown they designed a facility that, however functional inside, has no street presence and is strikingly insensitive to context. In today's high-performance architecture, the envelope, or facade, is just as important a part of a building's mechanical systems as it had been in the nineteenth century. At Barus and Holley it is not. Thermal massing, natural ventilation, and evaporative cooling towers may make a building enclosure work as a passive mechanical system when power is not available. None of these are part of the design of Barus and Holley. If the power goes out, the building is inoperable. Barus and Holley is a creature of cheap fossil fuel.

With a long shed north (Prince Engineering Laboratory) and a behemoth of a boxy building to the south (which offered the further indignity of a high window-less brick wall), it was left to the genius of a twenty-first-century firm to tie both together and in so doing give this end of Manning Walk a presence it sorely lacked.

74   Charles H. Giancarlo Engineering Laboratories
Payette Associates, 2001

The overscaled, two-story glass square that centers the concave limestone entrance to the Charles H. Giancarlo Engineering Laboratories is a clever throw of the dice; it closes with some panache the eastern end of the vista down Manning Walk, which previously had simply petered out. It is a classic Beaux-Arts gesture, and a necessarily large one given all the competing styles and sizes of the buildings on either side. The gamble works for several reasons: The brightness of the limestone, which is something of a light at the end of the Manning Walk, is so clearly a destination that you cannot help but be drawn forward. This is something of a blessing, since neither Prince Laboratory nor Barus and Holley makes a compelling claim as architecture worth a second glance. Even the trees on either side of the walk join the conspiracy by forming a vibrant green alley that propels you to your destination. The broad expanse of glass at the entrance introduces a welcome note of transparency not evident in the two buildings it links. Linking or bridging, in fact, turns out to be a design strategy that defines how this relatively small infill structure with big ambitions works both inside and out.

Once you pass through the front door, the almost classic repose of the exterior gives way to a surprising energy. The long ramp that leads from the front door is a circulation spine, which mitigates the varying floor elevations of the adjacent buildings. It also skillfully negotiates a 10-foot difference in grade from the front to the back. The clerestory windows at the top of the two-story walls on either side of the ramp (which really functions more like a bridge) and internal skylights are energy-saving tactics that reduce dependence on artificial lighting, while creating a pleasant ambiance within and visual links to the outside. Rather than hiding the structural skeleton with drywall, the bones and muscles are appropriately celebrated in a workplace for engineers: you can see what keeps the roof up and how opposing structural tensions are resolved to keep everything in place. Color is used expressively as visual punctuation in corridors and offices distinguished by transparency and spaciousness.

The lower level, which in many buildings is an orphan space, is opened up by the high ceiling. The ramp floats above covered with walnut paneling and a floor whose dark polished concrete looks like slate. The architects have subdued with a single, well-placed aim the bulk of the Goliath that is the Barus and Holley Building and distracted us from the remorseless long wall of Prince Laboratory. Recognized by their peers for their creativity, the firm received a Rhode Island Design Merit Award in 2002.

Before moving on, let us consider one of those touches that give a place soul. Although it is risky to devote copy to a single plant that may not have as long a shelf life as this guide, the small, almost shrub-like apple tree at the corner of Barus and Holley merits a few additional words. It is a graft of a descendent of Newton's apple, an antique strain called Flower of Kent, planted by Brown physics professor Humphrey Maris. The sculpture at the southwest corner of the building titled *King* is by Mario J. Kujawski (Class of 1966) and was given to the University by the sculptor as a gift at his graduation in gratitude for his education at Brown.

75 Henry Pearce House
Angell & Swift, 1898

Although the Henry Pearce House is frequently (and falsely) attributed to the mid-nineteenth-century American architect Henry Hobson Richardson, the master might have taken delight in this invocation of his spirit. All the elements are there, from the characteristic bold sweep of the Romanesque arches above the windows and the entry porch to the chunky, hand-hewn appearance of the rusticated stone walls. If a home is a man's castle, surely Henry Pearce built for himself a formidable schloss. All that is lacking is a moat. The house is a brass band of gables, chimneys, balconies, dormers, and a turreted tower around which the entire composition appears to swirl. Yet the whole thing hangs together, in no small part because of the heroic scale. There is plenty of room for all the geometry of circles, ovals, squares, rectangles, and triangles to peacefully coexist. Nothing is pinched. Every detail of this residence built for a prominent Providence banker is clearly meant to impress, if not to intimidate.

However, once past the front door of the castle-like exterior, visitors step into a jewel box of color,

Henry Pearce House

Center for Computation and Visualization

hand-tooled leather wall coverings, and crystal chandeliers. What keeps the richness upon richness from being disagreeably ostentatious is both the clearly defined and easy flow of the interior spaces as well as a refined taste that with great assurance orchestrates many diverse elements. Perhaps the most memorable space is the copper-clad conservatory, where daylight is filtered through a stained-glass grape arbor. It takes little imagination to picture late afternoons given over to the taking of tea. Along with the Maddock Alumni Center, the interior of the Henry Pearce House is a showcase for the fine furnishings produced by the designers and workmen steeped in the contemporaneous Arts and Crafts movement.

Brown bought the property in 1952. Currently occupied by the University's Division of Applied Mathematics, the Henry Pearce House is clearly treasured by faculty, students, and staff.

76   Center for Computation and Visualization

Philip Johnson, 1961; restoration, Lerner | Ladds + Bartels Architects, 2002

Originally built to house the IBM 7070 computer, which at the time was the most advanced computing system on the East Coast, the building was reassigned in 1988 to the Division of Applied Mathematics after the main data center moved to the basement of the CIT on Waterman Street. For an architect who aggressively promoted the International Style on these shores, Johnson is trying his hand, perhaps for the first time, at a neoclassical style, right down to porch, colonnade, and the series of Xs above the columns that suggest an entablature.[8] A decade later, he pursued with far greater vigor this latest wrinkle in his ever-evolving architectural palette when he received the commission to design Brown's List Art Building (Walk One).

Although Johnson's design is obviously modern, the scale is not at war with the residential character of the neighborhood. It is remarkable how much Johnson is able to achieve using the most minimal gestures, with the single and crucial exception of the expanse of glass at the front facing George Street. Part of this success may be attributed to how the building occupies its site. It perches like a temple on top of a stepped pyramid. The architect well understood that the experience of a building has a lot to do with procession, or how one approaches it.

In the first years of the twenty-first century, the building underwent a thorough renovation, including the replacement of the curtain wall, the removal of a staggeringly insensitive rooftop mechanical system, and the restoration of the lobby, which today includes a conference area in the western third of the space. A low bank of oak leaf hydrangeas laps at the front, offering an appropriate counterpoint to the geometry of Johnson's design. The tapestry that hangs in the lobby is a gift from the architect; the design is by the Armenian American painter Arshile Gorky. Viewed at night, the building glows like the small jewel it is. For renewing the life of this unusual and important building, the restoration architects received a 2003 Honor Award from AIA Rhode Island.

77   341 Brook Street

1901

333 Brook Street

1900

Like the Henry Pearce House, the pair of three-story buildings around the corner on Brook Street is representative of the Victorian affection for period styles. The difference between the impact of the Pearce castle and these two houses is in part a matter of status and money. Henry Pearce could afford a high-end architecture

333 Brook Street

firm whose reputation was earned by the work it did for affluent clients. The owners of 341 Brook Street, William and Louise Chandler (and no doubt the nearby neighbors down the block at 333 Brook Street), were clearly of more modest means. Also, even though only a few years had passed since Pearce built his house, residential design was moving in a new direction toward Colonial Revival, although in these two houses, it does not quite get there.

Instead, both clients received a hybrid composition that straddles the flamboyance of Queen Anne and the paradoxically more modern tradition-leaning Colonial Revival style. Queen Anne features common to both are porches and balconies that open the interior of the house to the outside; the contrast of materials on the exterior (compare the shingled gable end with the brick—341— and clapboard—333—of the first two stories); and the details that seem to be applied in the manner of ornaments according to whatever struck the architect's fancy—a third-story Palladian window at 341 and the street-facing gable end of 333 that looks like an overblown triangular piece from a child's collection of building blocks. The use of different building materials—shingles, brick, and clapboard— and the decorative flourishes most evident on the porches are a gift of the Industrial Revolution's cornucopia of inexpensive manufactured pieces. The Colonial Revival touches are evident in the relative restraint and symmetry of both houses, especially 341 with its paired dormers and chimneys and the central gambrel dormer, which echoes the gambrel gables at either side of the roof.

Neither grand nor imposing, both houses are evidence of the aesthetic pleasure derived from something put together competently and with care. These are the kind of background buildings with porch gliders and swings that give a neighborhood soul. Currently they house the Department of East Asian Studies.

78 Malcolm S. Forbes Center for Modern Culture and Media Studies
1930

Unlike late nineteenth-century architects and builders, who freely mixed, matched, and reinterpreted period styles, the next generation who designed the Colonial

and Federal Revival residences and public buildings in the decades leading up to World War II were careful historians. Critics and clients alike expected a scholarly knowledge that appreciated the subtle difference between a Palladian and a more delicate Adamesque detail. This preoccupation with the nation's early design legacy carried with it the seeds of America's historic preservation movement, a development that came to full flower in the restoration of Colonial Williamsburg, a project funded by Brown alumnus John D. Rockefeller Jr.

This did not mean architects were prisoners of history. Their role was to suggest a particular period, not to be the slave of it, and to use the

Malcolm S. Forbes Center

latest construction techniques and materials. The freedom to improvise was especially true of the interiors. After all, the demands of a twentieth-century client (think indoor plumbing) were different from those of his or her great-great-grandparents. In response to the twentieth-century lifestyle of its owner, the sequence of rooms in a building like this one is more spacious and free-flowing. In addition, architects now had to accommodate the demands of the automobile. Rather than fronting north on George Street, the main entrance at the Forbes Center is on the east side away from the sidewalk used by pedestrians. This allowed easier access for guests and visitors arriving by car, which could then be conveniently parked out back. Also, by rotating the long end of the house away from Brown Street, the architect is able to fit more building on a relatively narrow lot.

In 1991, a gift by Timothy C. Forbes (Class of 1976) created the Malcolm S. Forbes Center for Modern Culture and Media Studies now headquartered in this George Street house.

79 Edward W. Kassar House (formerly Nancy K. Bishop House)
1894

Gould Annex
1982

Department of Mathematics Complex
William Kite Architects, 1990

Built for Nancy K. Bishop, who was related by marriage to the Civil War General Ambrose Burnside (noted for the exuberance of his unusual facial hair), the three-story gambrel-roofed building steps back from the flamboyance of the earlier Queen Anne style. The symmetrical array of individual elements on either side of the two-story pedimented entry is evidence of a new spirit that was shaping the houses on College Hill. Yet although the original house seems to be anticipating the national obsession for Colonial American houses and furnishings, the execution of the detailing and scale often seem wrong, especially the overwrought entry with its colossal Ionic columns and the hint of a Richardsonian arch.

It was admirable of Brown to keep and take care of what is a significant neighborhood landmark. As large as the house is, it nevertheless had its limits. The need for additional space was first addressed by what was initially called the Gould Laboratory but is now simply the Gould Annex, which housed a computer science laboratory and an auditorium. Given the rapid evolution of computer science, the program required larger quarters and moved out, but the auditorium stayed and has been reworked into an attractive space. The challenge of weaving together the disparate parts of the complex while creating additional square footage for the Department of Mathematics was given to the same firm that a decade later shepherded the award-winning restoration, renovation, and repurposing of Pembroke's

Sayles Gymnasium into the Smith-Buonanno Hall (Walk Four). On the Thayer Street side, the architects created a new handicap-accessible main entrance and reorganized the first floor to improve internal circulation.

Their main intervention was a new three-story building with a separate recessed entrance on George Street that steps back from the historic house but is connected by a glass bridge at the rear of both buildings. Thus old and new are joined, yet remain visually distinct and engage in a playful dialogue. Compare, for example, the shed dormers of the one with the gable dormers of the other. The front facade of the George Street building is residential in scale and seems to recall elements of the Queen Anne style common in the neighborhood yet updated to a contemporary idiom. There is a similar contrast of materials: the decorative use of molded brick; the suggestion on the eastern side of glass-enclosed conservatories; and the exaggerated hip roof and projecting eave also on the east side. Most of the action happens in the middle of the front or north face and on the east side. The west facade is appropriately fairly neutral so as not to compete with or upstage its older neighbor. It is a skillful piece of work that earned the architects an AIA Rhode Island Honor Award (1994).

To move to the next and final stop of this Walk, do not take Thayer Street. Instead, go to the rear of Kassar and step onto the path that runs between George and Benevolent Streets. It leads to yet another of Brown's restfully intimate vest-pocket oases, Benevolent Community Park. If it is a sunny day, sit on a bench, unplug your headset, watch the play of sunlight on leaves, and enjoy the moment before moving across Benevolent Street to the Watson Institute.

80 Thomas J. Watson Jr. Institute for International Studies and Starr Plaza
Rafael Viñoly, 2002; landscape design, Signe Nielsen

In choosing Rafael Viñoly for this three-story, 56,000-square-foot building, Brown was for the first time commissioning design talent from foreign shores (a Uruguayan architect educated in Argentina). This was an inspired choice for an international program whose sleek but not dogmatic late modernist projects gained an international reputation for excellence. Did Brown receive the full magnitude of this star's power? The answer may depend on what part of the building you look at—front, back, or inside.

The front presents the most challenging countenance. It pays homage to the industrial tropes of the International Style: the straight lines, the absence of organic forms (no curved lines here), the steel frame and cantilever construction, the use of contemporary manufactured materials, such as steel and glass. What immediately capture the eye are the odd windows that jut out from the facade. Is this a reinterpretation of the bay windows common to nineteenth-century northern residential architecture? Perhaps the architect is reminding us that windows do more than simply facilitate the movement of light and air, that they are also decorative.

Thomas J. Watson Jr. Institute for International Studies

That said, these windows are in fact functional. The bottom pane or base of the windows is operable. Once open, the window is a small scoop, pulling fresh air inside. Sudden windswept downpours pose no threat if a window is left open, because the glass above keeps the rain from blowing in.

Louder criticism, or at least unhappiness, has been voiced over the architect's choice of brick, which has been attributed to the University's possible request that the Watson Institute blend in with the brick of the nearby Wriston and Gregorian Quads. However, at the time Viñoly was also working on Philadelphia's Kimmel Center (2001), which, like the Watson Institute, is an exercise in brick, steel,

and glass. Perhaps Viñoly chose brick simply because he was exploring ways of working with the material.

Existing records indicate the design went through a number of fairly drastic changes, which early into the process included a large winter garden in the center. What remained a constant throughout the various redesigns was a tree. The entrance stepped back to acknowledge a towering, beloved elm nicknamed "Elmo." Unfortunately, the year after the Watson Institute opened, Elmo sickened and died. Absent the graceful green arches of Elmo's branches at the front entrance, which was stepped back to embrace the large tree, this side of the building now seems a bit harsh, even cold. (Interestingly, this is also a criticism leveled at the Kimmel Center.) Maples have since been planted on Elmo's grave. As these grow, they should create the dialogue the architect intended between the building's severe linear geometry and nature's ever-changing forms. By way of recompense for the departed Elmo, when students return in the fall, the maples offer a vivid scarlet splash, a hue not part of an elm's palette.

Inside, the winter garden proposed in preliminary designs survives in smaller form as an atrium that during the day is flooded with light. Glass sky bridges obliquely cross the space to give quick access to either side of the second and third levels. Angling the sky bridges keeps them from looking like glass stumps and injects a welcome bit of energy into the austere detailing (black slate floors, stainless-steel railings, and birch trim), which to some eyes may seem a bit too upscale and corporate. The ramp from the first to the second floor is the most curious element. Too steep as initially designed to pass code, the incline of the ramp had to be broken into steps. This was unfortunate: unless one approaches the ramp running, an awkward shuffle is required to move up or down at a normal pace.[9]

It is at the rear elevation and the sides that the architect of the theaters for New York's Jazz at Lincoln Center (2004) makes the transition from cold to cool. The glass boxes or cubes are magical exclamation points that leap out from all that brick, not unlike water rushing over boulders or crystalline stalagmites from a rocky floor. A writer has aptly likened the two-story box that houses a library reading room to a medieval turret, from which the occupants have a privileged view of the neighborhood. When the sun goes down, the boxes become literal and figurative representations of the enlightenment the University seeks to send out into the world.

Starr Plaza, the green bamboo-fringed yard behind Watson, is a wonderful gift. It is as much a learning space as the classrooms, media center, and research facilities inside, although unlike these, the plaza is fitted out for the staging of a performance or a party. The tall stalks of the bamboo respond to and join the play of the winds, a gentle yet, in its way, a strong counterpoint to the architecture's hard edges. In histories that explore the early days of Brown, landscaping is typically a footnote. However, by the twenty-first century, the landscape architect has come to be appreciated both as a valued and credited partner in place making. Indeed, it is impossible to take the full measure of the architecture of Brown without close attention to the spaces in between.

1 R. M. Kliment and Frances Halsband, *Campus Heritage at Brown University: Preservation Priorities* (Providence: 2006), 102.

2 Brown University, Press Release Archives, John Hay Library, 224a, 1961.

3 Jacob Reidel, "Unbuilt Brown" (senior thesis, Brown University, 2002), 65. Additional information about the evolution of the Sciences Library design (including an explanation for the gravel pit on the north, Waterman Street side), along with illustrations, can be found in his discussion of the project, "The Tower in the Pool," 64–67.

4 The Talloires Declaration composed at an international conference in Talloires, France, is a ten-point action plan for incorporating sustainability and environmental literacy in teaching, research, operations, and outreach.

5 For more information about the University's progress toward shaping a more energy-efficient campus, see: www.brown.edu/Departments/Brown_Is_Green.

6 "The Science Center: A Bold Concept," *Brown Alumni Monthly*, October 1960, 7.

7 Brown University, Press Release Archives, John Hay Library, 224a, 1961.

8 Reidel, "Unbuilt Brown," 61. See Reidel's discussion of the evolution of Johnson's design, which shows a scaling back of the architect's original proposal.

9 Reidel, "Unbuilt Brown," 91.

The South Residential Campus

Wayland Arch, Wriston Quad

Dormitories are "unnatural" and a waste of money.
—President Francis Wayland [1]

If we are to have a genuine liberal college, we must have a care for the living conditions of our students. Their education is received not only in the classroom and the library but from all the contacts with their fellows and from their daily surroundings. We must regard the dormitories, therefore, as an important part of our educational project.
—President Henry Merritt Wriston [2]

Housed on the upper floors of University Hall, Brown's first students were kept somewhat removed from the world, the better, it was thought, to focus their minds on their studies. In a more practical vein, faculty and proctors could keep an eye on their charges and check youthful spirits when they got out of hand. However, there was a larger, more liberal concept that drove Brown's commitment to be a residential college. It informed the very heart of what succeeding administrations believed to be their mission. More than learning a craft or trade, an education at Brown and Pembroke would be about shaping the whole person. This meant integrating study with life, something that could only be accomplished, most administrators and faculty agreed, by living together in a community.

Although always a challenge, Brown was able to house its students while the University's rate of growth was relatively slow. However, the stage was set for a crisis in the decade immediately after World War II. During the Depression, dormitory construction had ground to a halt. Resources were focused on maintaining the existing facilities. As the need for additional housing arose, it was met by leasing and buying a variety of buildings on College Hill, while the fraternities provided additional beds and living spaces. After the war, this piecemeal approach was no longer an option. A mounting flood of students streamed through the Van Wickle Gates thanks to the G.I. Bill of Rights. By the late '50s, a second, even larger wave was in the making—the baby boom. If Brown were to continue to be a residential institution committed to what in effect was the idea of family, it needed to build beyond the relatively leisurely pace that had characterized the prewar years. Walk Four explored the University's response on the Pembroke campus. This Walk follows the impact of Brown's response in providing new housing for underclassmen and graduate students.

81   Wriston Quad
Thomas Mott Shaw of Perry, Shaw, Hepburn, Kehor & Dean, 1952; landscape design, Mary Elizabeth Sharpe

In his letter to alumni, quoted at the opening of this Walk, Brown's eleventh president was reaffirming Brown's historic commitment to be a residential college. More than a response to a pressing need to house returning veterans and the oncoming baby boom, Wriston saw a vast expansion of the University's residential facilities as a strategy to move Brown beyond a well-regarded regional institution to one that could hold its place on an international stage. To transform vision to reality, Wriston and Brown required three things: money, land, and a plan.

When in the first years of the twentieth century President Faunce decreed Brown's architectural brand would henceforth be Georgian or Colonial Revival, he and the Corporation had chosen what at the time was perceived as the quintessentially American architectural style. Think of it as a nostalgic reference to an idealized past when America forged an identity distinct from that of Europe. A rediscovery and celebration of that past took fire with the 1876 Centennial Exposition in Philadelphia. In the years that followed, America's ascent to the world stage and the nation's success in World War I validated the popular taste for "made in the U.S.A." In the midst of the Depression and the rise of fascism, Americans found comfort in the simple grandeur and democratic sentiment expressed in our national style, whether they were eating at Howard Johnson's or serving on a local board responsible for building a new high school.

The restoration and reconstruction of Colonial Williamsburg in the depths of the Depression reflected and reinforced this drive to reconnect with an idealized past. Reference to Colonial Williamsburg is particularly pertinent to the design of the residential complex the University was about to build: the principal donor, Brown alumnus John D. Rockefeller Jr. (Class of 1897), had underwritten Williamsburg's restoration; and it was the Boston firm of Perry, Shaw & Hepburn that carried it out, the same firm with which Wriston and the Brown Corporation already had a long and productive relationship. The elements were in place for a clone of Colonial Williamsburg on College Hill.

Even with Rockefeller's support, Wriston's vision of a Colonial Revival residential quad did not receive a free pass. First, there were the neighbors who did not share Wriston's enthusiasm for a major shredding of the Hill's historic residential fabric. At several points in its history, Providence was per capita one of the wealthiest cities in America. The evidence of this wealth was its architecture, especially the treasures on College Hill. Wriston's bulldozer would raze fifty-one buildings, including houses, shops, and the historic Thayer Street School. The irony of honoring the nation's architectural legacy by replacing the real thing with replicas was not lost on those who opposed the scheme. Nor did Wriston endear himself to the neighbors (much less the South) when he referred to the project as the "greatest slum clearance since Sherman burned Atlanta."

Wriston Quad in winter

Wriston felt heat from another quarter and was equally prickly in his response. In a report to the Corporation in 1946, he writes:

> We might just as well face the fact that there is more theology in modern architecture than in modern religion. We are presented with dogmas about what is modern and what is not modern which have no functional substance whatever. There are conventions as rigid and designs as imitative in the so-called modern as in the so-called traditional styles....The statement that we live in the twentieth century and therefore should not use an eighteenth century style is meaningless.[3]

Clearly, Wriston was reacting to the stirrings of Modernism, a new international style, much of it, he noted with barely hidden scorn, "transplanted from Germany." German transplant Walter Gropius (1883–1969) and his disciples might have been radically reshaping the Harvard campus 55 miles up the road in Cambridge and garnering praise in the architectural and popular press, but Wriston would have none of it. For the moment, neither would Brown. Since at the time there was no preservation legislation on the books that might have forced costly litigation, the building of the residential village that would become Wriston Quad went forward and it would be wrought in brick.

When the first students arrived in 1952 at Wayland Arch, the front door of the new complex, they found nine dormitories, or "houses," with hipped dormers arranged around two closed greens, Patriots Court and Hughes Court. The latter provide, respectively, strong east–west, north–south axes, which terminate in classic Beaux-Arts fashion at a large refectory that anchors the entire composition.

Wriston Quad and the statue of Caesar Augustus

Regardless of where Brown men lived on campus, and whether or not they belonged to fraternities, their meal plan took them into the Sharpe Refectory or "the Ratty," a large, high-ceilinged square capable of filling over 1,500 stomachs at a single sitting. As administrators had discovered over the years, neither chapel nor classroom nor even athletic field was so effective an agent of community as food.

The dormitories are named for two Brown presidents and seven alumni. The refectory, which honors the University's great patroness, Mary Elizabeth Sharpe, opened with separate dining alcoves for the members of fraternities who from this time forward were required to be housed in University buildings. This was not a move to diminish the prestige and influence of fraternities. Quite the contrary. President Wriston believed fraternities bred student leaders and loyal alumni. But two issues had to be addressed: greater University (i.e., adult) supervision was called for and the tendency to foster a sense of exclusivity had to be curbed. To nurture the positive potential of the fraternities, Wriston used architecture as tool of social engineering: By living under one roof, fraternity and nonfraternity men would forge a stronger, more unified community. The University would be in a stronger position to monitor student exuberance. And the architecture would also ensure a more egalitarian experience, even if there were separate entrances and fire doors in the halls that kept the members of the fraternities and the independents separated from one another: whether occupied by a fraternity brother or an independent, one room was pretty much like the next.

Ersatz Colonial Revival though the architecture may be and too perfect by half, the new quad works rather well as an urban plan. There is a pleasing domestic scale about the whole ensemble, which not coincidently echoes the architecture of Brown's first residential facilities, University Hall and Hope College, right down to the alignment of the brick called "University Hall bond." No one building stands alone, not even the Ratty. Rather, all the pieces relate to one another. The curving paths that follow the gentle slope of the land from Brown Street to Thayer Street, the varied landscaping carefully selected by Sharpe to provide interest in every sea-son, the thoughtful placement and the scale of the buildings, the ample flagstone terraces that serve as outdoor rooms—all show the power of a good plan to pull the various pieces into a coherent whole. Moated and gated though it may be, Wriston Quad provided the stage upon which a vibrant student community has emerged.

Four short footnotes before heading east to the Graduate Center. The bronze statue of Caesar Augustus that now stands on the east end of Hughes Court lost his arm during the great hurricane of 1938. Given in 1906 by Moses Brown Ives

Goddard, Caesar was relocated in 1952 from his previous site in front of Rhode Island Hall. The three gates in the fence surrounding the quad (the Morgan Witter Rogers [Class of 1914], the Cincinnati, and the Edward Leo Barry Gates) are gifts honoring, respectively, an alumnus, a city, and a popular swimming coach. Diman House was the first truly coed dorm (1968). Finally, is the irony intentional that Wayland Arch, the entrance to Brown's largest residential dorm complex, is named after Brown's fourth president, who described such projects as a waste of money? To honor the president who guided the University through the Depression and World War II, and with growing reputation into the postwar years, the Corporation named the new quad after Wriston upon his resignation in 1955. The dedicatory plaque in Wayland Arch reads: *Si monumentum requiris circumspice*, an appropriate borrowing from the inscription on the wall above his tomb in St. Paul's Cathedral that commemorates the great English architect Sir Christopher Wren, "If you seek his monument, look about you."

82   The Graduate Center
Jean Paul Carlhian of Shepley, Bulfinch, Richardson & Abbott, 1968

Although Brown has awarded advanced degrees since 1886, graduate students were for many years stepchildren in an academic family that emphasized under-graduate education. Graduate students found lodging were they could. Excellent in many ways, the Graduate School conspicuously lacked a home that would promote community. This need was decisively addressed by Brown's twelfth president, Barnaby Keeney (1955–66), who before he became president had been dean of the Graduate School. Convinced that graduate education would increasingly play a role in the United States maintaining its economic and military competitiveness, Keeney was an effective advocate of the Graduate School. During his tenure as dean and then president, the number of graduate students nearly tripled. It was largely through his efforts that they at last gained a home of their own.

   With a substantial loan from the Federal Department of Housing and Urban Renewal, the University broke ground in 1966 on what had been a parking lot—not merely broke, but excavated: the first two stories are below street level. As a result, the six-story dormitories appear to be more in scale with the surrounding residential neighborhood. The relative modesty of what is in fact a large complex is further enhanced by the brick cladding (which is nicely textured), heavy planting, the breaking into smaller pieces of what could have been an oppressive block of masonry, and deep setbacks from Charlesfield, Thayer, and Power Streets. After many stormy encounters with the residents of College Hill during the previous ten years, the Graduate Center attempts to be a deferential neighbor.

   Entered at the third-floor level via elevated walkways, the roughly cruciform residential towers are arranged around a four-story building originally designed to be a commons. Each of the four residential towers consists of four slender inter-locking wings that radiate from a central core with four units of graduate students

The Graduate Center

per floor. The architect's intent was to give the graduate scholars a welcome privacy for their research. The four-story commons, along with outdoor terraces, would enable those group encounters that make a community. Some have even suggested the relationship of the surrounding towers to the central commons is like that of chairs arranged around a community table.

But the commitment to privacy for the residents is the rub: All these thoughtful gestures notwithstanding, including the dynamic swirl of the sculptural spiral staircase that leads to the base of the central building or Tower E, cannot erase a pervasive fortress-like isolation. Unlike Wriston Quad or even the neighboring Gregorian Quad, it is not a neighborhood you casually walk through unless you belong there. The wall that surrounds the Graduate Center only reinforces the sense of this being a moated castle. Perhaps that was the intent. The interior has its own issues, which also begin with admirable intentions. Rather than housing all the residents in one block with long, double-loaded corridors, the architect pursues the model of separate entries around the central stairwell. Intimate, yes; however, the interiors come off feeling cramped; the rooms, monastic cells.

From the inventive way of handling the mass to the textures and color of the brick, the Graduate Center is a collection of good intentions that do not quite come together. But this is not necessarily the last word. Elsewhere on campus we have seen how an inspired design team can transform even the most stubborn spaces. Both the Graduate Complex and the Pembroke dorms that opened in the 1960s are candidates for similarly skillful interventions that will, among other desirable improvements, admit more daylight and provide breathing room for interaction.

83   Vartan Gregorian Quad
Davis, Brody & Associates, 1991

The modernist flat roofs of the Graduate Center yield to the pitched, gable-end roofs of what seems to be a reprise of the Colonial Revival aesthetic that shaped Wriston Quad. Among the largest construction projects built on campus during the tenure of Vartan Gregorian, and named after Brown's beloved sixteenth president, the design roots of this residential complex in fact tap into something quite different, late twentieth-century postmodernism with its emphasis on image over substance and the eclectic borrowing of historical details.

Following the example of the Graduate Center, the architects of Gregorian Quad break what is a large, if not overbearing, residential complex into smaller pieces. They designed two L-shaped buildings laid in opposition to one another around a central courtyard with a four-story hyphen, or hinge, at the jog of the easternmost L. This is the quad's front door. Unlike the Graduate Center across the street, Gregorian is easily entered, which is encouraged by the late-night opportunities for a quick bite at Josiah's snack bar. Eschewing modernist flatness, the roofs nervously erupt into a series of gable-ended dormers beneath which the facade makes timid steps out from the property line. Windows do not march like Prussian soldiers around the walls in rigid, unvaried lines, but are tightly choreographed to give an illusion of variety. Facades are broken up by occasional groupings of shallow metal bays. Elevations are also varied, from four to six stories.

Clearly an effort has been made to try to park the architectural equivalent of a battleship in a yacht basin. The effort only serves to draw attention to the fact the quad is not residential but institutional, and not inspired in the bargain. Gregorian Quad persuasively demonstrates that the conventions of Neo-Colonial or Georgian architecture can be stretched just so far. In a complex whose size is made possible by modern innovations in structural steel and curtain wall construction, the result is ungainly. What may be intended as playful, ironic allusions to the architecture of University Hall and Hope College subvert both contemporary and Colonial. The architects split the difference between the familiarity of tradition and the hard edges of formal modernism on a clearly tight budget, finding little favor, no doubt, with either camp.

Vartan Gregorian Quad

The Walk continues west to the corner of Charlesfield and Brown Streets. However, before moving on, pause for a moment. The intersection where Gregorian, the Graduate College, Wriston, and Viñoly's Watson Institute meet is a unique opportunity to test Mies van der Rohe's proposition that "God is in the details." The detail being tested here is the brick. The cladding of Wriston is the competent execution of architects striving for historical accuracy with a conscious echoing of the brickwork at University Hall. That of the Graduate College is a creative exploration of colors and varied textures; it rewards the close observer with small but well-earned pleasures. The Watson Institute offers yet another variation on the language of brick: its smooth precision communicates the larger message of an architect who values order and clarity. The language of Gregorian unfortunately takes a road too often traveled; it speaks of value engineering where the overriding concern is to hold down costs.

84   Andrews House (formerly James Coats House)
Ogden Codman, 1901

At the beginning of this guide, we caught a whiff of the Ogden Codman restrained aesthetic in the two ground-floor rooms of the Maddock Alumni Center—Brian and Lanpher. At the former residence of the industrialist James Coats, we get Codman in full bore in the only building he designed in Providence.

Both inside and out, the three-story Georgian Revival house is Exhibit A of the assured upper-crust aesthetic advanced by Codman and his friend, the American novelist Edith Wharton in what has been called one of the most influential books about decoration and architecture ever published in the United States. *The Decoration of Houses* (1897) was a reaction to the wave of brownstone houses built on the East Coast from 1865 to 1895, a style both authors deplored as dark and somber. (The period has since earned the disparaging moniker "the Brown Decades.") Codman and Wharton were even more critical of the prevailing interior décor—dark stained woodwork, heavy curtains and carpets, overstuffed furniture, lace doilies, and a wilderness of bric-a-brac.

Just as influential English art critic and writer John Ruskin had railed against the artificial symmetry of late eighteenth- and early nineteenth-century architecture (Manning Hall would be an example) in favor of the "organic" architecture one sees in the University's Nicholson House and Lyman Hall (Walks One and Three), Codman and Wharton took up arms against what they saw as vulgar conspicuous consumption as well as a lack in contemporary homes of rational and clear floor plans. "Codman shared my dislike of these sumptuary excesses, and thought as I did that interior decoration should be simple and architectural," Wharton once wrote.[4] Upper-crust and a passionate Francophile, Codman believed the interior and exterior of a house should convey a single design concept, one that ideally would be carried out by the same architect: A house had to be more than a useful container of stuff. It had to exhibit good taste. And the educated architect rather than the

Andrews House

client who paid for the architect's services would be the one to determine or at least recommend what constituted good taste.

Tasteful it surely is, and surely of a size to house a large family, frequent long-term guests, and a retinue of staff to clean, cook, and coddle the Coats family that built it. Codman designed a house that on the outside is defined by three parts: a stately front on Brown Street with a gable pedimented entry porch; an indented hyphen midway with a bump-out two-story brick bay facing south to Charlesfield Street; and the rear of the house, which duplicates in details and massing the front. The overall composition suggests an accordion. Clearly the front is formal; the middle, social; and the rear devoted to service functions and probably children. Thus, every activity of the house is carefully orchestrated.

Brown bought the house in 1922 and used it as a Faculty Club. In 1939, the club relocated one block west to the corner of Magee and Benevolent Streets. The University then repurposed the mansion's twenty-nine rooms into a fifty-bed infirmary named after President Elisha B. Andrews (Brown's eighth president). In its present antiseptic incarnation, not much besides the elaborate moldings, grand stairway, and ample spaces of the interior remains to convey the elegant residence Codman designed for his wealthy client.

85   Annmary Brown Memorial
Norman M. Isham, 1907

The other surviving structure on the superblock cleared for Wriston Quad is part art gallery, part crypt, and a bit odd. The one-story granite structure with a low hip roof and impressive bronze doors designed by Austin Hayes (depicting allegorical

Annmary Brown Memorial

Annmary Brown Memorial, interior

Graves of Rush Hawkins and Annmary Brown Hawkins, Annmary Brown Memorial

representations of Art and Learning) was commissioned by General Rush Christopher Hawkins for his wife. It served as the final resting place for the granddaughter of Nicholas Brown. Seventeen years later, Hawkins took up residence next to his wife. The general's choice of architect for this unusual project was Norman Isham (1864–1943), who was educated at Brown (Class of 1886). In the course of his career, Isham developed a reputation as one of America's first architectural historians and preservationists. Isham's expertise in historic structures was in fact consulted when University Hall was restored shortly before World War II. Among the relatively few buildings attributed to him, most of which are private homes, the Annmary Brown Memorial is unique—in many ways.

The windowless structure is divided into two art rooms, a personal treasure room, an office, a rare book room, and, at the east end, a gated tomb in which the general and his wife are buried. Every year on March 9, the birthday of Annmary Brown, fresh flowers are placed on her grave, a practice her husband started during his lifetime. That the bodies of Hawkins and his wife were his museum's final accessions echoes John Fowles's novel *The Collector* (1963).

First opened to scholars in 1907, the Annmary Brown Memorial was deeded to Brown in 1948. Today, the library is open free to the public from 1 PM to 5 PM, Monday through Friday, during the academic year. Featured are rotating exhibitions from Hawkins's collection of European and American paintings spanning the seventeenth through the twentieth centuries. Other collections formerly housed in the Memorial, including 521 books published before 1501, are now located in the John Hay Library. The love letters between husband and wife written while Hawkins fought in the Civil War (he led his own private regiment) are also kept in the Hay; however, they are not accessible to scholars or anyone else. Eccentric to and beyond the end, Hawkins stipulated they be kept under lock and key, never to be read.

86   Keeney Quad
Thomas Mott Shaw, 1957; landscape design, Mary Elizabeth Sharpe; restoration and renovation, DiMella Shaffer, 2013

Across the street, Colonial Revival is again in the saddle. Like the Quads of Wriston and Gregorian, the period facades are no more than a skim-coat on a series of steel and concrete block boxes. Behind the brick and pediments, the rooms and halls are contemporary fireproof construction, all in service to durability, utility, and economy. Here and at Wriston Quad, the choice of a Colonial Revival design vocabulary was as much about creating a domestic composition in a residential neighborhood as it was about promoting the University's eighteenth-century brand. However, housing some six hundred students in low-rise buildings on a pinched site was a challenge. Not having the acreage for a parklike academic village like Wriston Quad, Thomas Mott Shaw had to make every square foot work. He does this by pushing the ensemble of six dormitories as far out to the property line as he dares, except on the side facing Benevolent Street, which steps back behind a shallow landscaped lawn.

What follows is a checklist of some of the more conspicuous gestures that help break up a massive assemblage of bricks. Elevations range from two to five stories. All around the perimeter, multistoried gable-ended pavilions step out tentatively from the plane of the rectangular complex. The gables themselves are a lighter brick and have small oxeye windows at the center. Like the gables, tall brick chimneys break the line of the roof to give a vertical thrust. Whereas the foundations of the lower buildings are brick, those taller than three stories are faced with stone to suggest the strength needed to accommodate the greater weight of the larger buildings. The downward slope of the site from Brown to Benevolent Streets is an opportunity for the architect to increase the height of the buildings at the west end.

Ultimately the challenge of squeezing Brown's largest building into a tight lot proved too much for the architect. Whereas at Wriston there was room to orchestrate the buildings into a sequence of compression and relaxation not unlike that of a village, at Keeney Quad the composition is resolutely institutional and inert. There is nothing like Wayland Arch, which provides a focal-point entry to Wriston Quad. Instead, the way into Keeney Quad is through one of two tunnellike arches leading to courtyards that are in effect cul-de-sacs; short of escaping through an emergency fire exit, there was no way out as originally designed except to retrace one's steps. The moat and iron fence that run along Brown Street are hostile and anti-urban

Everett House, Keeney Quad

in the extreme. Recognizing the shortcomings and challenges of the design, and responding to the continuing challenge of building community for what is now a coed campus, in 2012 the University's Corporation approved an overhaul of Keeney Quad and student housing in general. What in the original configuration had seemed an advantage—that one could circumnavigate the interior of the entire complex in the manner of a token on a Monopoly board—felt impersonal to the residents. The plan being advanced by the University envisions a radically reconfigured collection of three, not six, distinct buildings to house incoming freshmen. Entrances will be gained through the courtyards, which will also be given a face-lift to bring life to these relatively underused spaces. Existing lounges have been expanded, and three new ones added on the top floors to serve as informal study and social spaces. When complete, the quad will seem less a barracks and more like a collection of residential colleges.

Unveiled during the 1982 Commencement ceremonies when the quad was named for President Keeney, the words of the commemorative plaque seem uniquely prescient: *Scientia est infinita*. The quotation taken from the *Summa Theologiae* of St. Thomas Aquinas translates, "knowledge is infinite"; that is to say, to cease learning is a sign of ignorance. Keeney Quad is learning from its mistakes.

The clearing of yet another historic neighborhood reignited a conflict still simmering after the building of Wriston Quad. This time the residents of College Hill adopted a strategy that would have long-term implications for the relationship between Brown and the neighborhood. Helped by local historian and preservationist Antoinette Downing and John Nicholas Brown Jr., they created the Providence Preservation Society. Under a grant from the Federal Department of Housing and Urban Renewal, and with the cooperation of the city, the Society published in 1959 a landmark document, *College Hill: A Demonstration Study of Historic Area Renewal*. The architect William Warner (1929–2012) was one of the principal authors of the study and in succeeding years a decisive force in the reimagining and revitalization of downtown Providence. Far from gathering dust, the study led to action—the designation of College Hill as a historic district and the creation of the city's Historic District Commission. Henceforth, before Brown made any changes that affected buildings within the district, the University would have to negotiate with the Commission. Over the years since its publication, the landmark document and the Providence Preservation Society have served as a bridge to bring the neighborhood and the University closer together.

87   Seth Adams House
c. 1823; restored and west side gallery added,
Lerner | Ladds + Bartels Architects, 2003

The Brown Faculty Club / Zachariah Allen House
Alfred Stone, 1864; dining room wing, Ira Rakatansky, 1980

Hope Club
Gould & Angell, 1885; additions 1911 and 1921;
west side renovation and addition, Walsh Architect, 2003

Located across and down the street from Keeney Quad, these buildings are another opportunity to take in at a single glance three of the most important residential styles that are the glory of the architecturally rich nineteenth century—Federal, Italianate, and Queen Anne. The first of these, the Seth Adams House, on the northwest corner of Benevolent and Brown Streets, shows off the skill of the city's early carpenter builders who drew upon the contemporary published drawings of Greek architecture. This two-and-a-half-story clapboard house exhibits all the characteristics of late Federal design, America's first truly national style: elegant, austere, and symmetrical down to the paired chimneys on either side of the gable roof and

Seth Adams House

the double set of stairs leading to the front door. The side lights that frame the door, along with the south-facing windows, yield cheerfully sun-filled rooms, which are especially welcome in the short daylight hours of a Providence winter.

Currently, the building houses the Sarah Doyle Women's Center, which was established in 1974 and initially housed on the other side of the

The Brown Faculty Club / Zachariah Allen House

campus at 185 Meeting Street. The extraordinary Sarah Doyle was a local figure who gained national prominence as one of this nation's most eloquent and effective voices for the rights of women, including access to higher education. We will meet her again early in Walk Nine. The present building includes a modest addition on the west side, the Sarah Doyle Gallery.

At the southwest corner of the same block, the Zachariah Allen House introduces us to the next major style that shaped residential design on College Hill. Developed in the early years of the nineteenth century by English architect John Nash, Italianate design quickly became the rage among England's rising middle class. The style took some time to cross the Atlantic, but cross the Atlantic it did, thanks to the work of American architect Alexander Jackson Davis (1803–1892). However, more than fashion shaped the house. Technological advances in everything from brick to gas lighting and central heating transformed both the size and shape of this and other houses built around the time of the Civil War. Heated solely by individual fireplaces, modest homes, like the earlier Seth Adams House, had to be fairly snug to conserve heat. The latest central heating and lighting innovations available to the architect of the Allen House opened the way for larger, deep rooms and higher ceilings. Another benefit of technology was the proliferation of manufactured parts. The architect or builder could go to a catalog and order an increasingly large array of decorative elements. This gave architects greater freedom to improvise both inside and out, a freedom abetted by a client who clearly had more money to spend than the owner of the Seth Adams House.

Several obvious markers of an Italianate house (besides a pronounced verticality) include wide eaves, the brownstone belt course, and the balustraded front porch. This was the first Providence commission for Alfred Stone, whose firm went on to become one of the city's most sought-after in the decades after the Civil War. The house carved out a unique niche in the city's history as the site in 1881 of the first telephone call in the state between industrialist and amateur scientist Zachariah Allen (Class of 1813) and Alexander Graham Bell, who dialed up from Boston. Brown acquired the house in 1938 and one year later opened it as the new home of the University's Faculty Club. The garden that connects the club with Maddock Alumni Center on the other side of the block is a landscaping grace note that facilitates interaction between alumni and faculty. Before moving down Benevolent Street, do not miss the bronze bear in the garden to the left of the front

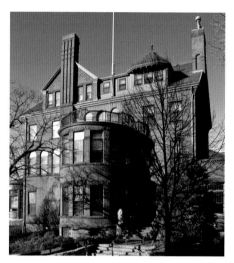

Hope Club

door. A gift of the late Rhode Island Senator and passionate Brown alumnus Theodore Francis Green (1867–1966, Class of 1887), this particular species of bear is a replica of a fountain that once existed in Bresslau, Germany.

One block farther west stands what is reputed to be the first building in America specifically built as a private gentleman's club. Whereas the earlier Italianate Faculty Club retains the symmetry and, relatively speaking, the simplicity of classical architecture, the Hope Club is a bracing brick confection of Queen Anne, Richardsonian Romanesque, and Scottish Baronial styles. Set high upon its lofty perch, the four-story club is a persuasive advocate of the more-is-better approach to life. The architecture and the design of the interior public spaces acknowledge wealth but are never ostentatious or vulgar. Every element is handled with knowing taste, from the expanse of stained glass that illuminates the central staircase to the darkly polished carpentry of the staircase itself, whose spindles engage the banister and the stairs like the strings of a harp. The high-ceilinged lobby that fills out the front bay could not be more welcoming, especially on a cold winter's night when a pile of logs is blazing in the grand fireplace.

The materials used on the surface of the modern addition on the west side are sympathetic to the original building and provide additional amenities, such as a brightly lit dining room that looks out to Providence, and a workout room in the basement. Even if you do not venture inside, take this opportunity to look closely at the two-story bay that pushes out from the front. At the left just above the stone of the foundation, you can make out the path of blood-red masonry that rises smokelike in steps up the wall and feeds into the base of the chimney, then gains speed, pierces the cornice, and shoots out of the top of the gable. Why did the architect spend so much time on what is in effect an exhaust system? Because, fortunately, he could.

The empty space between the Hope Club and Benefit Street is the one discordant note. While offering a fine view of downtown Providence, such spaces are obviously not part of the original fabric of College Hill. Where they occur, they are a sign that something has been torn down. A house in fact existed on the corner of Benefit and Benevolent. Built in 1853 for Edward Pearce, it was designed by Providence architect Thomas Tefft (1826–1859, Class of 1851). The property was acquired by the Hope Club and the house was demolished around 1960 for a parking lot.

88　First Unitarian Church
John Holden Greene, 1816

Parish House
*Stone, Carpenter & Willson, 1878; restoration, Irving B. Haynes and
Associates, 1966; addition, Centerbrook Architects and Planners
with James Barnes Architects, 2002*

The First Unitarian Church is a way-finder on the southwest side of College Hill.
Whether you stand at the edge of downtown Providence or look toward the north
from the harbor, the magnificent 200-foot steeple focuses the eye as surely as
a compass needle points north. (The steeple bell is the largest cast by the foundry
of Paul Revere and Son.) Gifted local carpenter and architect John Holden Greene
(1777–1850) had good reason to produce what many consider his most important
building: he was a member of the congregation, and from his well-placed pew at the
front of the sanctuary (number 75), he could survey the entire interior during the
Sunday service.

Like the First Baptist Meeting House, Greene's building marries a
horizontal, nonhierarchical, almost square evangelical meeting house with an
attached Anglican soaring steeple at the west end. Greene studied James Gibbs's
Book of Architecture (1728) for ideas before he set pen to paper. Like a consummate
musician, he took the plans he found in Gibbs and improvised using baroque (the
richly three-dimensional forms), Classical Revival (the monumental broken pediment

First Unitarian Church

supported by four engaged Doric
columns), Federal (the finials on the
outside and the delicate ornamental
fans on the ceiling of the sanctuary),
and Gothic notes (the tracery of the
rounded, three-part pointed arch
window below the pediment). A more
academic early twentieth-century
revivalist architect would not have
taken such liberties; fortunately
Greene did not know better or care.
The result is an entirely original and
exhilarating composition, a history,
if you will, of the evolution of one
hundred years of architectural styles,
from the beginnings of the city's
history to contemporary times.

How did the architect value
this gift to his congregation and
Providence? Clues may be found in

the decorative elements of the frieze above the entrance: in between the triglyphs (grooved projecting blocks) bloom clusters of oak leaves and acorns, ancient symbols of strength, honor, longevity, and steadfastness. The urns at the edge of the roof and clock tower appear to have flames shooting out of them. These are allusions to the resurrection: the flame is the soul rising to Heaven from the ashes of death. Perhaps they also allude to the spark of Greene's genius escaping mortal clay.

By all means, go inside. After the bold fireworks of the exterior, the interior (also designed by Greene, right down to the curved mahogany pulpit) does not disappoint. The coffered, shallow saucer dome supported by four Corinthian columns; the center ceiling medallion; the graceful fan details that fill in the four ceiling corners—these are just some of the pleasures equally accessible to the worshipper or the lover of architecture. The organ case (c. 1850) at the rear of the sanctuary was designed by Thomas Tefft. The handsome clock mounted on the balcony just below the organ console is a powerful reminder to those in the pulpit that brevity is not only the soul of wit; it is the mark of a well-crafted sermon.

The nineteenth-century Parish House and the twentieth-century Parish House addition (both, like the church, built of granite) demonstrate how to be deferential but not slavish to architecture of an earlier period. In 2003, the Parish House addition was the recipient of an Urban Design Citation from AIA Rhode Island.

89 President's House (formerly Rush Sturges House)
William T. Aldrich, 1922; garden design, Beatrix Farrand

If a certain durability or permanence characterizes what the University built for students and faculty, what the University built for the president is a notable exception. When the College's very first facility was under construction in the 1770s, a residence was built nearby for the president, designed presumably by the same architect or carpenter / builder. The two-and-a-half-story brick house is depicted in early prints and stood close to the site of the 1872 Gate on Prospect Street. In 1840 the building was moved to a location farther down College Hill on College Street, where it stood until 1936, when it was torn down by the Rhode Island School of Design.

A new house was erected on land donated by the ever-generous Nicholas Brown at the corner of Prospect and College Streets. Used by Brown presidents until 1900, the house was then repurposed as a refectory. This, too, was torn down in 1908 to make way for the John Hay Library. A few years earlier (1901), President Faunce had moved into a new home at 180 Hope Street, designed by Hoppin & Ely (the same firm that designed the Van Wickle Gates). When this was abandoned in the late 1940s for the present house on Power Street, the property on Hope Street was used by the Department of Physics until it was torn down in the 1960s to make way for the Barus and Holley Building.

A graduate of MIT and the École des Beaux-Arts, the architect of the Power Street house, William T. Aldrich (1880–1966), was well connected to the financial, political, and diplomatic establishment of his day, whose tastes ran to finely executed period houses. That Aldrich was the son of a powerful Rhode Island U.S. senator and a seasoned yachtsman no doubt further recommended him. The brick house he designed for a prominent Providence lawyer and his wife is a fine example of work done by a careful student of period styles. It looks like the first cousin of Andrews House on Brown Street, although Aldrich had a larger lot to build on, so the house sprawls down the slope of College Hill. The garden at the back was designed by Beatrix Farrand (1872–1959), who was no less connected to the power elite of her day. It would be difficult to commission a more gold-plated couple than the team of Aldrich and Farrand. It is a reminder that whereas during much of the period covered by this guide social connections were useful to a young man of talent, for a similarly talented woman, they were essential.

Although Farrand did major work at many colleges and universities, including Yale and Princeton, she is not well represented at Brown, unless one considers the influence she clearly had on Sharpe. A design genius, who modestly referred to herself not as a landscape architect, but a landscape "gardener," Farrand, like Sharpe, made extensive use of native plants that were easily cared for and would provide interest all four seasons of the year. These elements of her distinct style were well suited for college campuses where, until recently, activity tended to be confined to the colder months of the year. Also she believed that landscaping should complement rather than overwhelm architecture. She was the niece of novelist Edith Wharton and was related to the storied Jones family (as in "keeping up with the Joneses"), so Farrand, like Sharpe, had the social credentials to overcome the limitations placed on her gender in the professional world. Indeed, she was one of the eleven founders of the American Society of Landscape Architects and the only woman.

Once the five Sturges children had grown, the large house was sold to Brown in 1949 at a cost far below its true value, a gift from the family to the University.

President's House

Today the house serves as the president's residence and hosts guests of the University, heads of state, stars of film and stage, and scholars from around the world.

The next stops on this Walk bring us to a pair of exceptionally important houses. The first is a conservative summing up of currents that shaped residential design in the eighteenth century; the second looks forward to the passion for period styles that inspired the aesthetic pyrotechnics of Victorian architecture.

90 John Nicholas Brown Center for Public Humanities and Cultural Heritage (Nightingale-Brown House)

Caleb Ormsbee, 1791; stables and bowling addition, Thomas Tefft, 1855; library, Richard Upjohn, 1864; landscape design, Olmsted & Olmsted, 1890; restoration, Jackson, Robertson & Adams, c. 1920s; second restoration, Haynes / de Boer Associates, 1991

Directly south of the President's House is one of America's most important examples of eighteenth-century residential architecture. The main part of what is today the John Nicholas Brown Center for Public Humanities and Cultural Heritage was designed by the gifted carpenter-builder Caleb Ormsbee. Little is known about the self-taught Ormsbee beyond his dates (1752–1807), the fact that the better-known Providence architect John Holden Greene was apprenticed to him, and that Ormsbee designed two National Historic Landmark homes in Providence, the Thomas P. Ives House (1806) and this house for Captain Joseph Nightingale. Nightingale made his fortune as a partner in a Providence shipping firm that in addition to transporting slaves, engaged in the China trade. Perhaps this is alluded to in the curious design of the upper roof balustrade, composed of plain sticks between the rails intersecting in an intricate pattern referred to as "Chinese."

Unlike such eighteenth-century commercial centers as Boston; Philadelphia; and Charleston, South Carolina, the early American residential design of Providence is typically somewhat old-fashioned, or to use the term favored by architectural historians, *retardataire*. The Nightingale-Brown House is no exception. The symmetrical composition of the house, both inside and out, and the individual design elements are common to mid-eighteenth-century Georgian domestic architecture—e.g., the rusticated window surrounds, the three-part Palladian window above the entrance, the bold heavily beveled quoins (the stone-like blocks of wood that mark off the corners of the building), the turned balustrade on the roof with urn finials on the posts, and the gable-on-hip roof itself. Ormsbee clearly learned his craft not only from the widely read architectural pattern books, but also from his experience as a carpenter-builder. This is a man whose "school" was the construction site. Yet, if the currency of Ormsbee's art is old-fashioned, its value as seen in this magnificent house is calculated in gold.

In 1814, Nicholas Brown Jr. purchased the property from Nightingale's heirs. Although succeeding generations of the family turned to various prominent

John Nicholas Brown Center for Public Humanities and Cultural Heritage

architects for additions and remodeling, Ormsbee's original design is largely intact, no doubt a reflection of the fact the house was owned by one family for five generations, a truly remarkable legacy. However, neither the site nor the house was frozen in time. The first notable change occurred in 1853 when the next head of the family, John Carter Brown (1797–1874), engaged Thomas Tefft. Tefft's contribution to the legacy of the property was a new brick stable and carriage building directly behind the main house. Perhaps out of youthful eagerness to speak the language of a more contemporary aesthetic, the vocabulary Tefft chose was not Georgian, but Italianate. Around 1858, a two-story addition constructed of wood that this time matched the style of the house was built on the south side of the house. This expanded the first-floor kitchen and dining rooms, while creating a loggia between them that covered the side entrance. This too could have been designed by Tefft, although no supporting documentation exists.

Perhaps the most noteworthy addition that had future implications for the University is the library at the northeast corner of the house. This was designed by the architect of St. Stephen's Church, Richard Upjohn, and built during the Civil War. Like the addition on the south side, the one-story wing appears both in material (clapboard) and style to be a part of the original late Georgian house. It was here that Brown, an ardent bibliophile, assembled his remarkable collection of Americana, which after his death eventually became the nucleus of the John Carter Brown Library. Approximately three decades later, Frederick Law Olmsted designed a new landscape plan, much of which is still evident today.

A passionate advocate of modern architecture *and* historic preservation, his grandson, John Nicholas Brown Jr., played a leading role in the shaping of the University in the second half of the twentieth century. A direct descendant of the man who had purchased the house from Nightingale, he promoted twentieth-century masters like Philip Johnson and I. M. Pei while he was the influential chairman of Brown's Planning and Building Committee. At the same time, he invested heavily in redecorating the interior of the house in a Colonial Revival style and later was an advocate for the preservation of the architecture of College Hill. The last generation of the Brown family to live in the house included his son, John Carter Brown III, who became the director of the National Gallery of Art and the head of the United States Commission of Fine Arts.

Upon the death of Anne S. K. Brown in 1985, the largest extant wood-frame eighteenth-century residence in the United States became part of Brown University. After an eight-year painstaking restoration that essentially dismantled and rebuilt the house, it reopened as the John Nicholas Brown Center for Public Humanities and Cultural Heritage. An idea of the value of the more than 900 decorative furnishings collected by five generations of the Brown family can be grasped by the fact that the sale of a single piece, a unique block and shell secretary crafted in Newport, financed the restoration. (In 1993, a reproduction of the secretary was made for the house by Alan Breed.) There are many treasures left to see in this extraordinary house, including elaborately carved plaster moldings throughout the house and the hand-painted wallpaper by the stairs. A National Historic Landmark (1989), the Center is open to the public Monday through Friday 8:30 AM to 5 PM. During the summer, the hours are 8 AM to 4 PM.[5]

91   The Annenberg Institute for School Reform / Thomas P. Hoppin House

Alpheus C. Morse, c. 1855; major rehabilitation and restoration, Robinson Green Beretta, 1983

If there is one place on campus haunted by ghosts, Hoppin House may be it. This is the site of Mrs. Anna Hoppin's childhood home, a rather grand 1789 wooden residence built in the late Georgian style for Joseph Nightingale's business partner, John Innis Clarke. (The apparent resemblance noted at the time between the two houses suggests the Innis Clarke residence might also have been designed and built by Ormsbee. However, there are no surviving records.) In 1849, the eighteenth-century house was completely destroyed by fire. Only Anna Jenkins, 17, and her brother Moses, 15, were saved, having been awakened by the barking of the family dog, Black Prince, who had broken his chain to warn the family. Three years later Anna married the Providence artist Thomas Hoppin, and the couple built their three-story house on the site of Anna's former home, this time of fire-resistant brick. Her husband created a life-size bronze sculpture of Black Prince, which the couple called *The Sentinel*. Originally stationed on the lawn in front of the house, *The Sentinel* today greets visitors to the Roger Williams Park Zoo.

As an aspiring artist from a wealthy Providence family, Hoppin made the Grand Tour of Europe before settling down in marriage. So had Alpheus C. Morse, who would eventually design one of the University's most significant buildings,

Thomas P. Hoppin House

Sayles Hall. Given the tightness of the circle of wealthy Americans abroad, it would not be out of the question if Hoppin and Morse first made their acquaintance on foreign shores. Whatever the case, culturally and socially both architect and client had much in common: each was aware of what was fashionable among the moneyed classes on the Continent; each was eager to bring that knowledge back home. When Morse returned to Providence from his immersion in the social, scientific, and aesthetic currents reshaping Europe, Hoppin was his first client.

Like at the Maddock Alumni Center (Walk One), the somewhat austere exterior of the H-shaped block of the house hides the lavishness inside, much of which remains, including outstanding examples of wood paneling and intricate plaster molding. (However, the original crystal chandeliers were later sold and taken to Hollywood.) Clearly, Hoppin House was designed for gracious living in a manner that reflected the union of two sizable fortunes. Among the more notable features are the separate entrances. Pedestrians entered from John Street up a paired flight of stone stairs to the one-story brownstone porch; those arriving by carriage disembarked at the foot of the far more impressive three-bay brick arcade on the east side. The carriage entrance, with its statue of Flora in the second-floor niche, together with the rather impressive stable and carriage house that form a courtyard at the rear or north end, marks this as the "way in" for guests attending dinner parties and fancy dress balls. The precedent of a carriage entrance was not lost on succeeding generations, at least those who had the resources to build a grand house.

Separate entrances for foot and carriage traffic had an impact on the interior circulation and layout of the rooms. The main or center hallway of houses built during the first decades of the new Republic—the Nightingale-Brown House, for example—runs down the center of the house from the front to the back with the living spaces arranged symmetrically on either side. There is a central hallway running south to north in Hoppin House, but the rooms on either side do not match. Although the spaces on the west side of the central hall are equally divided into three large drawing and dining spaces, the east side consists, from front to back, of a large room, a separate stair hall at the center, and a smaller room and corridor leading to the kitchen wing at the rear. This half of the house is more utilitarian.

The west side of the hall is far more sumptuous, since this is where guests and visitors were entertained. The ceiling of the room on the southwest corner is grained to resemble wood. Like all the corner rooms, there is a fireplace. However, whereas the fireplaces in the other rooms have heavy, decorated iron hearth surrounds and carved marble mantles, in this room the mantelpiece gives full voice to the Victorian love of color and texture. At the center is a projecting lion mask nested in a sinuous garland of grapes and vines. The marble of the fireplace facing is pink, while that of the hearth itself is black. The adjoining room continues the fireworks with walls that feature raised plaster moldings with rococo leaf detailing at the top and bottom. The elaborately carved white marble fireplace above which floats a large mirror provides a wonderful focus for the candlelight that illuminated the many dinner parties at the Hoppin mansion.

The massive stairway at the center of the house deserves a second look for a number of reasons. For one, it helps to delineate the change in taste that separates a grand late eighteenth-century house, like Nightingale-Brown, from a similarly grand residence built around the time of the Civil War. At Nightingale-Brown, the stairs align with the central hall and lead directly to the second floor. At Hoppin House (as well as at the Maddock Alumni Center and Nicholson House, Walk One), the main stairs are pulled back from the front door and positioned in a separate space around an open well at the center of the hall, where they twist and coil to the upper stories. It is massive, masculine, and pulsing with energy. To a greater or lesser degree, architecture accommodates and mediates our experience of space, motion, and time. American architect Antoine Predock describes architecture as "processional and ceremonial." Nowhere is this aspect of a building's design more forcefully seen than in the manner in which movement is choreographed within a structure, especially from one level to the next. This architectural feature, the stairway, can simply be utilitarian and the sense of procession and ceremony minimal. But when handled as it is here at Hoppin House (and the Granoff Center, Walk Five), it is the star performer around which the rest of the architecture turns, commanding both our attention and admiration.

While Anna and Thomas Hoppin were alive, their home played a glittering role in the city's artistic community, quickly gaining the reputation as the "House of 1,000 Candles." But the house could never quite shake off the dark legacy of its past. The statue of Flora above the carriage entrance is not simply a reference to a classical figure, but more poignantly to Anna's sister, who perished in the fire that destroyed the family home. She was last seen at a window with a pitcher in her hand.[6]

One of the finest Italianate residences in Providence, Hoppin House was placed on the National Register of Historic Places in 1973, and since 1993 has been the home of the Annenberg Institute for School Reform. The University's southernmost academic building on College Hill, Hoppin House is today no longer something of an outpost, but midway between the College Hill campus and Brown's evolving engagement with the city's historic Jewelry District, which will be the subject of Walk Nine after a tour of Brown's athletic facilities.

1   *Thoughts of the Present Collegiate System in the United States* (Boston: Gould, Kendall & Lincoln, 1842), 112–31.

2   Henry Merritt Wriston, *Educational Housing, Providence, Rhode Island* (Providence: Brown University Press, 1946), 13. In this document, Wriston sets out the guidelines that will shape the design of Wriston Quad. He also explains his reasons for bringing the fraternities on campus.

3   Henry Merritt Wriston, "University Architecture," from *Wriston Speaking: A Selection of Addresses* (Providence: Brown University Press, 1957), 81.

4   Edith Wharton, *A Backward Glance* (New York: D. Appleton-Century Company, 1934), 107.

5   Additional information about the Nightingale-Nicholas Brown House in the National Register of Historic Places Registration Form published by the National Park Service prepared by Jean A. Follett and Robert P. Emlem, 1988.

6   The discussion of the Thomas P. Hoppin House owes much to the Historic American Buildings Survey prepared in 1961 by Antoinette Downing and Elvira Gowdey, published by the National Park Service. Additional information was developed by the National Register of Historic Places Nomination Form, 1972.

The Athletic Complex and Playing Fields

> [T]he college is…losing scholarship by the very great interest…in boating and
> baseball. [O]ur business will be to reduce the evil to its least practicable limits.
> —President Alexis Caswell [1]

> A measure of risk in playing a game nurses courage and adds to the moral value
> of the game.
> —President Elisha Benjamin Andrews [2]

For Brown's sixth president, baseball and rowing were not simply a distraction;
they were an evil to be actively resisted. His successor had a different perspective.
A liberalizing force—he did, after all, encourage the education of women at
Brown—President Andrews agreed with his contemporary Theodore Roosevelt
that physical culture contributed to the cultivation of a sound mind: Americans
were growing soft; high time to toughen up. There was also a practical reason
to encourage students to run, kick, row, throw, and hit each other with sticks,
College administrators hoped athletics would provide a safety valve for the kind
of high spirits that provoked the following reflection from a long-suffering
member of the University's staff:

> From 1877 to 1881 was probably the greatest time in the history of the college
> for cane-rushes, bonfires, blowing of fish-horns and explosions of gunpowder.…
> When material was scarce, the students would take a mattress from a bed or an
> old couch, saturate it with oil, and watch for a good opportunity to light it a short
> distance from the buildings.[3]

In the end, sports came to be appreciated as a pursuit that had as much
to do with building character as channeling youthful spirits. This was the
background behind the construction of a pair of outstanding buildings, Lyman
Gymnasium, which led the University's expansion east, and Sayles Gymnasium,
the second building on the new Pembroke campus.

As organized sports became increasingly popular, both Lyman and Sayles
Gyms were increasingly inadequate. Since larger facilities required more land,
new construction was pushed farther from the center of the campus. Besides the
inconvenience of getting from the classroom to the locker room and back, this
had at least two consequences. Away from the architectural traditions of both
the men's and the women's colleges, architects were working with a blank slate.
Apart from the need to construct sturdy, flexible, and spacious facilities capable
of accommodating large crowds, they were free to experiment. However,
freedom posed its own challenges. Would the new buildings aggregate in such
a way as to define a clear sense of place? What would the investment say about

Brown Stadium press box, c. 1950

the University's priorities? And perhaps the most pressing issue, how would these buildings be paid for?

A major development was the purchase in 1957 of Dexter Asylum, 39 acres and a short walk from the Pembroke campus. This would be the canvas on which a modern athletic complex would be sketched. This tour explores the path followed by Brown at Dexter Asylum and the building of Meehan Auditorium.

Meehan Auditorium
Perry, Shaw, Hepburn & Dean, 1961

By acquiring Dexter Asylum, the University gained a parcel more than four times the acreage of the original eighteenth-century campus. With all this land within easy walking distance of the Pembroke campus, Brown's athletic director at the time, Paul Mackesey (1947–1962, Class of 1932), envisioned not only a hockey rink but also a new gymnasium, a swimming pool, a field house, soccer and lacrosse fields, tennis courts, and a track. It was a long wish list that lacked only two critical prerequisites: an overall plan and, more immediately, the money to match Mackesey's and Brown's ambitions.

It was in the context of a tight budget and the rush to build a modern multipurpose facility for a growing student body that the large drum that is the George V. Meehan Auditorium took shape. Somewhat surprisingly, the project was given to the firm most associated with Brown's decades-long commitment to Colonial Revival architecture. In developing his design, the architect drew on two traditions, classic and modern. At its heart, the building offers spectacle in the round; in other words, it is an update on a Roman coliseum. Meehan also references a '60s fascination with domed structures. Think the geodesic domes of Buckminster Fuller (1895–1983). At the University of Virginia a similar facility, University Hall (1965), was constructed and christened by students the "pregnant oyster." The circular form provides optimal sight lines for spectators whatever the event, be it a hockey game, a banquet, or Brown's annual Commencement on those rare occasions when it rains.

Meehan Auditorium under construction

Meehan Auditorium

Meehan is one of those buildings that respect those who use them but not those who pass by. It is serviceable but perhaps a bit dull. However, peel away the skin, and a far more interesting building is revealed. Named for the Providence business executive who provided a half million dollars for its construction, Meehan is an engineering tour de force.

Photographs taken at the time of its construction show a roof that is a spiderweb of steel trusses, with thirty arched cantilever ribs 104 feet long. At the top of the dome, the converging ribs were field-welded to a 14-foot-diameter compression ring. Prefabricated pie-shaped roof sections were hoisted in place over the skeletal framing. The self-supporting dome is a fascinating exercise of thrust and counterthrust that combines great strength with light weight. This is architecture or, more to the point, engineering that is technologically exciting and, when stripped to the bone, wonderfully sculptural. Unfortunately, the whole thing is hidden behind a bland skin, which reveals little of the excitement inside, whether it is the engineering that went into constructing the building or the final minutes in a hotly contested hockey game between Brown and Yale.

93 Olney-Margolies Athletic Center
Daniel F. Tully, 1981

After the opening of Meehan Auditorium, Brown needed a field house. Plans were drawn up in 1967 by Spanish architect Félix Candela (1910–1997), who designed the 1968 Summer Olympics dome in Mexico City. Had the Candela design been built, it would have been an engineering marvel, a cage of the thinnest reinforced concrete covered with a bright copper skin. Ambitious but also too expensive for Brown, which was wrestling with financial challenges. Plans for a field house were put on hold.

Nearly fifteen years later, during the presidency of Howard R. Swearer (Brown's fifteenth president), a very different building opened its doors and was hailed by the magazine *Engineering News-Record* as one of the ten most noteworthy engineering structures in the world! No doubt the honor stemmed in part from the fact that the facilities inside Olney-Margolies—basketball, volleyball, and tennis courts; a six-lane 200-meter track; batting and golf cages; and more—are all contained under a column-free, 180-foot-span concrete roof whose 1.8-acre surface is covered with artificial turf that serves as a playing field for soccer, lacrosse, and football practice when the field below is too muddy for play.

The product of a "design-build" competition (i.e., the design and construction are carried out by a single entity), Olney-Margolies is named after Joseph Olney and Moe Price Margolies (both members of the Class of 1936). Built of reinforced concrete on steel forms, this is another athletic facility distinguished less by its envelope than its size, durability, and engineering. The straightforwardness of Olney-Margolies no doubt recommended it to the administration at a time when the University was living on an extremely tight budget. Of some architecture it can be said that no expense was spared; at Olney-Margolies no savings were overlooked. It was Frank Lloyd Wright who said that whereas doctors can bury their mistakes, the only advice architects can give a client is to plant vines. Brown has instead planted a row of trees along the blank wall that is Olney-Margolies. Over time, these will weave the austere facility into the a newly coherent quad.

94   Paul Bailey Pizzitola Memorial Sports Center
Eggers Group, 1988

By the 1980s, what had been the University's main athletic facility, the four-story Colonial Revival Marvel Gymnasium on Elmwood Avenue, had outlived its usefulness. After a short grace period, the building was torn down in 2002. The great bronze bear that had stood on a pedestal outside the front of the gym migrated (pedestal and all) to a new lair between the Faunce Arch and Salomon Center for Teaching. And the gold-leafed cupola atop Marvel was put into storage. It will reappear later on this Walk.

The new gym, named in honor of Paul Bailey Pizzitola (Class of 1981), was designed by one of America's leading architecture firms. Founded in 1903 by John Russell Pope (the Beaux-Arts-trained architect who designed the Jefferson Memorial and the National Gallery in Washington, D.C.), the Eggers Group employed none of the Classical Revival vocabulary nor the Beaux-Arts handling of space or urbanity. Instead, despite all the land Brown had at its disposal, this 2,800-seat multipurpose gym is uncomfortably squeezed into the tight space between Meehan Auditorium and the Olney-Margolies Athletic Center. The totality of the facility's envelope is less than the sum of its parts. The smooth undulating white paneled front is so understated as to seem more wall than building. In respect to the rest of what is a rather large structure, this side of the building seems laminated to the large box behind it. The long strip of small square windows high up on the wall are less sources of light—in either direction—than decorative elements to relieve the blankness of the surface plane. The way in, like that of Lyman Gymnasium, is off center, but what in Lyman is dramatic is here purely functional.

If Pizzitola is coolly aloof at the front, it is positively indifferent to the neighborhood on the Lloyd Avenue side. Pedestrians and motorists approaching Hope Street confront on the left a tall red windowless metal structure. From this angle, the building could be a warehouse or storage facility, except for what is arguably the most interesting feature—the canopy or hat on top of the roof. It is Teflon-coated fiberglass, a translucent material that admits daylight onto the four all-weather tennis courts below. The glow that seeps through the fiberglass at

Paul Bailey Pizzitola Memorial Sports Center

night adds a bit of pizzazz to what is otherwise a dark site. That said, by day the face Pizzitola shows to the world is disappointingly pedestrian.

By 1988, a traditional open quadrangle that included the now demolished Smith Swim Center (1973) had emerged and was christened the Erickson Athletic Complex. The name honors Wendell R. Erickson (Class of 1919), a catcher on Brown's baseball team and a steadfast supporter of Brown athletics. However, instead of fronting on a green space of paths, trees, and grass, the complex faced out to a parking lot. Neglecting its rich heritage of institutional buildings arranged around a park, Brown by default adopted as its model the suburban shopping strip. The possibilities inherent in this space to become a more traditional campus quad that would tie these disparate buildings together and create a real sense of place were not realized until the end of the opening decade of the twenty-first century. This is the story told by the next stop.

However, if time and curiosity permit, walk through the space between the Pizzitola and Olney-Margolies and head a short distance to the tall, windowless brick building that fronts on Lloyd Avenue. This is Brown's Central Heat Plant. The architecture is surprisingly and agreeably sculptural. Brown Professor of History of Art and Architecture Dietrich Neumann explains the unusual quality of such a humble structure by identifying it as a fragment of the original proposal architect Candela had designed for the site. It is a reminder that a humble material like brick can be transformed in the hands of an architect with a strong design sense even when the building is meant to serve a purely utilitarian end.

Nelson Fitness Center

95 Jonathan M. Nelson '77 Fitness Center
Katherine Moran Coleman Aquatics Center
David J. Zucconi '55 Varsity Strength and Conditioning Center
Ittleson Quadrangle
Robert A. M. Stern Architects, 2012; landscape design, Todd Rader + Amy Crews

Since World War II, the coherence of many established campuses has been challenged by a zeitgeist-obsessed approach to their development based on disciplinary methods of art history that has led to the view that new buildings are the environmental equivalent of art objects in a museum, each reflecting a prevailing stylistic trend deserving of representation. As a result, in place of a shared community of buildings, there is now all too often cacophony resulting from a competition between ideologies and isms.
— Robert A. M. Stern [4]

Each generation renegotiates the balance between yesterday and tomorrow. For Brown, this has meant treasuring the legacy of its unique identity, while acknowledging changing needs and the tidal pull of shifting cultural values. Throughout its history, this dynamic has been reflected in the University's architecture. It appears in stark terms in two of the most recent additions to the Brown campus.

If not a leap, the Granoff Center (Walk Five) is certainly a bold step by an internationally recognized firm that positioned Brown among the architectural avant-garde. By contrast, the new Jonathan M. Nelson '77 Fitness Center, designed by America's most well-known "Modern Traditionalist," Robert A. M. Stern, looks over its shoulder to the now demolished Marvel Gymnasium and grafts a new "historical" building onto a neighborhood that has a mixed and varied architectural history. The building that now stands on the south side of the Ittleson Quadrangle rises to the challenge of meeting what everyone agreed was an urgent need for a new athletic facility. Certainly the site with its mix of unrelated buildings confronting a parking lot fit the definition of a complex problem. Jonathan M. Nelson (Class of 1977) liked the idea of a facility more in keeping with the Colonial Revival look of Marvel Gym; the candidate to do the job was Robert A. M. Stern Architects. This led to a neotraditional proposal that envisioned a single large structure on the site designed to serve three distinct purposes: a fitness center for the student body, a pool, and a varsity athletes' fitness room.

The Stern building acknowledges and contributes to the transformation of the entire quad. The trio of older buildings—Pizzitola, Meehan, and Olney-Margolies—may stir fond memories for what went on inside the opaque walls; however, the architecture of these facilities could not have evoked an artistic response. The new athletic complex does. By day and by night, there is an energizing transparency throughout that brings the outside in and the activity of the inside out. Compare how people enter and leave the various buildings that frame the Ittleson Quad. The generous two-story arched main entrance at the Nelson Fitness Center, opening underneath the center pediment, focuses the energy of coming and going, recapturing the sense of drama sometimes lost in post–World War II buildings where it can be difficult to locate the front door. For those arriving by bike or on foot, the Nelson Fitness Center is clearly a destination, the real way into the athletic quad, especially after a small section of the old Dexter Asylum wall (1832) was removed to increase the building's visibility from the street. At night, the brightly lit clock of the old Marvel Gymnasium cupola, which was brought out of storage and reset atop the roof, is a way-finding beacon.

Within this Neo-Colonial skin beats a contemporary heart that is no stranger to computer-aided design. Take the Katherine Moran Coleman Aquatics Center, which is the slightly smaller middle or second element of the three-part facility: the million-gallon, 56-meter state-of-the-art pool is heated by an array of 168 hybrid solar panels, the largest in the country at the time of its installation, and the first of its kind at a university. Under the full sun, the system as designed has the potential not only to heat the pool but to light the building.

The third element of the composition and the smallest at the rear or eastern end, the David J. Zucconi '55 Varsity Strength and Conditioning Center is a gift to the University's varsity athletes. Within the grasp of their strong and capable hands is an array of state-of-the-art equipment. Admission is gained directly from the playing fields through the tall arched, multipaned glass entry beneath the gable-ended bay.

Aside from the urbanity, which engages the neighborhood, and the engineering, the complex offers expansive views through the large windows of the Nelson Fitness Center, a pleasant distraction as one chases calories on a treadmill or stationary bike. The transparency is an aesthetic and philosophical plus; it helps to erase the wall between inside and out, making the building less dependent on artificial lighting. Since the Nelson Fitness Center, the largest of the three elements, is situated like a locomotive at the front and steps slightly into the Ittleson Quad, it effectively masks what is in fact a very large building. This helps the structure to fit more easily into the residential scale of the neighborhood. The term for the brickwork's decorative patterning seems to be derived from Greek by way of French to suggest "bejeweling." Bejeweled the brickwork certainly is, especially on the walls that face Hope Street and the quad. The way this material is handled evokes memories of some of the more outstanding examples found on the Brown campus, especially on Victorian buildings like Slater Hall.

The Ittleson Quad green between the Nelson Fitness Center and Meehan Auditorium may prove to be the most transformed and transformational innovation at the Erickson Athletic Complex. More than any single building, the open green gives definition to the Quad and contributes to the overall life and vitality of both this particular site and the University. It gathers the individual buildings into what might be styled a community or village. Named after Brown trustee H. Anthony Ittleson (Class of 1960), the newest of Brown's outdoor living rooms replaced the parking lot and is designed to be a catalyst for the kinds of conversations between buildings and park that are one of the great treasures of the University. As envisioned by the Kliment / Halsband master plan, Ittleson Quad is now a welcoming space in which to linger for students and the neighborhood alike. As the new landscaping matures, the full power of this space as a magnet for community will be felt. The before and after of Ittleson Quad illustrates how landscape design is not simply decoration or a mute accessory to architecture. It guides how we perceive individual buildings as well as how they relate to one another. This is the last destination of this tour of the Athletic Complex and the nearby neighborhood. For those who have access to a car or bike, there are two additional stops.

96   Brown Football Stadium
Gavin Hadden and Paul Cret, 1925

To chart the distance between the sport of scholarly athletes and modern pro football, read the speech President Faunce delivered at the dedication of the Brown Football Stadium: "To clean sport and fair play; To the development of a sound mind in a sound body; To the loyalties of the game leading to the loyalties of life; To forgetfulness of self in devotion to the team; To respect for all opponents whether they lose or win; To the comradeship of American colleges."

By the 1920s, football at campuses across the country had moved from game to passion bordering on craze. The songs, pennants, chrysanthemum corsages, hip flasks, and raccoon coats defined in the popular mind what college was about. In 1921 a committee was established to raise funds for modern facilities. This initiative led to the development of a 30-acre athletic complex approximately a mile from the main campus. Facilities included the Aldrich Baseball Field, Marvel Gymnasium, and a football stadium, the design of which was overseen by one of the world's leading architects, the French-American Paul Cret (1876-1945)—the same Beaux-Arts-trained architect who advised Brown about the design of Lincoln Field, who later in his distinguished career was awarded a Gold Medal by the American Institute of Architects.

Brown Football Stadium

Brown Football Stadium, rear view

Designed to seat nearly 28,000 spectators (which is one measure of the popularity of the sport at Brown), the stadium straddles the middle distance between Classical Revival and a more austere modernist interpretation of the style. Viewed from outside, the arches that support the trapezoidal south stand have an almost surreal quality, like the arches of the painter Giorgio de Chirico's metaphysical town squares. Rather than the more expected oval coliseum seating, the grandstand is a massive wedge that narrows as it descends to the field. The original intent of the architects was for the north stand to be a mirror image of the south. The onset of the Depression curbed this vision. Today, there is something of a faded romantic quality about the stadium, as if the facility wanted to become more classical in the sense of a Roman ruin.

The next and final stop on this extended tour takes us south to the Seekonk River waterfront and the site of the oldest organized sport at Brown.

97 Hunter S. Marston Boathouse
Butler & Rodman, 1967; renovation, 1994

The Hunter S. Marston Boathouse reminds us of the tie between the University and the prosperous harbor that underwrote its birth. The first residents of University Hall would have looked out to the Providence River and to the head of Narragansett

Hunter S. Marston Boathouse

Bay. Today, such a view is reserved for those whose offices are on the top floors of the Sciences Library or who come down to the Seekonk River to row in its waters or watch a race.

The present boathouse is the latest of a series of facilities that have supported a sport organized in 1857. The first boathouse was a casualty when a gale blew up Narragansett Bay in 1869 and swept away the wharf and float. The next hundred years was a litany of fire and flood, until the University acquired the former plant of the Saltesea Packing Company. Several remodelings, the most significant of which was in 1994, have yielded a modern facility that has well served a string of winning teams.

1 Report to the Corporation, 1870; Martha Mitchell, *Encyclopedia Brunoniana* (Providence: Brown University Library, 1993), 44.

2 *Annual Report to the Corporation*, 1895; ibid.

3 Mitchell, *Encyclopedia Brunoniana*, 521.

4 *On Campus: Architecture, Identity, and Community*, ed. Peter Morris Dixon (New York: Monacelli Press, 2010), 13.

5 Andrew Jackson Downing, *The Architecture of Country Houses* (New York: D. Appleton & Co., 1859), 317–18.

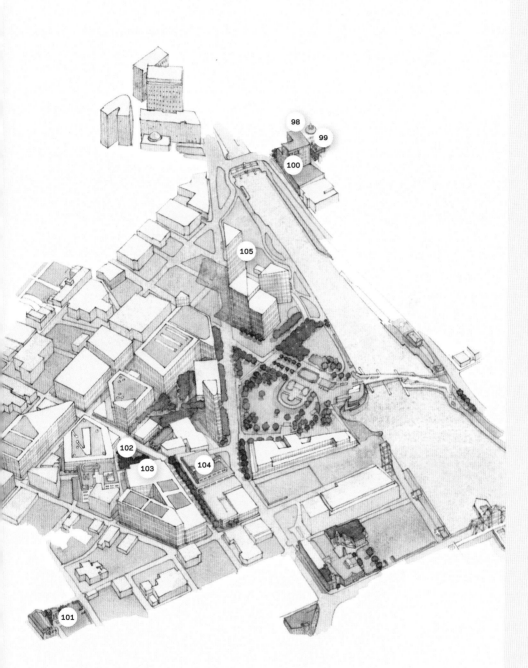

The footbridge and riverfront park at center
are projected for completion in late 2015.

That as a College is about to be built in Providence…it should be built in such a Place and part of the Town, as it will at once be the most commodious for the College and beneficial for the Public. These are the only objects, in our opinion, that should demand the attention of the Committee.
— Certain citizens of Providence, to the Committee appointed for determining the Sport, or Place in Providence, where the College is to be built, 1770 [1]

In 1770 the college moved to Providence where the next five Commencements were held in Mr. Snow's Meeting House.[2]

In 1746, dissidents from the First Congregational Society, located on Benefit Street, packed up their belongings and headed to open land on the west side of the Providence River. Their leader was a charismatic preacher, the Reverend Joseph Snow Jr. The site chosen for the congregation's house of worship was a largely undeveloped knoll at the head of an Indian trail, which today is Weybosset Street. (The earlier history of the Indian trail is preserved in the name *Waubosset*, which is native Narragansett for a river crossing where three trails meet.) Trust in God was of course paramount, which is what guided the Reverend and his flock to the first high piece of ground not likely to be flooded by the periodic great storms that roared up the bay and choked the Providence River. Secure on the high ground, Mr. Snow's Meeting House was destined to play a small but nevertheless colorful footnote in the University's larger history.

After the young College moved from Warren, Rhode Island, to Providence, there was no place in the city large enough in which to hold Commencements. At least not quite yet. That would come a few years later, when the First Baptist Meeting House opened its doors. President Manning, a Baptist, turned to his friend, a Congregational minister, and Reverend Snow graciously welcomed the College's first graduating students. As the young men of these first Commencements marched up Weybosset Street, people from all over Rhode Island poured into Providence for what was the colony's first holiday. They came to watch, be part of the ceremony, and listen to the graduates who filed into the church to declaim in Latin and Greek on topics that increasingly took a patriotic tone. Few, if any, understood what was being said. No matter: those who listened were proud and impressed. Rhode Island, which was still somewhat of a pariah among the New England colonies for its tolerance of opposing beliefs, could now boast an institution dedicated to higher learning, and the College was located not in Newport, which had coveted this honor, but in Providence.

However, before the first shovel of earth was turned, the question was exactly where in Providence would the College be built? What detractors referred to as "the Mountain," or at the time more prosaically known as Prospect Hill, was not the unanimous choice. In a polite yet pointed letter written to the committee charged for determining the site, a group of citizens opposed to locating the College on the Hill wrote: "The Memorial of us the Undersigners Sheweth: That as a College is about to be built in Providence, we have it such at Heart, that it should be built in such a Place and part of the Town, as will at once be most commodious for the College, and beneficial to the Public." The letter went on to say:

We have observed with the utmost concernment a Disposition in divers people to have the College Edifice erected upon an almost inaccessible Mountain; and our concern is the greater as this Measure appears to be promoted by some principal Gentlemen, and large Subscribers.[3]

The "Gentlemen" were of course the Brown brothers, who in this instance, as in so much else, got their way: the College Edifice was built on the Mountain.

Reverend Snow's Meeting House was torn down in the 1830s and replaced with a new building designed by the carpenter architects Barnard Eddy and John Newman. They found inspiration for their striking Greek Revival design in those bibles carefully studied by America's first architects, the popular architectural pattern books. With its large gilded dome, the house of worship they built is today a familiar downtown Providence landmark within sight of Brown's Warren Alpert Medical School. The proximity of the two suggested the underlying narrative that shapes this final Walk: With an increasing presence on the west side of the river, the University has come down from the Mountain to the very site proposed by those who had opposed the move to College Hill.

At the beginning of the twentieth century, Providence led the nation in the manufacture of jewelry. The need to supply a steady stream of educated owners, innovators, and businessmen was the inspiration for the science buildings that arose on campus in the years between the Civil War and World War I. The center of the industry was in that part of the city bounded by Clifford Street on the north, Point Street on the south, Empire Street on the west, and the river on the east. Work was typically carried out in large buildings that housed a number of small firms. As the area evolved in the late nineteenth and early twentieth centuries, the large manufacturing buildings clustered at the perimeter, whereas the middle was distinguished by small residential lots. This was the high-water mark of the city's manufacturing prosperity, a prosperity that paid for many of the grand houses on College Hill.

Succeeding decades saw an accelerating erosion of the city's industrial base, a decline hastened by the devastating floods of the 1938 and 1954 hurricanes. The construction in the 1960s of the massive I-195 interchange that sliced through the Jewelry District and across the river through the south end of College Hill administered an exhaust-choked coup-de-grace to formerly vibrant and productive neighborhoods. What was not demolished was left to languish in the shadow

Warren Alpert Medical School, atrium

of graffiti-splashed highway off-ramps. As early as the 1990s, Rhode Island's Historical Preservation & Heritage Commission and others began to agitate for tearing down and relocating the interchange south. Among those whose voice was especially persuasive was Providence architect William Warner, whose vision some years earlier for recovering the waterfront and reconnecting the downtown with McKim, Mead & White's imposing capitol had a rejuvenating impact on the city. Might a similar transformation be possible on the south side of downtown if the interchange were realigned?

Strategically located between the downtown and College Hill, the vacant land under the interchange was increasingly appreciated as a valuable piece of real estate. If the interchange were in fact moved, a hole in the city's fabric could be repaired, knitting together close-by neighborhoods that had been torn apart on both sides of the river. In 2006, construction began on the "IWAY," a realignment of I-195 that moved the interchange out of the Jewelry District and the southern flank of College Hill. The stage was set for major reinvestment in this quarter of the city that would be the engine to drive the emergence of a lively neighborhood, and Brown was prepared.

The University's *Strategic Framework for Physical Planning* showed that by consolidating the core, Brown could in the short term meet the needs of the increasing number of students entering the University's new programs in science and research. However, for the long term, the architects recognized that if the University were to be a leader in the emerging knowledge economy, Brown's need to grow could not be realized on the limited land available on College Hill. A 2010 Kliment/Halsband proposal, *Jewelry District Area Plan*, directed the University to look across the river to accommodate two million square feet of growth over the next twenty-five years. An especially striking feature of this document is that it outlines a vision that does not erase what was left of the area's industrial buildings. Rather, it celebrates an important chapter of twentieth-century American architecture whose embrace of modern building materials and simple utilitarian forms was admired and widely imitated around the world. The *Jewelry District Area Plan* also envisioned significant public open space, encouraged mixed use, and reimagined both the existing streets leading to downtown and future pedestrian access to College Hill.

South Main Street (Joseph Brown House, Old Stone Bank, Benoni Cooke House, and 121 South Main Street)

98 Joseph Brown House
Joseph Brown, 1774

As he had in conceiving the First Baptist Meeting House, Joseph Brown consulted the pages of the well-thumbed architectural pattern books to design his own home. Historians suggest Brown's source for the curiously appealing facade that fronts South Main Street could have been Colen Campbell's *Vitruvius Britannicus* (1717) or Plate P of William Salmon's *Palladio Londinensis* (1748). Joseph had access to both, since his brother, Nicholas, was the city's first librarian. The exterior appearance of the house bears the mark of a man eager to make a strong statement about his position and the position of the Brown family in the growing community. For interior details, Brown was no less the connoisseur, carefully pursuing what would be recognized as quality and the height of fashion. For example, the finely wrought two-story wood mantel originally located in the front part of the house is a simplified version of one shown in James Gibbs's *Book of Architecture* (1728), Plate 91, which Brown owned.

The exuberance of what was built, with its distinctive baroque ogee (i.e., double curve) gable that faces the street, is what one might expect of a man proud of his taste and craft. Never, however, is the utilitarian sacrificed to mere fashion. The difference in the materials used on the South Main Street facade (brownstone on the lower story, brick from there on up) is not a simple matter of giving variety to the composition. It tells us the original entrance was not at street level, but at the *piano nobile,* or what we would call the second floor. This is clear from lines on the brownstone that show traces of what had been a double flight of stone steps. Locating the main floor one flight up was not only the custom of houses built during the Renaissance and adopted in the new world by Joseph Brown; it made great sense at a time when Towne Street (as South Main Street was called) was the city's chief commercial artery, one that was unpaved and, depending on the season, ground up by hundreds of wagon wheels and horses into a noxious mud or dust.

Brown's house was also his place of business. It was here that he and his brother John organized the Providence Bank in 1791, the first financial institution in Providence and the predecessor of what became the Old Stone Bank. Sixteen years after Joseph's death in 1785, the house became the headquarters of the bank. To make it easier for customers to conduct business, the paired stairs and second-floor entrance were removed. What had been the front door was replaced by a window. An old drawing shows the original condition of the front of the house, including a suggestion that the distinct ogee lines of the gable were repeated in the pediment above the original second-floor doorway. The house is still used by the Brown family, perhaps a record for a building to be held so long by one family.[4]

99   Old Stone Bank
C. G. & J. R. Hall, 1854; Stone, Carpenter & Willson, 1898

Benoni Cooke House
John Holden Greene, 1828

That the final Walk of this guide should exhibit yet another, indeed, perhaps the most exuberant example of the shape-shifting nineteenth-century firm of Stone, Carpenter & Willson, as well as a house from the talented eighteenth-century amateur architect Joseph Brown, seems an appropriate place to pause before leaving the Hill.

As originally designed, the Providence Institution for Savings (predecessor to the Old Stone Bank) was a modest one-story, three-bay granite affair. However, the city's increasing prosperity called for a major expansion. In rising to the challenge, the architects performed an extraordinary piece of surgery, splitting the older building in two pieces, moving the south half (to the site of the demolished twin of the present Benoni Cooke House), and inserting into the space that was opened up the architects' interpretation of Rome's Pantheon. The patient survived and prospered. The reconfigured structure with its impressive Corinthian columned

Benoni Cooke House

portico is the building we see today. The low gold-leafed and verdigris dome that looks vaguely Asian is no less a College Hill and Providence landmark than the steeples of the First Baptist and Unitarian churches.

One door south stands the neighboring Benoni Cooke House, the remaining twin of what had been a pair of houses designed by the city's leading carpenter-architect for two business partners, Benoni Cooke and Isaac Brown, who were brothers-in-law. Whereas Joseph Brown addressed the issue of South Main Street's dust and noise by centering his front door on the second floor, John Holden Greene accomplished the same end by using to advantage the steep slope of the Hill and locating the facing entrances on the north and south sides of the respective houses. In between the two was a driveway from South Main Street that emptied into a semienclosed service court. Guests arriving by horse or carriage would enter either house at ground level; those approaching from the street climbed up a steep flight of stairs. It is a clever tour de force. The elegant porch framed by slim Ionic columns leads to a front door that is complemented by a necklace of side lights and fanlights above, sure hallmarks of Federal-style architecture. Greene bears no responsibility, however, for the first floor "greenhouse" at street level. It was added in 1982.

In 1995, Brown purchased the Old Stone Bank and the adjacent Benoni Cooke House. This seemed a unique opportunity to pull both properties together into a larger complex for the University's excellent but remote Haffenreffer Museum of Anthropology, located in Bristol, Rhode Island. As explained by President Vartan Gregorian: "The city's rich ethnic and cultural diversity makes Providence an appropriate permanent home for the Haffenreffer's collections, and the museum's long-standing commitment to education and outreach will make the Old Stone site a great asset for Providence schools." However, the cost of renovating both buildings proved daunting. After thirteen years, Brown sold both properties in 2008, while leasing the Benoni Cooke House for administrative purposes.

100 121 South Main Street
Edward Larrabee Barnes, 1984; park design, M. Paul Friedberg; conference room renovation, Architecture Research Office, 2011

Whatever issues Joseph Brown might have faced in building his home are not a matter of record. The same cannot be said about the modern eleven-story commercial building on the west side of South Main Street. The protracted struggle leading up to the construction of the somewhat boxy high-rise had all the elements of a television drama. The cast included the rich and powerful, preservationists and politicians, the media and the public—all in a heated controversy that was seasoned by the occasional anonymous death threat to the client in the dead of night. This is not an exaggeration.

Recognizing the sensitivity of the site at the very moment Providence was rediscovering its waterfront and constructing a river walk, the developers (the Old Stone Corporation) held a limited competition that drew some of the nation's leading designers. The architect who landed the commission was Edward Larrabee Barnes, who later in his career would be the recipient of an AIA Gold Medal. When Antoinette Downing (the nationally respected doyenne of Providence's powerful preservation community) learned Barnes had been selected for this project, she remarked the job had been given to an architect who was doing the most sensitive contextual work in the country. Living up to his reputation for sensitivity to site, Barnes took his cue from the city's historic but now largely demolished commercial waterfront with its brick warehouses. On what was a large, windswept parking lot, he developed a design that featured two opposing low-rise brick buildings whose facades pulled back in a series of steps from an open landscaped space. The buildings would have framed a view from the water of three historic buildings on the east side of South Main Street: the 1774 Joseph Brown House, the 1828 Benoni Cooke House, and, in the middle, the Old Stone Bank.

The scheme was roundly attacked, and a second design was developed, also clad in brick. Although most of those who had fought against the first proposal were

121 South Main Street

pleased with the architect's thoughtful response to their concerns, this new scheme ignited a lawsuit, this time from the west side of the river. Barnes's third design is the building we see today. It combines the square feet of the architect's first proposal, which called for two buildings, and bundles them to create a single high rise on the south end of the site. The part of the parcel to the north became a park. Since the new building no longer referenced the warehouses, brick was beside the point and in any case not especially appropriate for an eleven-story building. Instead, the gray granite of the Barnes building echoes the granite of the historic Old Stone Bank.

This did not mean Barnes abandoned a consideration of context; he simply looked in another direction—first, to the Benoni Cooke House directly across the street. But the way the older building is referenced comes as something of a surprise. Imagine if the cube that is Benoni Cooke could somehow be levitated into either the tall square void at the northeast street-level entrance or into the two-story void in the northwest corner at the top; it would slide as neatly into either space as a folded letter into an envelope. Barnes did something very interesting here: with a nod across the street, he took the box so favored by twentieth-century Modernist architects and cut great pieces out of it to relieve the relentless squareness of the form. It is a gesture that was increasingly adopted by architects who in the later years of the twentieth century pulled, pushed, and hacked away at plain geometry, a task made easier by computer-aided design tools. The various squares and rectangles on the west face of the Benoni Cooke House (look at the windows and the lintels above) may have also influenced the building's detailing. The pattern could just as well be an allusion to the checkerboard pattern of the Old Stone Corporation's logo. According to him, Barnes had more distant prospects in mind when he anchored the two shades and textures of gray granite squares onto the building's steel frame: he was inspired by the proportions of one of the base sides of the top spire of the Unitarian Church steeple just up College Hill.

A similar attention to the smallest detail is evident in the craftsmanship of the building both inside and out. The two-story conference room at the top is a stunning space that offers spectacular views of the city, the harbor, and College Hill. (In 2011, the room was renovated by Architectural Research Office as the seminar room for the Institute of Computational and Experimental Research in Mathematics, a newly created math institute funded by the National Sciences Foundation.) Unlike too many contemporary commercial buildings built for a quick return on the dollar, there are many fine details and a generosity of space throughout. This is not a building that was meant to be torn down. Rather, it is the work of a skilled architect and a client willing to pay for excellence. That said, it is a shame Barnes's first scheme did not go forward. The present building is open to the criticism it is too large for the site. The park is a nice consolation for what was not built. But during the colder months, it is darkened by the shadow the building casts.

The acquisition of 121 South Main was an important step toward realizing the third guiding principle of the University's 2003 *Strategic Framework for Physical*

Planning. The first two principles involved developing circulation infrastructure and consolidating the core. Both inspired the creation of The Walk that today connects the Pembroke campus with Simmons Quad. The third principle set a course for Brown's future growth beyond College Hill. With 121 South Main, Brown acquired first-class research and office space for the University's School of Public Health and math institute. The move to South Main Street confirmed Brown's growing engagement with the city, which continues to unfold most dramatically in the Jewelry District.

101 Phenix Iron Foundry Machine Shop
1848

Like the Benoni-Cooke House on the east side of the river, the Phenix Iron Foundry is not owned but leased by Brown; and like the House, the Foundry is important on several counts: It is a milestone in the transformation of the United States from an agrarian society to an industrial power. Also the first American textile-printing machines were manufactured here, which helped Providence dominate the textile industry. Established in 1830, the Foundry quickly grew in size, ultimately covering some two acres by the end of the nineteenth century. In 1903, the business failed and the plant was bought by the Narragansett Electric Lighting Company, which eventually tore down most of the structures, with one exception, this two-and-a-half-story stone building, the Elm Street Machine Shop.

And what a wonderful building it is: Form and function are skillfully integrated; the prose of utility is seamlessly married to the poetry of aesthetic delight. Notice how the slightly recessed arched openings at the north end, which accommodated hoists, proportionally decrease in size from the ground level to the top floor. There is a pleasing balance and symmetry echoed by the placement of the windows, also somewhat recessed. This allows for an ever-changing play of light and shadow across the planes of the wall. The size of the windows also changes as

Phenix Iron Foundry Machine Shop

one's eye travels up the wall: on the ground floor, they are 20 over 20; one flight up, they are 16 over 16; then, 8 over 8 at the very top in the gable end. These basically functional gestures give what is a low structure a vertical lift. Above the cornice on the long sides, a clerestory monitor adds to the generous amount of natural light that enters the building. The many openings on every side also enhance rapid air exchange, no small consideration in a manufacturing plant.

The stone walls of the Foundry are load-bearing and, therefore, thicken at the bottom to support the structure. But even here, necessity becomes a virtue: The stone—the varied colors of which are attractive in their own right—is both randomly cut and seemingly randomly positioned. This is a building designed and built to last. True, the location in the city demanded that even a factory building show some attention to durability and quality, if only for prestige. After all, the owners were not a distant corporation, but were members of the community and often lived close by. Whatever prompted the owners to build well, they left for future generations a resource, a gift that does not often come to mind when looking at most suburban post–World War II commercial and industrial buildings.

Identified in 1994 by the Providence Preservation Society as one of the city's ten most endangered historic properties, the Phenix Iron Foundry and the community have been beneficiaries of Brown's leasing and restoration. The building has been given the needed breathing space to develop a passionate constituency that will insist on its survival as part of one of the nation's first thematic local historic districts. The University has preserved a well-designed structure that can now play a role in the rebirth of the Jewelry District as a productive, healthy, and sustainable twenty-first-century neighborhood.[5] The building is currently the home of Brown's Division of Advancement.

102 Laboratories for Molecular Medicine / Doran-Speidel Building
Monk & Johnson, 1912; five-story addition on Bassett Street, 1965; renovation Tsoi Kobus, 2004

The five-story Doran-Speidel Building is typical of the solidly built early twentieth-century industrial architecture that sprang up at the margins of older American cities. The embrace of modern construction materials and methods (steel and concrete), the use of standardized manufactured parts, the lack or minimal appearance of decorative features, the horizontality of the massing, and the flexible interior spaces that could be easily reconfigured in a matter of days if not hours—basic elements of early twentieth-century American industrial architecture—were to become the unornamented, straightforward vocabulary of the midcentury International style.

Although the names of the architecture firms of record are cited where available, the design of the modern factory had as much to do with the technical skills of engineers. Certainly that is true of the design and construction innovations that enabled great advances in productivity and efficiency: a horizontal building minimized the need to go up and down stairs; raw materials were easily brought in and

Laboratories for Molecular Medicine /
Doran-Speidel Building

finished products quickly shipped out; the fireproof construction gave industrial solvents and other materials nothing to feed on; and the high ceilings and large windows provided light and ventilation for the workers who, in this factory, produced pocket-watch chains, and later the "twist-o-flex" expandable metal watchbands that made the Speidel brand a household name.

All these advances were made possible by structural engineers.[6] Chief among these innovators was Claude Allen Porter Turner (1869–1955), a Rhode Island native who received a patent in 1908 for an innovative flat-slab support system, known as the Turner or Spiral Mushroom System found here in this building. When it first appeared toward the end of the nineteenth century, reinforced concrete floor construction was based on traditional beam and girder framing elements. Turner's innovation was to recognize that the thick beams could be eliminated if reinforcement were placed in the floor slab, extending from column to column. His approach was named the "Mushroom System," because of the shape of the column heads that enclosed the reinforcement that tied the column and the floor slabs together. The fact that mushrooms spring up overnight further recommended the name to a system that could be constructed with remarkable speed.

In short, although the Doran-Speidel Building is rather plain on the outside, it had good bones: the floors were strong and could bear heavy loads; the interior spaces were high and open, which allowed them to be easily reconfigured and upgraded; and the exterior nonstructural walls with their large windows were as much about glass as masonry. Not to be overlooked was the fact that the recycling of older buildings here and on College Hill advanced Brown's commitment to make its physical plant a model of sustainability. Indeed, 70 Ship Street, the first building Brown acquired in the Jewelry District, was also the first building studied as part of a joint project launched in 2011 by Brown and the University of Rhode Island to collect quantifiable data on how the goal of developing a sustainable designed environment was playing out.

Initially, there were some doubts about the wisdom of Brown's move into the neighborhood at a time when I-195 was still in place. When the Doran-Speidel building was repurposed for the University's Molecular Medicine program, the University's provost insisted a sign be put on the roof to signal speeding motorists that, yes, here was Brown. The sign is still there, but in the spring of 2011, the last truckload of rubble from the interchange pulled out of town. Instead of seeing the underbelly of I-195, students and faculty who came to 70 Ship Street in the fall in 2011 looked across the street to the freshly sown sod of a wide swath of land ripe for new development. For the first time they could see the river and beyond to the spires of College Hill.

103　Ship Street Square

Landscape design, !melk, with the Maguire Group and
Robert Silmon Associates, 2011

Throughout this guide, the narrative of Brown's architecture has paused at the small green spaces that are the University's gift to students, faculty, and neighbors. Recognizing that such a space inserted into the existing streetscape could serve as a town square around which new development would coalesce, Kliment Halsband Architects identified a lot at the intersection of Richmond and Ship Streets as the site for a green intervention. Far from arbitrary, the site straddles a potentially vital crossroads: the broad vehicular north-south route to and from downtown (Richmond) and the narrower east-west pedestrian-scaled path (Ship) students and faculty will take to the Hill once a proposed bridge across the river for pedestrians and bikers is in place. As the armature for a revitalized neighborhood, what has since been named Ship Street Square has the potential for doing for the Jewelry District what the College Green does for Brown.

In 2011, Brown retained !melk as lead landscape architect and urban design consultant. Their assignment was to shape the existing barren site into a welcoming and safe environment that would entice developers and investment. Conceived as a public plaza and events space, the ⅓-acre plot has become a staging ground for temporary pop-up retail, such as farmers' markets, food trucks, and craft fairs, as well as performance and cultural venues. Ship Street Square is also a unique opportunity to showcase and nourish the entrepreneurial talents of Brown, RISD, and Johnson and Wales students whose campuses are nearby. The ultimate goal is that over time, the energy collected and redistributed by Ship Street Square will generate a living, 24-hour academic, business, and residential community.

104　Warren Alpert Medical School of Brown University

1928; renovation, Ellenzweig Associates, 2011; lobby mural, Larry Kirkland;
streetscape design, !melk

Take a solidly constructed vacant building, a growing medical school, and the design skills of a talented architecture firm, add a generous donor plus a vision, and the result is the home for the Warren Alpert Medical School of Brown University. This new home is the first building of its kind dedicated to housing the core facilities for academic medicine under one roof. What comes as a welcome surprise is the Alpert Medical School has entered the neighborhood with arms wide open, not under armed guard. This building represents a leap forward in Rhode Island's growth as a major center for biotechnology and medicine.

The large windows that comprise approximately 70 percent of the exterior skin of what had been the headquarters of the Brier Manufacturing Company (producer of Little Nemo jewelry) became, in the hands of the architects, the signature of a modern medical facility distinguished by admirable transparency.

Warren Alpert Medical School, view from Eddy Street

Augmented by four LED panels on the side of the building facing College Hill, the Alpert Medical School glows brightly at night in a corner of the city that had long been in shadow. Continuing this openness to the neighborhood, the University committed a prime first-floor corner location not for offices, but a cafe. When the weather is fair, customers can carry their bagels and coffee across the way to the new Ship Street Square. To encourage foot traffic around the Medical School, sidewalks have been widened along Richmond Street from 4 to 13 feet, and trees have been planted to soften the hard edges of the industrial landscape, especially the adjacent parking garage. (Check out the blue-gray sidewalk paving blocks. Even the grates of the tree boxes designed by !melk have a surprising flair.)

The neighbors are not the only ones who benefit from this openness. To encourage interaction and connectivity among students and faculty, the architects punched a sunlit glass atrium through the center of the building. The resulting open space functions like an avenue for students arriving from College Hill and those headed back from the heart of the Jewelry District to the College Green. The creation of the atrium was also an opportunity to replace the concrete columns of the original structure with structural steel. This preserved the industrial feel of the building while providing the necessary strength to shoulder the insertion of two-story lecture halls.

The building also houses the Clinical Skills Center (sixteen suites providing training in diagnosis and patient interaction), a 10,000-square-foot state-of-the-art anatomy suite, case study rooms, a bookless digital medical library, and computer labs. A commons on the third floor overlooking the atrium is a pleasant space for faculty and students to connect and converse. The 2,000-square-foot rooftop terrace on the fourth floor is designed for informal gatherings and special events. From here, faculty, students, and guests have a commanding view out to the waterfront and College Hill.

105 Office of Continuing Education and the Office of College Admission
Architect unknown; renovation, Durkee, Brown, Viveiros & Werenfels Architects, 2012

In trying to weigh the significance of everything built, there are times when it is best to relax and allow that a building may just be a building, and not architecture with a capital A. This would describe the new home of Brown's Office of Continuing Education on Dyer Street.

Formerly a local U.S. immigration field office, this decidedly nondescript two-story structure was slated for demolition in 2005, to be replaced by a nine-story office building with a residential and hotel component. But that was at the height of the real estate casino days. When the market went bust, the project was shelved. That might have been the end of the story except for Brown's entry into the Jewelry District. The downturn in the economy proved to be an opportunity to purchase a 41,000-square-foot building that could be repurposed to accommodate the University's growing commitment to continuing education, while providing more spacious and accessible digs for Admission. At the same time, a clever design intervention by a firm committed to smart growth and sustainability could and does contribute to the overall revitalization of the Jewelry District by making the building available to the community for lunchtime and evening lectures. Further, the repurposing of the Dyer Street property became a clever tactic in the University's drive to reduce its carbon footprint; not only is an existing building reused, the trucks that would have hauled tons of debris to a landfill site stayed idle.

Office of Continuing Education and the Office of College Admission

The architects of this Providence firm have sensibly opened up the interior, welcoming both natural light and interaction among students and faculty. The tall, south-facing windows look out to a tree-shaded green space. At night, the brightly lit lobby filled with adult students communicates life and energy to a corner of the Jewelry District that had been dark. Inside, the architects have exposed the guts of the HVAC system. It is something of a contemporary cliché, but in this unremarkable building, it provides visual interest. The interiors are largely variations on the white, but punctuated by bright splashes of bold color on the walls themselves and the furnishings.

In the near future, the Continuing Education and Admission offices and the other facilities of Brown's Jewelry District campus will be within walking distance of the proposed pedestrian bridge linking the downtown to College Hill. The new bridge will straddle the piers of the roadbed that had carried the traffic of the now relocated I-195. Stripped to its bones, a fragment of the highway that had sliced through the old Jewelry District and divided the city will now be an artery of new life. The practical yet visionary businessmen who fought to have a college in their upstart town would, no doubt, have appreciated the double irony.

1 William Greene Roelker, "The Browns and Brown University," *Brown Alumni Monthly* XLIX, no. 4 (December 1948), 4.

2 Martha Mitchell, *Encyclopedia Brunoniana* (Providence: Brown University Library, 1993), 157.

3 Roelker, "The Browns and Brown University," 4.

4 Additional details about the Joseph Brown House are found in the National Park Service Historic American Buildings Survey prepared by Osmund R. Overby, 1962.

5 A brief history of the rise of Providence as a major industrial center can be found in "Providence Industrial Sites," a 1981 document prepared by the Rhode Island Historical Preservation & Heritage Commission. See in particular chapter III, beginning at page 4.

6 Information about reinforced concrete construction gathered from a 2011 exhibition Vertical Urban Factory: The Concrete Factory: Reinforced Concrete Systems, January 12 – July 27, 2011, at New York's Skyscraper Museum.

To me an institution is a biological unfolding, is a sacred living organism
whose roots are buried deep in the past and whose branches spread out, always
in unpredictable fashion, into the sky above.[1]
—Ninth president, William Herbert Perry Faunce (1899–1929)

It is always old Brown and it is always new Brown. I am here to greet the new
Brown of this era, to hail the dawning of a new day full of the brightest promise.[2]
—Chief Justice Charles Evans Hughes, Class of 1881.
   Commencement speech, 1937.

In the decades following World War II, Brown spent energy, resources, and
good will in an on-again, off-again struggle with its College Hill neighbors over
new construction. In the decades since, the relationship between Brown and its
neighbors on College Hill has grown closer, with all the challenges and opportunities that come with the recognition of a shared destiny. This transformation
is reflected not only in renewed dialogue between Providence and the University,
but also in the way Brown is today shaping its campus and embracing the city's
rich architectural legacy. For all their differences, the ideal city on the Hill
and the real city of Providence are rediscovering they share the urban impulse
of bringing different people and ideas together to make community.

   Each generation will over time see a different Brown. Change is the
inevitable outcome of life. Change is how we adapt to and embrace the future.
What should not change if the University is to maintain its unique identity
is the belief expressed in the *Preamble to the Charter of 1764* that "discharging the
office of life with usefulness and reputation" is what an education at Brown
is about. If that remains the guiding principle, then what is built will not simply
keep out the rain; the architecture will delight the eye, nourish the soul, and
sustain a special sense of place.

1 Martha Mitchell, *Encyclopedia Brunoniana* (Providence: Brown University Library, 1993), 222.

2 Ibid., 300.

The Van Wickle Gates, detail of the University seal

Acknowledgments

This guide would not have been possible were it not for the gracious support of the Brown Alumni Association Board of Governors, the Maddock Alumni Center Committee, and the Office of Alumni Relations. Special thanks are also offered to former Board of Governors presidents George Billings '72 and the late Joseph Fernandez '85; to current Brown Alumni Associate Board of Governors president Nancy Chick Hyde '80; to past Maddock Alumni Center Committee chairs Gail Solomon '76 and Kenneth McDaniel '69; long-time Committee member Paul "Jay" Maddock '72; and to an emeritus member of the University's Corporation and former Maddock Alumni Center Committee member Joan Wernig Sorensen '72, who championed the guide.

Our grateful acknowledgments must go to Brown Chancellor Thomas Tisch '76, for his intellectual insights; to Brown President Christina H. Paxson, for her wonderful foreword to the guide; and to Brown Professor Dietrich Neumann, for his insightful introduction.

We owe a sincere debt of gratitude to architect Frances Halsband for generously sharing the research that was the basis for Kliment and Halsband's *Strategic Framework for Physical Planning.* The invaluable works of historians Walter C. Bronson, William H. Jordy, and William McKenzie Woodward '75 MA, as well as that of Brown University archivist Jennifer Betts and sports archivist Peter Mackie '59, provided insight and sound reference. *Encyclopedia Brunoniana* provided endless historical facts, stories, and anecdotes—special thanks to its author, the late Martha Mitchell, the University's former archivist. A special thank you goes to architect Leslie Armstrong; Brown's assistant vice president for planning, design and construction, Michael McCormick; and Todd Rader of Todd Rader + Amy Crews, Architecture Landscape Architecture, LLC. The manuscript drafting was aided by former trustee Scott Burns, Heather Ewing, Edward F. Sanderson, and Forrest MacCormack.

Our gratitude to Raymond Rhinehart '62 for his eloquent writing, Walter Smalling Jr. for his artful photography, and to Tom Gastel for his exquisite watercolor maps. We thank the staff of Princeton Architectural Press, especially Dan Simon, Benjamin English, and Jan Cigliano Hartman, for their expertise. Finally and ultimately, we must praise Office of Alumni Relations Vice President Todd Andrews '83, who led the guide through its conception and development, and Alumni Relations Director Jill Rossi, who deserves tremendous credit for managing the creation of this guide from start to finish.

Wayland Arch

Bibliography

Barry, Jay, and Martha Mitchell. "A Tale of Two Centuries: A Warm and Richly Pictorial History of Brown University, 1764–1985" *Brown Alumni Monthly* (1985): 10–33.

Barry, John M. *Roger Williams and the Creation of the American Soul: Church, State, and the Birth of Liberty*. New York: Viking, 2012.

Bradley, Betsy H. *The Works: The Industrial Architecture of the United States*. New York: Oxford University Press, 1999.

Bronson, Walter C. *The History of Brown University 1764–1914*. Providence: Brown University, 1914.

Codman, Ogden, Jr., and Edith Wharton. *The Decoration of Houses*. London: B. T. Batsford, 1898.

Conley, Patrick T. *An Album of Rhode Island History, 1636–1986*. Norfolk, Va.: Donning Company, 2000.

Downing, Andrew Jackson. *The Architecture of Country Houses*. New York: Dover, 1969.

Downing, Antoinette Forrester. *Early Homes of Rhode Island*. Richmond, Va.: Garrett and Massie, 1937.

Elfland, Carolyn W., Martha J. Kanter, Daniel R. Kenney, and Reed Kroloff, "Campus Architecture: The Good, the Bad, and the Future in Campus Design." *Chronicle of Higher Education*, 52, no. 34 (April 28, 2006): B28.

Emlen, Robert P. "Picturing Brown: The First Views of the College." Providence: Brown University Library and University Archives, 2012. Also available at www.library.brown.edu/cds/images_of_brown/emlen/.

Eschenbacher, Herman. "When Brown Was Less Than a University but Hope More Than a College." *Brown Alumni Magazine* (February 1980): 26–32.

Haefeli, Evan. *New Netherland and the Dutch Origins of American Religious Liberty*. Philadelphia: University of Pennsylvania Press, 2012.

Halsband, Frances. "Charles Klauder's Brilliant Invisible Hand." *Chronicle of Higher Education* 51, no. 29 (March 25, 2005): B24–25.

Huxtable, Ada Louise. "Symbols of Our Nation." *Wall Street Journal*, September 21, 2011.

Jordy, William H. *Buildings of Rhode Island*. New York: Oxford University Press, 2004.

Kasson, John F. *Civilizing the Machine: Technology and Republican Values in America, 1776–1900*. New York: Hill and Wang, 1999.

Kliment Halsband Architects. *Campus Heritage at Brown University: Preservation Priorities*. Providence: Brown University, 2006. Also available at www.brown.edu/Facilities/Facilities_Management/docs/newsletter/Campus_Heritage_2006.pdf.

———. *Jewelry District Area Plan*. Providence: Brown University, 2010.

———. *Strategic Framework for Physical Planning Brown University*. Providence: Brown University, 2003. Also available at www.brown.edu/Facilities/Building_Brown/resources/Brown_Stategic_Framework_Book.pdf.

Kliment Halsband Architects, Todd Rader + Amy Crews Landscape Architecture. "The Walk: A Proposed Design for the Extension of the Brown University Campus Joining Lincoln Field and Pembroke Green." Providence: Brown University, 2004. Also available at www.brown.edu/Facilities/Building_Brown/resources/Walk_2004.pdf.

McCabe, Anthony. "The College Buildings in Other Days." In *Memories of Brown: Traditions and Recollections Gathered from Many Sources*, edited by Robert Perkins Brown, Henry Robinson Palmer, Harry Lyman Koopman, and Charles Saunders Brigham. Providence: Brown Alumni Magazine, 1909.

Mitchell, Martha. *Encyclopedia Brunoniana*. Providence: Brown University Library, 1993.

Munro, Walter Lee. *The Old Back Campus at Brown*. Providence: Haley & Sykes, 1929.

Ossman, Laurie, and Heather Ewing. *Carrère & Hastings: The Masterworks*. New York: Rizzoli, 2011.

Rappleye, Charles. *Sons of Providence: The Brown Brothers, the Slave Trade, and the American Revolution*. New York: Simon & Schuster, 2006.

Reidel, Jacob. "Unbuilt Brown." Senior thesis, Brown University Department of History of Art and Architecture. Providence: Brown University, 2002.

Robinson, Ezekiel Gilman. *Ezekiel Gilman Robinson: An Autobiography*. Edited by E. H. Johnson. New York: Silver, Burdett and Company, 1898.

Roelker, William Greene. "The Browns and Brown University." *Brown Alumni Monthly* XLIX, no. 4 (December 1948): 3–8.

Ruskin, John. *The Stones of Venice*. Edited by J. G. Links. New York: Da Capo Press, 1960.

Scully, Vincent, Jr., Catherine Lynn, Erik Vogt, and Paul Goldberger. *Yale in New Haven: Architecture and Urbanism*. New Haven, Conn.: Yale University, 2004.

Stern, Robert A. M. *Robert A. M. Stern: On Campus: Architecture, Identity, and Community*. Edited by Peter Morris Dixon, Alexander Newman-Wise, and Jonathan Grzywacz. New York: Monacelli Press, 2010.

Tolles, Bryant Franklin, Jr. *Architecture & Academe: College Buildings in New England before 1860*. Hanover, N.H.: University Press of New England, 2011.

Turner, Paul Venable. *Campus: An American Planning Tradition*. Cambridge, Mass.: MIT Press, 1984.

United States Department of the Interior, National Park Service, National Register of Historic Places Inventory: Nomination Form, Form 10-300 (December 1968), "Corliss (George H.) House," Providence, William Slater Allen, 1959.

United States Department of the Interior, National Park Service, National Register of Historic Places Inventory: Nomination Form, Form 10-300 (July 1969), "First Baptist Meeting House." Providence, Patricia Heintzelman, 1962.

United States Department of the Interior, National Park Service, National Register of Historic Places Inventory: Nomination Form, Form 10-300, "Joseph Brown House." Providence, Osmund R. Overby, 1962.

Vertical Urban Factory: Reinforced Concrete Systems, an exhibition at the Skyscraper Museum. New York, January 12–July 27, 2011.

Wayland, Francis. *Thoughts on the Present Collegiate System in the United States*. Boston: Gould, Kendall & Lincoln, 1842.

Woodward, William McKenzie. *PPS/AIAri Guide to Providence Architecture*. Providence: Providence Preservation Society, 2003.

———. *Providence: A Citywide Survey of Historic Resources*. Edited by David Chase. Providence: Rhode Island Historical Preservation Commission, 1986.

Wriston, Henry Merritt. *Educational Housing*. Providence: Brown University Press, 1946.

———. *Wriston Speaking: A Selection of Addresses*. Providence: Brown University Press, 1957.

ADDITIONAL RESOURCES

In 2006, a catalog of the trees and shrubs of the entire Brown campus was compiled by Professor of Biology Emerita Annette W. Coleman: www.scribd.com/doc/46675154/Brown-Guide-to-Trees-and-Shrubs.

The campus in spring